ICIW 2016

The Eleventh International Conference on Internet and Web Applications and Services

May 22 - 26, 2016

Valencia, Spain

ICIW 2016 Editors

David Lizcano, Universidad a Distancia de Madrid - Udima, Spain
Dirk Labudde, University of Applied Sciences Mittweida, Germany

Printed from e-media with permission by:

Curran Associates, Inc.
57 Morehouse Lane
Red Hook, NY 12571

Some format issues inherent in the e-media version may also appear in this print version.

Printed by Curran Associates, Inc. (2016)

International Academy, Research, and Industry Association (IARIA)
412 Derby Way
Wilmington, DE 19810

Phone: (408) 893-6407
Fax: (408) 527-6351

petre@iaria.org

Additional copies of this publication are available from:

Curran Associates, Inc.
57 Morehouse Lane
Red Hook, NY 12571 USA
Phone: 845-758-0400
Fax: 845-758-2633
Email: curran@proceedings.com
Web: www.proceedings.com

TABLE OF CONTENTS

ICIW 2016

Foreword

The Eleventh International Conference on Internet and Web Applications and Services (ICIW 2016), held between May 22-26, 2016, in Valencia, Spain, continued a series of co-located events that covered the complementary aspects related to designing and deploying of applications based on IP&Web techniques and mechanisms.

Internet and Web-based technologies led to new frameworks, languages, mechanisms and protocols for Web applications design and development. Interaction between web-based applications and classical applications requires special interfaces and exposes various performance parameters.

Web Services and applications are supported by a myriad of platforms, technologies, and mechanisms for syntax (mostly XML-based) and semantics (Ontology, Semantic Web). Special Web Services based applications such as e-Commerce, e-Business, P2P, multimedia, and GRID enterprise-related, allow design flexibility and easy to develop new services. The challenges consist of service discovery, announcing, monitoring and management; on the other hand, trust, security, performance and scalability are desirable metrics under exploration when designing such applications.

Entertainment systems became one of the most business-oriented and challenging area of distributed real-time software applications' and special devices' industry. Developing entertainment systems and applications for a unique user or multiple users requires special platforms and network capabilities.

Particular traffic, QoS/SLA, reliability and high availability are some of the desired features of such systems. Real-time access raises problems of user identity, customized access, and navigation. Particular services such interactive television, car/train/flight games, music and system distribution, and sport entertainment led to ubiquitous systems. These systems use mobile, wearable devices, and wireless technologies.

Interactive game applications require particular methodologies, frameworks, platforms, tools and languages. State-of-the-art games today can embody the most sophisticated technology and the most fully developed applications of programming capabilities available in the public domain.

The impact on millions of users via the proliferation of peer-to-peer (P2P) file sharing networks such as eDonkey, Kazaa and Gnutella was rapidly increasing and seriously influencing business models (online services, cost control) and user behavior (download profile). An important fraction of the Internet traffic belongs to P2P applications.

P2P applications run in the background of user's PCs and enable individual users to act as downloaders, uploaders, file servers, etc. Designing and implementing P2P applications raise particular requirements. On the one hand, there are aspects of programming, data handling, and intensive computing applications; on the other hand, there are problems of special protocol features and networking, fault tolerance, quality of service, and application adaptability.

Additionally, P2P systems require special attention from the security point of view. Trust, reputation, copyrights, and intellectual property are also relevant for P2P applications.
On-line communications frameworks and mechanisms allow distribute the workload, share business process, and handle complex partner profiles. This requires protocols supporting interactivity and real-time metrics.

Collaborative systems based on online communications support collaborative groups and are based on the theory and formalisms for group interactions. Group synergy in cooperative networks includes online gambling, gaming, and children groups, and at a larger scale, B2B and B2P cooperation.

Collaborative systems allow social networks to exist; within groups and between groups there are problems of privacy, identity, anonymity, trust, and confidentiality. Additionally, conflict, delegation, group selection, and communications costs in collaborative groups have to be monitored and managed. Building online social networks requires mechanism on popularity context, persuasion, as well as technologies, techniques, and platforms to support all these paradigms.

Also, the age of information and communication has revolutionized the way companies do business, especially in providing competitive and innovative services. Business processes not only integrates departments and subsidiaries of enterprises but also are extended across organizations and to interact with governments. On the other hand, wireless technologies and peer-to-peer networks enable ubiquitous access to services and information systems with scalability. This results in the removal of barriers of market expansion and new business opportunities as well as threats. In this new globalized and ubiquitous environment, it is of increasing importance to consider legal and social aspects in business activities and information systems that will provide some level of certainty. There is a broad spectrum of vertical domains where legal and social issues influence the design and development of information systems, such as web personalization and protection of users privacy in service provision, intellectual property rights protection when designing and implementing virtual works and multiplayer digital games, copyright protection in collaborative environments, automation of contracting and contract monitoring on the web, protection of privacy in location-based computing, etc.

We take here the opportunity to warmly thank all the members of the ICIW 2016 Technical Program Committee, as well as the numerous reviewers. The creation of such a broad and high quality conference program would not have been possible without their involvement. We also kindly thank all the authors who dedicated much of their time and efforts to contribute to ICIW 2016. We truly believe that, thanks to all these efforts, the final conference program consisted of top quality contributions.

Also, this event could not have been a reality without the support of many individuals, organizations, and sponsors. We are grateful to the members of the ICIW 2016 organizing committee for their help in handling the logistics and for their work to make this professional meeting a success.

We hope that ICIW 2016 was a successful international forum for the exchange of ideas and results between academia and industry and for the promotion of progress in the field of Internet and Web applications and services.

We are convinced that the participants found the event useful and communications very open. We hope that Valencia provided a pleasant environment during the conference and everyone saved some time to enjoy the charm of the city.

ICIW 2016 Chairs:

ICIW General Chair
David Lizcano, Universidad a Distancia de Madrid - Udima, Spain

ICIW Advisory Committee
Mario Freire, University of Beira Interior, Portugal
Steffen Fries, Siemens AG, Corporate Technology - Munich, Germany
Vagan Terziyan, University of Jyvaskyla, Finland
Mike Wald, University of Southampton, UK
Sergio De Agostino, Sapienza University of Rome, Italy
Kwoting Fang, National Yunlin University of Science & Technology, ROC
Renzo Davoli, University of Bologna, Italy
Gregor Blichmann, Technische Universität Dresden, Germany

Vincent Balat, University Paris Diderot - Inria, France
Ezendu Ariwa, University of Bedfordshire, UK

ICIW Industry/Research Chairs

Giancarlo Bo, Technology and Innovation Consultant- Genova, Italy
Ingo Friese, Deutsche Telekom AG - Berlin, Germany
Sven Graupner, Hewlett-Packard Laboratories - Palo Alto, USA
Alexander Wöhrer, Vienna Science and Technology Fund, Austria
Caterina Senette, Istituto di Informatica e Telematica, Pisa, Italy
Nazif Cihan Tas, Siemens Corporate Research - Princeton, USA
Jani Suomalainen, VTT Technical Research Centre of Finland, Finland
Samad Kolahi, Unitec Institute of Technology, New Zealand

ICIW Publicity Chairs

Sven Reissmann, University of Applied Sciences Fulda, Germany
David Gregorczyk, University of Lübeck, Institute of Telematics, Germany

ICIW 2016

COMMITTEE

ICIW General Chair

David Lizcano, Universidad a Distancia de Madrid - Udima, Spain

ICIW Advisory Committee

Mario Freire, University of Beira Interior, Portugal
Steffen Fries, Siemens AG, Corporate Technology - Munich, Germany
Vagan Terziyan, University of Jyvaskyla, Finland
Mike Wald, University of Southampton, UK
Sergio De Agostino, Sapienza University of Rome, Italy
Kwoting Fang, National Yunlin University of Science & Technology, ROC
Renzo Davoli, University of Bologna, Italy
Gregor Blichmann, Technische Universität Dresden, Germany
Vincent Balat, University Paris Diderot - Inria, France
Ezendu Ariwa, University of Bedfordshire, UK

ICIW Industry/Research Chairs

Giancarlo Bo, Technology and Innovation Consultant- Genova, Italy
Ingo Friese, Deutsche Telekom AG - Berlin, Germany
Alexander Wöhrer, Vienna Science and Technology Fund, Austria
Caterina Senette, Istituto di Informatica e Telematica, Pisa, Italy
Nazif Cihan Tas, Siemens Corporate Research - Princeton, USA
Jani Suomalainen, VTT Technical Research Centre of Finland, Finland
Samad Kolahi, Unitec Institute of Technology, New Zealand

ICIW Publicity Chairs

Sven Reissmann, University of Applied Sciences Fulda, Germany
David Gregorczyk, University of Lübeck, Institute of Telematics, Germany

ICIW 2016 Technical Program Committee

Mohd Helmy Abd Wahab, University Tun Hussein Onn Malaysia, Malaysia
Charlie Abela, University of Malta, Malta
Witold Abramowicz, Poznan University of Economics, Poland
Dharma P. Agrawal, University of Cincinnati, USA
Mehmet Aktas, Indiana University, USA
Grigore Albeanu, Spiru Haret University - Bucharest, Romania
Markus Aleksy, ABB AG, Germany
Mehran Alidoost Nia, University of Guilan, Rasht, Iran
Filipe Araujo, University of Coimbra, Portugal
Marcos Baez, University of Trento, Italy

Nidal AlBeiruti, University of South Wales, UK
Feda AlShahwan, The Public Authority for Applied Education and Training (PAAET), Kuwait
Josephina Antoniou, UCLan Cyprus, Cyprus
Eiji Aramaki, NAIST (Nara Institute of Science and Technology), Japan
Ezendu Ariwa, University of Bedfordshire, UK
Khedija Arour, University of Carthage - Tunis & El Manar University, Tunisia
Marzieh Asgarnezhad, Islamic Azad University of Kashan, Iran
Jocelyn Aubert, Luxembourg Institute of Science and Technology (LIST), Luxembourg
Nahed A. Azab, The American University in Cairo, Egypt
Panagiotis D. Bamidis, Aristotle University of Thessaloniki, Greece
Masoud Barati, Islamic Azad University - Kangavar branch, Iran
Bradley Barker, University of Nebraska-Lincoln, USA
Ana Sasa Bastinos, University of Ljubljana, Slovenija
Khalid Belhajjame, LAMSADE - Paris-Dauphine University, France
Luis Bernardo, Universidade Nova de Lisboa, Portugal
Siegfried Benkner , University of Vienna, Austria
Emmanuel Bertin, Orange Labs, France
Giancarlo Bo, Technology and Innovation Consultant- Genova, Italy
Christos Bouras, University of Patras / Research Academic Computer Technology Institute, Greece
Laure Bourgois, INRETS, France
Mahmoud Brahimi, University of Msila, Algeria
Tharrenos Bratitsis, University of Western Macedonia, Greece
Maricela Bravo, Autonomous Metropolitan University, Mexico
Ruth Breu, University of Innsbruck, Austria
Claudia Canali, University of Modena and Reggio Emilia, Italy
Dung Cao, Tan Tao University - Long An, Vietnam
Miriam A. M. Capretz, The University of Western Ontario - London, Canada
Jorge C. S. Cardoso, University of Minho, Portugal
Juan Carlos Cano, Universidad Politécnica de Valencia, Spain
Ana Regina Cavalcanti Rocha, Federal University of Rio de Janeiro, Brazil
Shiping Chen, CSIRO Digital Productivity Flagship (DPF), Australia
Xi Chen, Nanjing University, China
Zhixiong Chen, School of Liberal Arts - Mercy College, USA
Raja Chiky, ISEP Paris, France
Costin Chiru, University Politehnica of Bucharest, Romania
Dickson K.W. Chiu, University of Hong Kong, Hong Kong
Soon Ae Chun, City University of New York, USA
Paolo Ciancarini, University of Bologna, Italy
Marta Cimitile, Unitelma Sapienza University, Italy
Hugo Coll, Universidad Politécnica de Valencia, Spain
Gianpiero Costantino, Institute of Informatics and Telematics - National Research Council (IIT-CNR) of Pisa, Italy
María Consuelo Franky, Pontificia Universidad Javeriana - Bogotá, Columbia
Javier Cubo, University of Malaga, Spain
Roberta Cuel, University of Trento, Italy
Paulo da Fonseca Pinto, Universidade Nova de Lisboa, Portugal
Maria Del Pilar illamil Giraldo, Universidad de los Andes, Columbia
Maria del Rocío Abascal Mena, Universidad Autónoma Metropolitana - Cuajimalpa, Mexico

Kathia Marcal de Oliveira, University of Valenciennes and Hainaut-Cambresis, France
Massimo Marchiori, University of Padua & European Institute for Science, Media and Democracy, Italy
Jose Miguel Martínez Valle, Universidad de Córdoba, Spain
Barbara Masucci, Università di Salerno, Italy
Inmaculada Medina-Bulo, Universidad de Cádiz, Spain
Fuensanta Medina-Dominguez, Carlos III University Madrid, Spain
Christoph Meinel, Hasso-Plattner-Institut GmbH, Germany
Abdelkrim Meziane, DSISM CERIST, Algeria
Andre Miede, University of Applied Sciences Saarbrücken, Germany
Fernando Miguel Carvalho, Lisbon Superior Engineering Institute, Portugal
Serge Miranda, University of Nice, France
Sanjay Misra, Federal University of Technology - Minna, Nigeria
Mohamed Mohamed, IBM US Almaden, USA
Shahab Mokarizadeh, Royal Institute of Technology (KTH), Sweden
David Molik, Cold Spring Harbor Laboratory, USA
Stefano Montanelli, Università degli Studi di Milano, Italy
Arturo Mora-Soto, Mathematics Research Center (CIMAT), Mexico
Jean-Henry Morin, University of Geneva, Switzerland
Prashant R. Nair, Amrita University, India
T.R. Gopalakrishnan Nair, Prince Mohammad Bin Fahd University, KSA
Alex Ng, The University of Ballarat, Australia
Theodoros Ntouskas, Univeristy of Piraeus, Greece
Jason R.C. Nurse, Cyber Security Centre | University of Oxford, UK
Asem Omari, University of Hail, Kingdom of Saudi Arabia
Carol Ou, Tilburg University, The Netherlands
Federica Paganelli, CNIT - National Consortium for Telecommunications - Firenze, Italy
Helen Paik, University of New South Wales, Australia
Marcos Palacios, University of Oviedo, Spain
Grammati Pantziou, Technological Educational Institute of Athens, Greece
Andreas Papasalouros, University of the Aegean, Greece
Marcin Paprzycki, Systems Research Institute of the Polish Academy of Sciences, Poland
João Paulo Sousa, Instituto Politécnico de Bragança, Portugal
Al-Sakib Khan Pathan, UAP and SEU, Bangladesh/Islamic University in Madinah, KSA
George Pentafronimos, University of Piraeus, Greece
Mark Perry, University of New England in Armidale, Australia
Simon L. Podvalny, Voronezh State Technical University, Russia
Agostino Poggi, Università degli Studi di Parma, Italy
Jim Prentzas, Democritus University of Thrace - School of Education Sciences, Greece
David Prochazke, Mendel University in Brno, Czech Republic
Xiuquan Qiao, Beijing University of Posts and Telecommunications (BUPT), China
Ricardo Queiros, Polytechnic Institute of Porto, Portugal
Ivana Rabova, Mendel University in Brno, Czech Republic
Carsten Radeck, Technische Universität Dresden, Germany
Mustafa Rafique, IBM Research, Ireland
Khairan Dabash Rajab, Najran University, Saudi Arabia
Muthu Ramachandran, Leeds Metropolitan University, UK
José Raúl Romero, University of Córdoba, Spain
Albert Rego, Universidad Politécnica de Valencia, Spain

Stephan Reiff-Marganiec, University of Leicester, UK
Sven Reissmann, Fulda University, Germany
Werner Retschitzegger, University of Linz, Austria
Jan Richling, Technical University Berlin, Germany
Biljana Risteska Stojkoska, University "Ss. Cyril and Methodius", Macedonia
Thomas Ritz, Aachen University of Applied Sciences, Germany
Christophe Rosenberger, ENSICAEN, France
Gustavo Rossi, Universidad Nacional de La Plata, Argentina
Jörg Roth, Nuremberg Institute of Technology, Germany
Antonio Ruiz Martínez, University of Murcia, Spain
Marek Rychly, Brno University of Technology, Czech Republic
Gunter Saake, Otto-von-Guericke-University Magdeburg, Germany
Fatiha Sadat, Université du Québec à Montréal, Canada
Saqib Saeed, University of Siegen, Germany
Sébastien Salva, University of Auvergne (UdA), France
Demetrios G. Sampson, Curtin University, Australia
David Sánchez Rodríguez, University of Las Palmas de Gran Canaria (ULPGC), Spain
Maribel Sanchez Segura, Carlos III University of Madrid, Spain
Célio Santana, Universidade Federal de Pernambuco, Brazil
Antonio Sarasa, Universidad Complutense de Madrid, Spain
Ana Sasa Bastinos, fluid Operations AG, Germany
Claudio Schifanella, RAI - Centre for Research and Technological Innovation Turin, Italy
Holger Schwarz, University of Stuttgart, Germany
Jörg Schwenk, Ruhr University Bochum, Germany
Wieland Schwinger, Johannes Kepler University Linz, Austria
Didier Sebastien, ESIROI-STIM, Reunion Island
Florence Sèdes, IRIT Université Paul Sabatier Toulouse, France
Mohamed Sellami, ISEP Paris, France
Caterina Senette, Istituto di Informatica e Telematica, Pisa, Italy
Cássio Vinícius Serafim Prazeres, Federal University of Bahia, Salvador, Brazil
Omair Shafiq, University of Calgary, Canada
Asadullah Shaikh, Najran University, Kingdom of Saudi Arabia
Jawwad Shamsi, National University of Computer & Emerging Sciences - Karachi, Pakistan
Jun Shen, University of Wollongong, Australia
Sujala D. Shetty, Birla Institute of Technology & Science, Pilani – Dubai Campus, UAE
Zhefu Shi, University of Missouri-Kansas City, USA
Kuei-Ping Shih, Tamkang Unviersity, Taiwan
Patrick Siarry, Université Paris 12 (LiSSi) - Créteil, France
André Luis Silva do Santos, Insituto Federal de Educação Ciencia e Tecnologia do Maranhão-IFMA, Brazil
Florian Skopik, AIT Austrian Institute of Technology, Austria
Günther Specht, Universität Innsbruck, Austria
Vladimir Stancev, SRH University Berlin, Germany
Matthias Steinbauer, Johannes Kepler University Linz - Institute of Telecooperation, Austria
Michael Stencl, Mendel University in Brno, Czech Republic
Yuqing Sun, Shandong University, China
Jani Suomalainen, VTT Technical Research Centre of Finland, Finland
Sayed Gholam Hassan Tabatabaei, Isfahan University of Technology, Iran
Panagiotis Takis Metaxas, Wellesley College, USA

Nazif Cihan Tas, Siemens Corporate Research - Princeton, USA
António Teixeira, IEETA University of Aveiro, Portugal
Vagan Terziyan, University of Jyvaskyla, Finland
Pierre Tiako, Langston University - Oklahoma, USA
Leonardo Tininini, ISTAT-Italian Institute of Statistics), Italy
Konstantin Todorov, LIRMM / University of Montpellier 2, France
Orazio Tomarchio, University of Catania, Italy
Victor Manuel Toro Cordoba, University of Los Andes - Bogotá, Colombia
Vicente Traver Salcedo, Universitat Politècnica de València, Spain
Christos Troussas, University of Piraeus, Greece
Nikos Tsirakis, University of Patras, Greece
Radu Tudoran, Huawei European Research Center, Germany
Pavel Turcinek, Mendel University in Brno, Czech Republic
Yoshihisa Udagawa, Tokyo Polytechnic University, Japan
Lorna Uden, Staffordshire University, UK
Abel Usoro, University of the West of Scotland, UK
Samyr Vale, Federal University of Maranhão - UFMA - Brazil
Bert-Jan van Beijnum, University of Twente, Netherlands
Dirk van der Linden, Artesis University College of Antwerp, Belgium
Perla Velasco-Elizondo, Autonomous University of Zacatecas, Mexico
Ivan Velez, Axiomática Inc., Puerto Rico
Tommaso Venturini, King's College London, UK
Maurizio Vincini, Universita' di Modena e Reggio Emilia, Italy
Michael von Riegen, University of Hamburg, Germany
Liqiang Wang, University of Wyoming, USA
Norman Wilde, University of West Florida, USA
Alexander Wöhrer, Vienna Science and Technology Fund, Austria
Michal Wozniak, Wroclaw University of Technology, Poland
Rusen Yamacli, Anadolu University, Turkey
Sami Yangui, Concordia University, Montreal, QC, Canada
Beytullah Yildiz, Tobb Economics and Technology University, Turkey
Jian Yu, Auckland University of Technology, New Zealand
R. Zafimiharisoa Stassia, University of Blaise Pascal, France
Amelia Zafra, University of Cordoba, Spain
Sherali Zeadally, University of Kentucky, USA
Martin Zimmermann, Hochschule Offenburg - Gengenbach, Germany
Jan Zizka, Mendel University in Brno, Czech Republic

Copyright Information

For your reference, this is the text governing the copyright release for material published by IARIA.

The copyright release is a transfer of publication rights, which allows IARIA and its partners to drive the dissemination of the published material. This allows IARIA to give articles increased visibility via distribution, inclusion in libraries, and arrangements for submission to indexes.

I, the undersigned, declare that the article is original, and that I represent the authors of this article in the copyright release matters. If this work has been done as work-for-hire, I have obtained all necessary clearances to execute a copyright release. I hereby irrevocably transfer exclusive copyright for this material to IARIA. I give IARIA permission or reproduce the work in any media format such as, but not limited to, print, digital, or electronic. I give IARIA permission to distribute the materials without restriction to any institutions or individuals. I give IARIA permission to submit the work for inclusion in article repositories as IARIA sees fit.

I, the undersigned, declare that to the best of my knowledge, the article is does not contain libelous or otherwise unlawful contents or invading the right of privacy or infringing on a proprietary right.

Following the copyright release, any circulated version of the article must bear the copyright notice and any header and footer information that IARIA applies to the published article.

IARIA grants royalty-free permission to the authors to disseminate the work, under the above provisions, for any academic, commercial, or industrial use. IARIA grants royalty-free permission to any individuals or institutions to make the article available electronically, online, or in print.

IARIA acknowledges that rights to any algorithm, process, procedure, apparatus, or articles of manufacture remain with the authors and their employers.

I, the undersigned, understand that IARIA will not be liable, in contract, tort (including, without limitation, negligence), pre-contract or other representations (other than fraudulent misrepresentations) or otherwise in connection with the publication of my work.

Exception to the above is made for work-for-hire performed while employed by the government. In that case, copyright to the material remains with the said government. The rightful owners (authors and government entity) grant unlimited and unrestricted permission to IARIA, IARIA's contractors, and IARIA's partners to further distribute the work.

eRoDes: a Web-based Framework for the Development of Semantic-Enhanced Learning Objects

Pedro Álvarez, Sandra Baldassarri

Department of Computer Science and Systems Engineering
University of Zaragoza, Spain
Email: {alvaper, sandra}@unizar.es

***Abstract*—Learning objects are often created reusing multimedia resources available in the Web. The metadata of these new objects are usually annotated using semantic technologies. Nevertheless, some relevant challenges related to the creation of semantic-based metadata and their use in learning experiences are still open. The combination of solutions of service-oriented computing, Linked Data Cloud and semantic technologies allows to tackle these challenges. The result is *eRoDes*, a web-based and service-oriented framework able to semantically annotate learning objects in an automatic way and that provides services for the development of learning activities using these objects. *eRoDes* functionality has been tested in a subject of Computer Engineering's Degree at the University of Zaragoza during 2014-15. The results are reported and discussed.**

Keywords*–*Semantic annotation; learning objects; web services; e-learning.

I. INTRODUCTION

The Internet provides a huge amount of multimedia resources, such as videos, audio, web pages, documents, etc. These resources can be useful in the design and creation of new learning objects. However, in order to include these objects in teaching experiences it is necessary to previously describe their metadata, which consist of annotations that help users to classify, recover and share the learning objects. Semantic technologies have been integrated into e-learning systems to enrich these annotations and allow to improve the management of the learning objects stored into the repositories. Nevertheless, in the field of e-learning, some open challenges must be still addressed in relation with: the automation of semantic-annotation processes, the validation of annotations from the user's perspective, the linking of new learning objects with other Web-accessible resources, and the interoperability of solutions to access and exchange these objects.

In most of the studied semantic-based systems [1]–[7], the annotations are manually created by users' or by domain experts'. Nevertheless, they differ in the origin of the annotations. In several systems, annotations are based on the contents of the learning objects and are created using domain ontologies [3]–[7]. These systems are only able to work with video while other works deal only with textual resources [1][2]. Annotations, in these cases, could be indicators about the complexity for the learners to understand the concepts related with the learning objects [2] or pedagogical terms extracted from the text-based comments and manually added by the teachers to the learning objects [1]. On the other hand, there are some automatic annotation tools, but they are not focused in the contents. The annotations can be generated by assigning categories extracted from synthatic structures of the text [8] or, instead, they are generated after processing the multimedia resources in order to automatically extract visual features that provide knowledge about the contents [9][10].

Once the learning objects have been semantically annotated, it is necessary to validate the usefulness of these annotations for learners. Most of the manual annotation tools previously mentioned have not implemented feedback mechanisms to improve the annotations since they are supposedly created by experts. The system presented in [4] is an exception. There, the system monitors the interactions of the learners with the objects and with other participants and uses this feedback information to identify resources that could be improved. On the other hand, there are other approaches that propose the use of collaborative techniques to improve their annotations [11][12]. Learners review peers' annotations and provide ratings or comments that will be used to re-annotate the learning objects.

Finally, the annotation systems should use standard ontologies to describe the metadata of new learning objects. The use of standards makes the linking of new objects to other online resources easier. Although the existing systems are prone to work with proprietary ontologies, some works propose as an alternative the use of vocabulaires of the Linked Data Cloud [13] to link their annotations to external data sets [3][6][7]. On the other hand, the standarization also helps e-learning systems to access and exchange learning objects between them [14]. Unfortunately, most of the existing e-learning systems are monolithic solutions that integrate a non-web editor to create semantic annotations and a web browser or application to search and recovery the annotated objects.

eRoDes, acronym in Spanish of "crEación participativa de RecursOs Docentes Etiquetados Semánticamente" (collaborative creation of semantically annotated learning objects, in English), is a web-based and service-oriented framework that allows to semantically annotate learning objects and stores these objects and their Resource Description Framework (RDF) based annotations. Unlike other existing approaches, the annotation process is automatic, without users' or domain experts' interaction, it uses vocabularies of the Linked Data Cloud (the learning objects are linked to the DBpedia) and annotations are created from the content of different kind of resources (the text of a web page, or the audio of a video, for instance). This process has been implemented by integrating external web services, Linked Data algorithms and semantic technologies. Two different voting mechanisms are provided in order to validate and to improve the annotations that were automatically created. Moreover, *eRoDes* integrates a set of software components to design learning and teaching activities.

These components are basic functional units that work over the annotated learning objects and that have been implemented as services to facilitate their reusability and integration into e-learning applications or workflows.

In order to show the use of this framework, a learning activity is described. The activity is aimed to involve students in the creation of new learning objects: searching, classifying and assessing resources available in the Web. The created objects have been submitted to *eRoDes* to be semantically annotated and afterwards used in the teaching of a subject. Also, the students provided feedback in order to improve the annotations of new learning objects created by other students.

The remainder of this paper is organized as follows. Section II presents the architecture of *eRoDes* framework, while in Section III implementation's details are described. In Section IV, a complete learning-teaching activity is explained, including its phases and the results obtained. Finally, the most important conclusions are presented at Section V.

II. THE ERODES FRAMEWORK

Figure 1 depicts the high-level architecture of the *eRoDes* framework. It is a service-oriented system that has been implemented using web-based and semantic technologies. The framework provides two types of services: 1) Submission services that semantically annotate new learning objects and store them into the knowlegde database of *eRoDes*, and 2) Application services that automate some tasks of learning activities planned by teachers.

Students and teachers can submit new learning objects, such as text documents, PDF files, or videos, to the framework using the Moodle application or the *eRoDes* web-application. The submission services are implemented as a semantic annotation process that automatically annotate these objects before storing them into the knowledge database of the system. These annotations are generated from the content of each object and mapped on an ontology which was previously defined by the teachers or automatically created by the system from the teaching guide of the subject.

As it can be observed in the left part of Figure 1, this semantic annotation process consists of a linear pipeline of three stages: Resource preprocessing stage, Extraction of relevant terms stage and Annotation process stage. This pipe has been designed following the Pipes and Filters architectural pattern [15] in order to make easier the exchange and the recombination of filters, the rapid prototyping of pipes and the parallel processing of the different stages. The pipe was implemented by the integration of web-accessible services and libraries developed in the field of Semantic Web.

From the execution point of view, some stages could be computing intensive processes (more precisely, the speech-to-text translation of a video when its duration is long) or an user could request the annotation of a large collection of learning objects. Thus, the pipe components have been programmed to be optionally deployed in some of the distributed computing infrastructures at our disposal. For this purpose, the HERMES computing cluster hosted by the Aragon Institute of Engineering Research and the clouds provided by OpenShift and Amazon have been integrated in the *eRoDes* framework. This remote deployment is configured, executed and monitored by the mediation layer developed in [16]. This layer provides a transparent and easy-to-use access to the set of hybrid computing infrastructures. So that, these heterogeneous infrastructures are viewed as a whole by end-users.

On the other hand, the right part of Figure 1 shows the application services offered by the current version of *eRoDes*. An application service provides a coarse-grained functionality that will be used in learning activities by students or teachers. These services access and use the annotated objects that had been stored into the knowledge database of *eRoDes*. Until now, three student-oriented services and two prototypes of teacher-oriented services have been implemented in order to provide the following functionality:

- the validation of annotations service allows a student to improve the semantic annotations of a learning object,
- the ranking system helps students to assess the quality and usefulness of the objects submitted by other students,
- the understanding system allows to create a mind map that represents the understanding of a student after working with a learning object,
- the quality resource evaluation service is used by teachers to evaluate the quality of resources created by students,
- and, finally, the learning process evaluation service provides teachers with feedback about if students learn what they should when working with a specific object.

All these services expose their functionality as web services in order to make easier their integration in different applications. As it will be described in next section, the services for improving and ranking learning objects have been integrated into PyBossa [17], an open-source framework for crowdsourcing. With this tool, students will improve the semantic annotations of objects created during an activity or a course.

III. IMPLEMENTATION OF ERODES

In this section, the *eRoDes* main components involved in the semantic annotation of learning objects and the validation of these annotations are described in detail.

A. Semantic annotation process

The skeleton of the semantic annotation pipeline has been implemented in Java and is based on the Pipes and Filters pattern: each processing stage has been implemented as an individual component and the connections between stages as buffers that synchronize the data flow between adjacent components. These components and buffers are called filters and pipes, respectively. First, a version of this architectural pattern based on Java interfaces was programmed. Afterwards, all the filters and pipes that compose the pipeline have implemented these interfaces. The web-accessible services and the semantic libraries and technologies used in these implementations are described in detailed in the next paragraphs. This interface-based implementation makes easier the integration of components in the pipeline and their future update and maintenance.

The first stage of the pipeline is executed by the resource preprocessing component. A different preprocessing component has been programmed for each kind of input object.

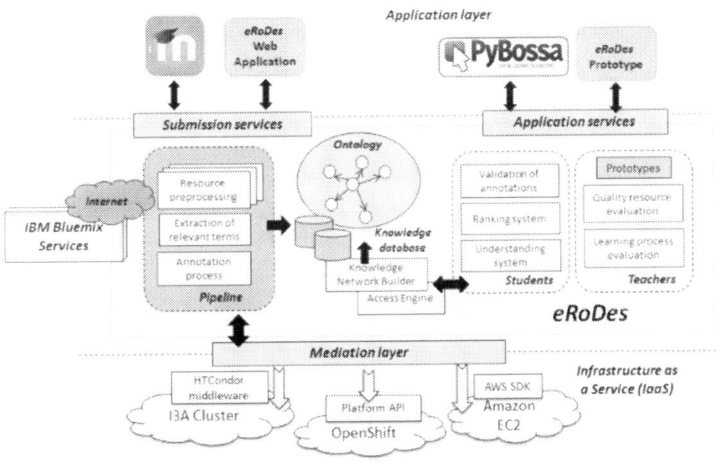

Figure 1. High-level architecture of the eRoDes framework

On the one hand, videos are preprocessed using the Java Audio Video Encoder (JAVE) library and a speech-to-text service provided by the IBM Bluemix platform [18]. Different alternative technologies have been studied in this stage. For video preprocessing, JAVE was compared with Xuggler [19], but, alghough both have similar features, JAVE proved to be simpler. Regarding speech recognition, several web services and libraries have been considered. One of the most known web services, Google Speech API was analysed. But the input audio is restricted to 15 seconds and the daily requests to 50 in the free version, while IBM Bluemix platform allows 3 minutes for the input audio time and there is not limit for requests. The CMU Sphinx library [20] was also considered in order of not depending on the web or on external services. However, quality and performance tests shown that IBM Bluemix platform is twice faster and offers 30% better accuracy in word recognition. In our implementation, JAVE extracts the audio of an input video and is capable of converting it to different formats. Then, the resulting audio file is sent to the IBM Web service to be transcribed into a text file. On the other hand, documents are preprocessed using Apache PDFBox library. The text of PDF documents is extracted and transcribed to an output text file.

Following, the extraction of the relevant terms stage has been implemented by integrating the Java Automatic Term Extraction toolkit (JATE). This toolkit provides a set of Automatic Term Recognition (ATR) algorithms that will be used to determine the most relevant terms of the text-based transcriptions [21]. We have selected the ATR algorithms capable of recognising both single-word and multi-word terms and that do not discard candidate terms only on the basis of frequency. The execution of each algorithm generates an output file that contains the recognised terms; then, these files are processed by an automatic voting component to select the most relevant terms. In our solution, two different strategies based on a weighted and majority voting have been combined: first, a weight is assigned for each recognised term based on its rankings and, then, the terms that received the greatest total weighted vote are selected.

Finally, the annotation process is responsible for annotating semantically the most relevant terms. This last stage integrates an implementation of the ADEGA algorithm [22]. ADEGA annotates each term by means of a RDF graph created from those instances of the DBpedia that are relevant in the resource domain. In our solution, the resource domain is defined from materials provided by the teachers, the guide or the slides of a subject, in order to link the annotations of learning objects with the context where they will be used. An RDF graph is created for each specific term and stored into a Virtuoso database [23]. Then, these graphs are used to classify the input learning resources, facilitating the search and retrieval of information.

B. Application services

The service for validating the semantic annotations of the learning objects is one of the most used application components. The validation of annotations consists of accepting or discarding each term that was automatically generated by the annotation pipeline. A web application, based on the front-end of PyBossa that allows students and teachers participate in the validation tasks, was programmed. A PyBossa microtasking project publishes the list of objects waiting to be validated. Registered users can access to these objects and check if the terms associated to a specific object correspond with its content. A term can be accepted/discarded or new terms can be optionally added. These decisions are then sent to the *eRoDes* validation service in order to improve the object's annotations and update the knowledge database of the platform.

Figure 2 shows the components involved into the validation system. A bridge component interconnects the web service with the PyBossa core. It translates the list of unvalidated objects returned by the service to a set of PyBossa tasks. These tasks are JSON objects with the information that needs to be completed by the user during the validation of annotations process.

A new task creator has been programmed to upload these tasks into the PyBossa core via its RESTful API. Then, these

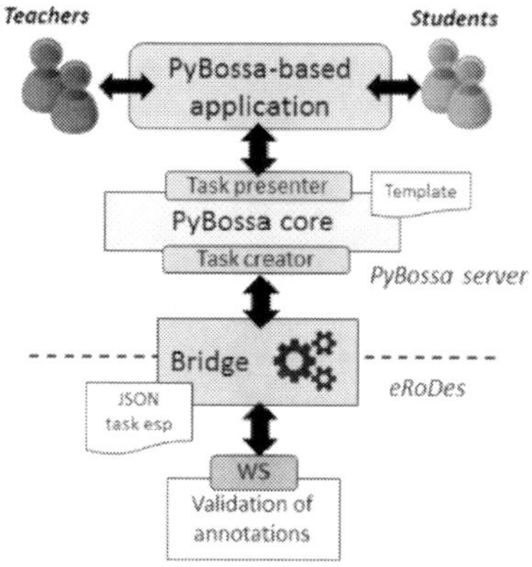

Figure 2. Validation based on the PyBossa framework

tasks are presented to students and teachers through a web-accessible interface which was previously created in a PyBossa server. We have reused an existing template for programming the task presenter, the module in charge of presenting the pending tasks and submitting the user decisions to the *eRoDes* framework. This presenter has been implemented in HTML and JavaScript. Finally, from the deployment point of view, the PyBossa server and the *eRoDes* framework are installed and run in the same server. Nevertheless, the API-based integration of services makes easier the possibility of configuring a distributed deployment.

IV. A LEARNING-TEACHING ACTIVITY BASED ON THE USE OF ERODES

In this section, an activity developed during 2014-15 in the subject Design of User-Centered Interfaces, of Computer Engineering's Degree is presented. The activity's objective is to involve students in the creation of learning objects. During the development of this work, students have to search, classify and assess teaching resources available in the Web and the resulting learning objects are stored in the *eRoDes* framework and used for teaching the subject.

A. *Phases of the activity*

The phases planned for the learning-teaching activity are shown in Figure 3. In the Initial phase, the teacher proposes some specific topics for the learning objects. These topics, together with the pdf document of the teaching guide of the subject, are sent to the *eRoDes* framework.

The objective of the First phase is the creation of the learning objects. At the beginning, the students are organized in groups of three (this number may be modified depending the class size) and a different topic is assigned to each group. This first phase consists of two sequential tasks: the resource searching and the developing of guide notes. In the first task each student individually searches resources and materials that could be useful to create the learning object. The teacher must previously define the maximum number of selected resources. Subsequently, the second task, performed in groups, involves the assessment of the resources contributed by each member of the group, in order to decide those materials that will be more suitable for the creation of the learning object, and, finally, to create it. In our proposal, a learning object consists of a limited set of resources and guide notes that determine how to use them for achieving the teaching objective. The guide notes allow to know, for example, the order in which the resources must be used, the knowledge that should be acquired with each one, or the relationship between the content of the different resources, among others. Finally, each group must submit the guide notes and the selected and discarded resources to *eRoDes* to be semantically annotated and stored into the knowledge database. Besides, a short explanation to justify the final decision of discarding an specific resource is required.

The Second phase of the activity consists of two individual tasks: the evaluation of guide notes and the activity assessment. In the first task, students must download the semantically annotated learning objects created with *eRoDes*. Then, each student must use these objects following the instructions provided by the guide notes developed by the other groups and has to evaluate their usefulness for learning the corresponding topic. This evaluation is based on peer review techniques. A PyBossa project has been created to interact with *eRoDes* and provides students a template to evaluate each learning object. The template also allows students to add or delete the semantic annotations of the downloaded resources, in order to improve these annotations in the *eRoDes* system. Once the evaluation is completed, in the assessment task students evaluate the activity by means of a questionnaire which gathers their opinion about their involvement in the activity, the experience of working in group, the strengths and weaknesses of the learning object created by their group, and about possible improvements in the planning and development of this kind of activities.

During the two first phases students must control the time dedicated to the planned tasks. A time tracking report is delivered to teacher at the end of the activity in order to know the effort dedicated by students. However, this information does not have influence over their final grades. In parallel, the teacher also evaluates the set of learning objects creating a reference evaluation, that will be used in the following phase.

Finally, the Third phase corresponds with the grading of the activity, in which the teacher determines the final marks for the work done by the students. This grading is based on the teacher's reference evaluation and the students' peer review. Besides, the teacher analyses the learning process and the questionnaire results in order to write a final report with the main conclusions and an activity improvement plan.

B. *Results*

There were 16 students in the subject during 2014-15, which have been organized in four groups of three persons and two groups of two persons. The six topics selected by the teachers were: Agile software methodologies and User eXperience design (UX Agile), Usability evaluation, Accessibility evaluation, Crowdsourcing methods, Adaptative design and Wearable interfaces. Each student of a group must search resources of a specific format, in order to have at least two or three different kind of resources.

Figure 4 shows an overview of the results of this experience. The first row represents the number of resources found by each group after completing the searching task. The teacher defined that the maximum number of resources per student was 6. In general, these resources were found using Google and Google Scholar, DuckDuckGo, and YouTube, being videos

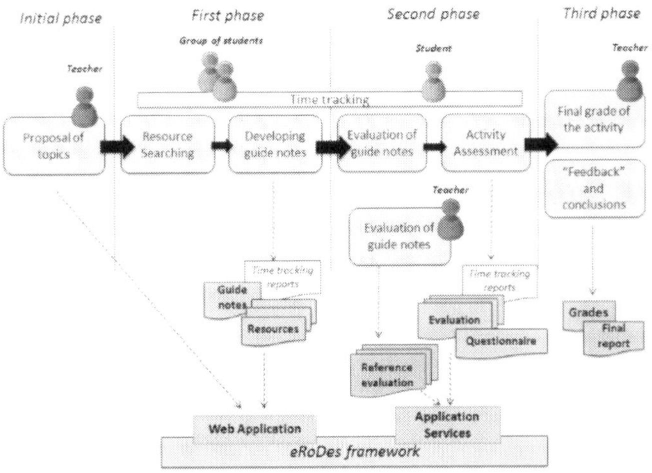

Figure 3. Phases of the learning activity

	UX Agile	Usability	Accessibility	Crowdsourcing	Adaptative design	Wearables	
Num. of found resources	15	25	23	18	18	11	Phase 1
Number of videos	7	6	4	6	2	5	
Number of documents	1	6	8	4	3	6	
Number of Web pages	5	8	4	8	11	0	
Number of tools	2	5	7	0	2	0	
Improved annotations	1	4	16	1	12	4	Phase 2
The students' gradings	8,6	7,1	7,9	7,3	6,2	8,5	
The teachers' gradings	8	6	9	7,5	5	9	
Hours per student (Phase 1)	5,3	2,75	4,25	1,4	5,8	4,25	Time tracking
Hours per student (Phase 2)	4,4	3,9	1,4	4,2	4,5	1,5	
Hours per group (Activity)	29,2	20	11,3	16,8	30,8	11,5	

Figure 4. Indicators related to the development of the activity

a 30% of resources. 55% of these resources were in English and 45% in Spanish. It must be taken into account that the topic had influenced over the format of found resources. For example, most of the Usability or Accessibility resources were tools. Finally, all the groups must select 7 resources to develop their guide notes. Once the First phase was completed, all the guide notes and resources were submitted to *eRoDes* to be semantically annotated by the framework. Figure 5 shows one of the graphs that were created to semantically annotate a video about Crowdsourcing methods. This video is available at https://www.youtube.com/watch?v=-38uPkyH9vI. The graph corresponds with the term Expertise which is a relevant concept extracted from the contents of that video. Its depth was limited to three levels of exploration and all types of relations were not explored. From the computational point of view, video annotation was the most compute-intensive operation. For example, if the speech-to-text service provided by the IBM Bluemix platform is invoked, the time needed to extract the text of an audio is proportional to the input video duration.

On the other hand, also the students's grading and the teachers's grading of each group can be observed at Figure 4 in rows 6 and 7. In general, both gradings are very similar and have been calculated from the rubric results. The aim of this rubric is to evaluate, mainly, the suitability of the selected resources, the usefulness of the guide notes, and the learning level that a student could achieve using them. Besides, 7 students proposed to modify some of the resource annotations via the PyBossa application: more specifically, the semantic annotations of 16 resources were modified, 103 resources had been submitted to *eRoDes*, and most of these changes belong to usability and accessibility resources.

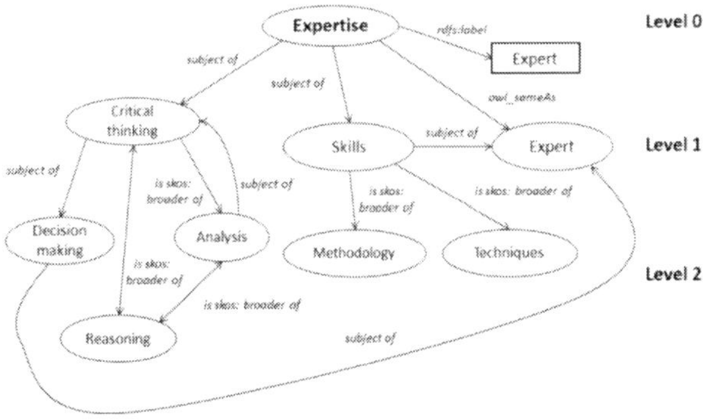

Figure 5. Graph example for the Expertise term

Finally, an overview of the time dedicated by the students is also presented. Rows 8 and 9 show the amount of hours individually dedicated to complete the first and second phase, respectively, while the hours dedicated in group to complete the whole activity is in row 10. In some cases the times reported by the students are below the time expected by the teachers. For example the time dedicated by the crowdsourcing, the accessibility and the wearable interfaces groups were insufficient. It is possible that some of these time trackings were wrong, since the students are not used to monitor their work hours. Therefore, in future activities, our rubric evaluation must be improved in order to detect these situations.

From the analysis of the results obtained from the questionnaires, the students evaluation and also during the development of the activity, some changes should be introduced in next courses. Following, the main proposals included in the activity improvement plan are summarized. Firstly, students must be trained in the gathering and assessment of resources and in the creation of guide notes. Teachers must define more precise instructions on how to make these tasks and provide students with meaningful feedback during the activity. An active role of teachers will help to improve the quality of guide notes and learning objects and, therefore, their reusability in this subject or in other similar subjects. Secondly, all the topics proposed to students should be equally motivating for them. And, finally, the evaluation of learning objects and their usefulness in the learning process must be students and teachers responsability. Besides, for the future course teachers have decided to replace the guide notes by a short-length video which will be created from learning resources found by the students.

V. Conclusions and Future Work

A new service-oriented framework to store and retrieval semantic-enhanced learning objects has been presented in this work. Its interface provides functionality to semantically annotate learning objects from a wide variety of formats. These annotations are automatically created from the contents of input learning objects and are expressed as RDF based graphs built from the DBpedia vocabulary. We selected the ADEGA algorithm because it obtained better results for precision and recall values than other semantic and DBpedia based annotation algorithms [22]. The system also provides functionality to validate the usefulness of these ADEGA-based annotations from the users' perspective. Nevertheless, the objective is not only to support the annotation and validation of learning objects, but also to facilitate their use in the development of learning activities. Application services facilitate the integration of the functionality of *eRoDes* into different e-learning applications.

As future work we are interested in improving the interoperability of *eRoDes* by the integration of standards for the description, discovery and retrieval of learning objects. We will also study the usability of our application to create new online learning contents by means of a System Usability Scale (SUS). On the other hand, another open challenge is to evaluate the quality of new learning contents and validate their usefulness in the learning and teaching process. On this regard, a first solution based on semantic technologies and graph algorithms is being tested in the same subject during this course. Also, a new *eRoDes*-based application able to provide feedback about the students' learning process is now under development.

Acknowledgment

This research has been supported by a grant of the Spanish Ministry of Economy and Competitiveness, Projects TIN2014-56633-C3-2-R and TIN2015-67149-C3-1-R, and the University of Zaragoza, Project PIIDUZ_15_175.

References

[1] S. Dehors, C. Zucker, and R. Kuntz, "Reusing Learning Resources based on Semantic Web Technologies," in Proceedings of 6th International Conference on Advanced Learning Technologies (ICALT). IEEE Computer Society, 2006, pp. 859–863.

[2] R. Farhat, B. Defude, and M. Jemni, "Towards a better understanding of learning objects' content," in Proceedings of 11th IEEE International Conference on Advanced Learning Technologies (ICALT). IEEE Computer Society, 2011, pp. 536–540.

[3] H. Qing Yu, C. Pedrinaci, S. Dietze, and J. Domingue, "Using linked data to annotate and search educational video resources for supporting distance learning," IEEE Transactions on Learning Technologies, vol. 5, no. 2, 2012, pp. 130–142.

[4] J. e. a. Jelena, "Using semantic web technologies to analyze learning content," IEEE Internet Computing, vol. 11, no. 5, 2007, pp. 45–53.

[5] C. Nithya and K. Saravanan, "Semantic annotation and search for educational resources supporting distance learning," International Journal of Engineering Trends and Technology, vol. 8, no. 6, 2014, pp. 277–285.

[6] S. Nayyar and S. Nagadevi, "Digital library service integration of educational videos using linked data and semantic web," International Journal of Computer Science and Information Technology and Security, vol. 3, no. 2, 2013, pp. 197–201.

[7] P. Phalle and S. Salunkhe, "Using linked data to context-aware annotate and search educational video resources," in Proceedings of 2nd International Conference on Emerging Trends in Engineering and Technology (ICETET-09), 2009, pp. 61–63.

[8] R. Faiz, B. Smine, and J. Desclés, "Relevant learning objects extraction based on semantic annotation of documents," in Proceedings of 2nd International Conference on Web Intelligence, Mining and Semantics, 2012, pp. 1–11.

[9] D. Cernea, E. Del Moral, and J. Labra-Gayo, "Soaf: Semantic indexing system based on collaborative tagging," Interdisciplinary Journal of E-Learning and Learning Objects, vol. 4, no. 1, 2008, pp. 137–149.

[10] A. Altadmri and A. Ahmed, "A framework for automatic semantic video annotation," Multimedia tools and applications, vol. 72, no. 2, 2014, pp. 1167–1191.

[11] M. Uncik and M. Bielikova, "Annotating educational content by questions created by learners," in Proceedings of 5th International Workshop on Semantic Media Adaptation and Personalization (SMAP 2010). IEEE Computer Society, 2010, pp. 13–18.

[12] I. Hsiao and P. Brusilovsky, "Modeling peer review in example annotation," in Proceedings of 16th International Conference on Computers in Education (ICCE 2008), 2008, pp. 357–362.

[13] "The Linking Open Data cloud diagram," URL: http://lod-cloud.net/ [accessed: 2016-04-12].

[14] D. Dagger, A. O'Connor, S. Lawless, E. Walsh, and V. Wade, "Service-oriented E-learning platforms: From monolithic systems to flexible services," IEEE Internet Computing, vol. May-June, 2007, pp. 28–35.

[15] F. Buschmann, R. Meunier, H. Rohnert, R. Sommerlad, and M. Stal, A System of Patterns. John Wiley and Sons Ltd., 1996.

[16] J. Fabra, S. Hernández, J. Ezpeleta, and P. Álvarez, "Solving the interoperability problem by means of a bus. An experience on the integration of grid, cluster and cloud infrastructures," Journal of Grid Computing, vol. 12(1), 2014, pp. 41–65.

[17] "PyBossa: the ultimate crowdsourcing framework," URL: http://pybossa.com/ [accessed: 2016-04-12].

[18] "IBM Bluemix: Create, Deploy, Manage Your applications in the cloud," URL: http://www.ibm.com/cloud-computing/bluemix/ [accessed: 2016-04-11].

[19] "Xuggle," URL: http://www.xuggle.com/ [accessed: 2016-04-11].

[20] "CMU Sphinx: an open source speech recognition toolkit," URL: http://cmusphinx.sourceforge.net/ [accessed: 2016-04-12].

[21] Z. Zhang, J. Iria, C. Brewster, and F. Ciravegna, "A comparative evaluation of Term Recognition Algorithms," in Proceedings of 6th international conference on Language Resources and Evaluation (LREC 2008), 2008, pp. 2108–2113.

[22] M. Lama, J. C. Vidal, E. Otero-García, A. Bugarín, and S. Barro, "Semantic linking of learning object repositories to DBpedia," Educational Technology and Society, vol. 15, no. 4, 2012, pp. 47–61.

[23] "Virtuoso Universal Server," URL: http://virtuoso.openlinksw.com/ [accessed: 2016-04-12].

Provenance-Aware Self-Healing Systems for Heterogeneous Computing Environments

Bahadır Dündar
Software Testing and Quality Evaluation Laboratory
TUBITAK
Gebze-Kocaeli, Turkey
email: bahadir.dundar@tubitak.gov.tr

Mehmet S. Aktas
Computer Engineering Department
Yildiz Technical University
Istanbul, Turkey
email: mehmet@ce.yildiz.edu.tr

Abstract— **Dependability is an important attribute for heterogeneous computing environments and their applications. The growing complexity and dependency of heterogeneous computing environments makes fault tolerance an appealing research area. In this study, we discuss the inability to forecast faults in large-scale execution traces. In addition, we discuss research challenges in self-healing capabilities for autonomic, dynamically coordinated smart-environments based on the supervision of continuous monitoring of execution traces. To address such limitations and research challenges, we introduce a methodology, in which the state data coming from heterogeneous computing environments, such as Internet of Things (IoT) devices, is monitored for predictive maintenance, optimization and dynamic provisioning.**

Keywords-self-healing capabilities; fault tolerance; dynamic replication; provenance; heterogeneous; IoT

I. INTRODUCTION

IoT depends on self-configured smart objects that have limited storage and processing capacity. These small objects are dynamically coordinated in a large-scale environment [1]. Platforms for connected smart objects are built by plugging heterogeneous computational entities together in highly dynamic configurations. Orchestration, management and monitoring of such devices and smart objects are fundamental fields of research, as the number of interconnected objects is supposed to reach several hundred billion. This brings up the need for suitable approaches to adaptation, reconfiguration and self-healing systems, made of entities whose common characteristic is precisely their heterogeneity. The current state of the art in these applications lacks self-healing capability, which is commonly used to refer the capability of self-recovery of systems. To achieve this capability, there are number of coordinating nodes to perform a particular task, running on heterogeneously distributed computing platforms whenever an adaptation is required to an abnormal situation.

In this paper, our first goal is to investigate research opportunities in self-healing capabilities of dynamically coordinated heterogeneous distributed computing environments based on the supervision of continuous monitoring of execution traces. To this end, we use provenance as the descriptor metadata of the execution traces taken from IoT application nodes. Our next goal is to propose a software architecture for fault forecasting/estimation on large-scale execution trace data. In order to address these goals, this paper identifies following concrete research objectives described as follows.

Objective 1: To determine how to achieve fault tolerance to support self-healing capabilities in heterogeneous computing environments.

Objective 2: To determine how to enable fault forecasting/estimation within the execution traces of activities happening among IoT application nodes.

Objective 3: To determine how to optimize self-healing capabilities by taking into account both user involvement and computing environment in heterogeneous distributed computing environments [2].

This paper introduces architectural guidelines for providing fault tolerance to heterogeneous computing environments, such as IoT application domains. To achieve fault tolerance, the use of provenance metadata is proposed.

The rest of the paper is organized as follows. Section II presents the literature summary. Section III presents various application scenarios to describe the scope of this research. Section IV presents our proposed system architecture for developing fault tolerance in an IoT application domain. Finally, Section V presents conclusion and future work of our paper.

II. LITERATURE SUMMARY

In a typical IoT application, a smart object is a lightweight component that has a clear, software-defined API through, which it can be controlled and managed at runtime, and dynamically provisioned in an elastic way. Autonomous composition of these smart objects leads to complex software ecosystems. In autonomous heterogeneous computing environments, such as IoTs, there are different units that can potentially be provisioned at runtime. Currently, there is a lack of adequate solutions to achieve resilient, dynamically coordinated IoTs.

The IoT components of these applications have end-to-end links and data storage with read/write access. We argue that in the IoT domain, if a number of IoT devices or IoT services has faults, these faults will lead to complete failure of the entire IoT application. Since our study primarily focuses on fault tolerance mechanisms for heretogenous computing environments, such as the IoT, we only review background work on fault tolerance for these applications running in heretogenous computing environments and consisting of different kinds of resource-limited devices. There are a number of previous studies that emphasize the importance of self-healing capability in IoT domains [3][4]. In light of this emphasis, we categorize and review the previous work as in the following paragraphs.

Deployment of IoT devices can be challenging. Fault tolerance has been addressed in several studies in this domain. These studies require deployment and re-configuration of the devices during the execution of IoT applications. However, these deployments require human intervention and must be performed by experts. In our study, we are interested in providing fault tolerance mechanisms that can run applications continuously, even in the case of individual node failure. Our approach is designed to run applications without stalling them. In this scenario, an IoT application can degrade gracefully under individual faults, but it can continue its execution.

In order to provide fault tolerance in the IoT domain, previous studies have used data replication techniques [5][6][7]. These studies have utilized both predefined replication and dynamic replication techniques. However, apart from the previous work, in our study we only focus on providing fault tolerance for services (instead of data replication) that are taking place in IoT applications.

Another approach for fault tolerance focused on service replication technique [8]. This was addressed for failover purposes. This approach only takes user requirements into consideration in deploying services onto multiple devices in order to recover failed services. In addition, this mechanism is tightly coupled with a middleware, and the number of replicated services is predefined. This approach does not support dynamic replication of services. In our solution, we introduce a loosely coupled fault tolerance mechanism to solve this problem. Our study aims at using a combination of both permanent and dynamic replication methods in order to optimize fault tolerance strategy in IoT domains.

With the increasing number of security attacks in the IoT domain, developing detection and prevention systems to protect the components has become essential [9]. There are some studies on detecting security attacks in the context of IoT [10][11][12]. We, however, are interested in the continuity of the entire IoT application, even under the condition of failure of individual work items. We are not concerned with preventing failures that may happen in individual IoT devices due to security attacks.

Arjun et al. proposed a framework for IoT devices in which these IoT devices can manage themselves with regard to their configuration and resource utilization [13]. However, this study focuses on a self-managing mechanism for individual IoT devices by controlling their behaviors. Additionally, this mechanism does not provide fault tolerance for entire IoT applications. Our study primarily focuses on fault tolerance for IoT applications, including multiple devices, which are coordinating with each other.

Self-healing systems should have the ability to protect themselves from possible failures. One of the methods of protecting systems from failures is to predict faults before they occur. There various types of fault prediction modeling techniques, such as Linear Regression, Naive Bayes Logistic Regression, Random Forests, Support Vector Machine and C4.5 are used in fault prediction [14][15][16]. These modeling techniques use different metrics, such as process metrics, source code text, socio-technical metrics, object oriented metrics, and line of code metrics [16][17][18]. In our study, we focus on existing machine learning algorithms that may lead to predicting/estimating fault incidents using provenance data.

III. APPLICATION USE SCENARIOS

In order to define the scope of the proposed research, we outline several application usage scenarios and various requirements of the desired self-healing system architecture. This section identifies several such scenarios, which differ in terms of the devices used, their number, granularity, and their interaction capabilities.

A. *Elderly surveillance*

This application aims at capturing important information from elderly people and sending it back to a central platform. It also serves as an agenda, reminder and telephone. Outside, it works as a global positioning system (GPS). The primary areas of application of the IoT in this scenario are shared with those in typical healthcare systems: tracking, identification and authentication, sensing and data gathering. This system works on a mobile platform, being dependent on availability of internet signal and energy. Moreover, it takes into consideration wearable sensors for acquiring vital information, which ship it to the mobile device via bluetooth, and from the device into the central, in real-time. Different sorts of services are coordinated with each other and composed to fulfill the system's functional requirements. The computational resources and battery power of these systems are limited, while communication technologies consume considerable amounts of energy. In this particular scenario, the IoT application should be capable of proactively predicting problems and should have fault tolerance. In this sense, the system should act (and react) in accordance with self-healing mechanism when detecting and predicting problems.

B. *Smart Cities*

The primary issue here is the way smart objects and sensors interact and are orchestrated with the families of electronic public services (EPS) that structure the urban network. A smart city is often characterized as instrumented, interconnected, and intelligent. Instrumented refers to the capacity to acquire real-world data using different types of channels like sensors, personal devices, medical devices, social networks, etc. Interconnected refers to the integration of data in an interoperable platform and its provision to and usage on different city services. Intelligent relates to the use of complex computational tools to deliver public value to city inhabitants. Due to the embeddedness of digital technology, citizens are more and more used to interacting with them on a daily basis, typically through mobile devices and wireless networks. Therefore, cities possess a wide range of digitally skilled users that are ready to use and benefit from the IoT to deliver EPS. However, the development of smart city initiatives faces some challenges, some of them falling clearly into the domain of applications of the heterogeneous computing platforms, such as IoT. In this scenario, we argue that these challenges in developing IoT applications are rooted in the lack of self-healing capabilities associated with such IoT applications. These capabilities are very beneficial, considering the growth of connected devices, as these applications are integrating many smart environments from different domains, such as transportation, health and e-participation.

IV. SYSTEM ARCHITECTURE

In this study, we present a self-healing mechanism for IoT application domain. Inspired by our application use scenarios, we argue that given an IoT application, if some devices or services failed, IoT application would be shut down. To this end, in this study, we introduce a failover mechanism to enable fault tolerance in IoT applications, so that the application can still continue its functioning (even in the case of few failed devices/services). This failover mechanism is introduced to address the aforementioned objective#1. We present a fault prediction/estimation mechanism that could estimate the present number and future incidences of faults. We refer the failover mechanism as the Self-Healing Mechanism Component. Within this component, we also take into account both user involvement and computing environment requirements to address the objective#3. In this study, we also introduce the use of existing solutions to a Provenance Service (i.e., Metadata Service for execution traces of activities) to enable fault tolerant IoT systems. This addresses the aforementioned objective#2. Figure 1 illustrates system architecture for fault tolerance. In this section, the components and their interdependencies are explained in detail, together with the employed research methods.

A. *Provenance Service*

Provenance is metadata, which is defined as the lineage of a piece of data or an activity. It keeps track of the lifecycle of an activity or data. In the presented self-healing methodology, provenance metadata will be used for providing fault tolerance. To this end, PROV-O Specification (W3C recommended data representation) will be utilized for provenance data representation [19]. In provenance data representation, ideal granularity of provenance and the types of information should be considered for self-healing purposes.

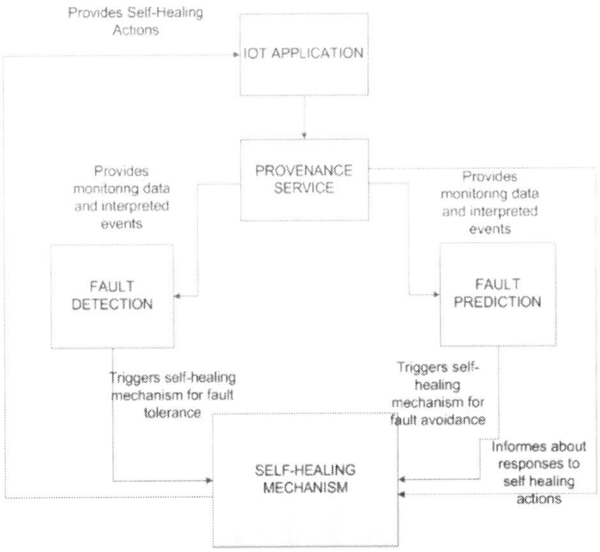

Figure 1. System Architecture

B. *Fault Detection and Prediction*

One of the aspects of a self-healing mechanism is to be able to protect itself from possible failures. To achieve this, we argue that the following research challenges should be taken into account.

The first challenge is data conversion. Provenance is graph-based data expressing the execution traces of activities. Since provenance data is represented in XML format, it is not suitable for data mining tasks. Distributed provenance graphs should be converted to a small-scale provenance graphs should be converted to a small-scale representation without information loss, so that they can be processed for fault prediction/estimation. Such a data conversion can be done by utilizing statistical features for performing the data conversion, without information loss for tasks like clustering of scientific workflow execution traces [20][21].

The second challenge is fault prediction/estimation. Existing machine learning algorithms that could lead to predicting/estimating fault incidents will be utilized. Within this challenge, one of the sub-goals of this study is to identify all possible faults that might occur in the aforementioned application domains. There could also be a case in which the provenance data conversion will not lead to good prediction/estimation capabilities; hence, big data processing approaches (Map/Reduce programming model) that can enable application of prediction/estimation algorithms on large-scale provenance data should be considered.

The third challenge is fault detection on runtime. To support accommodation to unexpected changes, change detection strategies should be carried out. Interdisciplinary research activities should be conducted, combining advanced data mining & knowledge discovery methodology with fault detection strategies based on models including smart environment' context and human-user factors. Basic principles of fault detection imply the exploitation of redundancy in order to detect inconsistencies on real data. Such deviations are used to generate alarms associated to unexpected changes and signatures described by them are used in the identification and isolation of possible causes. Models used for this purpose can be obtained from either first principles (transient models) or learned from data (following data mining, knowledge discovery approaches). Complex event processing (CEP) has been one of the widely used method utilized to facilitate runtime fault detection for IoT. CEP is used for controlling operational rules for each device taking part in IoT separately. Here, we aim at monitoring the overall rules regarding the coordination of many systems within an IoT context.

C. *Self-Healing Mechanism*

In this study, we argue that self-healing systems handle fault tolerance for dynamic coordinated IoT devices taking part in IoT application. Self-healing mechanisms autonomously identify erroneous service and manage the means by which the system is repaired. Resilience is considered as a property of coordinated IoT to be deeply studied to progress towards completely automated self-healing systems. Hereby, one can consider several strategies as follows: i) a failover mechanism by providing availability to facilitate failure recovery, ii) architectural adaptation and (automated) architecture reconfiguration, iii) manufacturing values and estimations to facilitate testing of the Self-Healing Mechanism component, and iv) providing online feedback to operators in case of potential/foreseen errors. Our approach to resilience is to provide a failover mechanism. To this end, we identify following sub-components of a self-healing mechanism: a) Failover mechanism, b) Messaging protocol and messaging bus, and c) Recovery. We describe each component as follows.

Failover mechanism: We use replication to achieve fault tolerance. The technique of replication is generally used in order to increase the dependability level of data hosting environments. There are two types of replication methods: permanent replication and dynamic replication. Permanent replication stores the copies of data permanently. However, in the dynamic replication method, the copies of data are created temporarily [22][23]. In the proposed self-healing mechanism, we are interested in replicating services and providing service redundancy for fault tolerance. Employment of a combination of both permanent and dynamic replication in providing resilient IoT applications should be considered in order to provide a minimum level of replication of services (to meet with desired fault tolerance), as well as an adjustable level of replication of services (in case some services tend to be more fragile).

Messaging protocol and messaging bus: In order to achieve a decentralized replication mechanism, messaging-based replication protocols should be used. These protocols will include messages like: a) selection of replica IoT devices for replica service (both active and idle), b) selection of new active replica services, c) live-state of existing IoT devices, and d) introduction of a new IoT device into the system. The use of a topic-based publish/subscribe-based messaging paradigm, as for messaging bus, provides one-to-one, one-to-many, and many-to-one communication channels among the IoT devices. In this approach, each participating IoT device will send a ping request (liveliness information) to the rest of the available network nodes through a publish-subscribe system. Each node will keep a vector of information on existing nodes and will refresh it periodically. Whenever a fault is predicted, a self-healing system is expected to self-optimize itself for fault avoidance. Here, our approach will take inputs from the Fault Prediction mechanism and readjust the replica service configuration (e.g., selection of new active replica service, increasing the replica service numbers, etc.).

Recovery: Recovery is another aspect of a self-healing mechanism. In our self-healing mechanism approach, a recovery mechanism will include actions to provide the system with one of the idle replica services (instead of the failed service) to bring the system to a known state of replication level. Here, we intend to use messaging-based protocols for recovery as well to achieve this.

An ideal self-healing system should implement the fault-tolerance related tasks, implicitly optimizing the use of resources of the system and the involvement of users. Users must be involved in the customization of recovery or tolerance of failures in the IoT applications that they generate. We argue that the proposed approach to model replication strategy should take into account the use of resources and involvement of users in the IoT environments.

V. CONCLUSION AND FUTURE WORK

We have discussed research challanges related to fault tolerance for IoT applications running in heretogenous computing environments. We reviewed background work on fault tolerance for these applications. We explained application use scenarios to define the scope of this study.

The expected contributions of this research can be outlined as follows. This study presents a fault tolerance methodology that could address the resilience requirements of IoT applications. It defines architectural constraints for building fault tolerance in IoT application domains and proposes a self-healing mechanism for IoT application domains. This approach includes the use of replication of services and utilizes topic–based, publish-subscribe messaging protocols to achieve fault tolerance.

In the future work, we will introduce a) a failover mechanism, b) machine learning algorithms to perform forecasting/estimations, c) a methodology to define the fault tolerance related tasks. Furthermore, we also plan on manufacturing values and estimations to facilitate testing of the Self-Healing Mechanism component and providing online feedback to operators in case of potential/foreseen errors.

ACKNOWLEDGMENT

We would like to thank Software Testing and Quality Evaluation Laboratory (YTKDL) of TUBITAK-BILGEM and Software Quality Laboratory of Yildiz Technical

University for supporting us and allowing us to use their computer facilities for this study. As always, we are really grateful for the help of the extended team of our department.

REFERENCES

[1] A. Botta, W. Donato, V. Persico, and A. Pescape, "On the Integration of Cloud Computing and Internet of Things", IEEE, 2014, pp. 23-30, ISBN: 978-1-4799-4357-9.

[2] U. Yildiz, P. Mouallem, M. Vouk, D. Crawl, and I. Altintas, "Fault-Tolerance in Dataflow-based Scientific Workflow Management", IEEE, 2010, pp. 336-343, ISBN: 978-0-7695-4129-7.

[3] N. Finne, "Towards Adaptive Sensor Networks," Dissertation for the degree of Licentiate of Philosophy in Computer Science, Uppsala University, 2011.

[4] T. Bourdenas and M. Sloman, "Starfish: policy driven self-management in wireless sensor networks", Proceedings of the 2010 ICSE Workshop, 2010, pp. 75-83, ACM 978-1-60558-971-8.

[5] J. Neumann, N. Hoeller, C. Reinke, and V. Linnemann, "Redundancy Infrastructure for Service-Oriented Wireless Sensor Networks", in 9th IEEE International Symposium on Network Computing and Applications (NCA 2010), IEEE Computer Society , July 2010, pp. 269–274, ISBN: 978-0-7695-4118-1.

[6] K. Piotrowski, P. Langendoerfer, and S. Peter, "tinyDSM: A highly reliable cooperative data storage for Wireless Sensor Networks", in 2009 International Symposium on Collaborative Technologies and Systems, IEEE, 2009, pp. 225–232, ISBN: 978-1-4244-4586-8.

[7] S. Ratnasamy, B. Karp, L. Yin, F. Yu, D. Estrin, R. Govindan, and S. Shenker, "GHT: A Geographic Hash Table for Data-Centric Storage," in Proceedings of the 1st ACM international workshop on Wireless sensor networks and applications (WSNA '02), ACM, 2002, vol. 5, pp. 78–87.

[8] P. H. Su, C. Shih, J. Y. Hsu, K. Lin, and Y. Wang, "Decentralized Fault Tolerance Mechanism for Intelligent IoT/M2M Middleware", IEEE World Forum on Internet of Things (WF-IoT), IEEE, 2015 pp. 45-50, ISBN: 978-1-4799-3459-1.

[9] R. Roman, J. Zhou, and J. Lopez, "On the features and challenges ofsecurity and privacy in distributed internet of things", Computer Networks, vol. 57, no. 10, 2013, pp. 2266-2279.

[10] F. M. Almeida, A. R. L. Ribeiro, and E. D. Moreno, "An Architecture for Self-healing in Internet of Things", UBICOMM 2015 : The Ninth International Conference on Mobile Ubiquitous Computing, Systems, Services and Technologies, IARIA, 2015, pp. 76-81, ISBN: 978-1-61208-418-3.

[11] H. M. Salmon, et al., "Intrusion detection system for wireless sensor networks using danger theory immune-inspired techniques", International journal of wireless information networks, vol. 20, no. 1, 2013, pp. 39-66.

[12] S. Raza, L. Wallgren, and T. Voigt, "SVELTE: Real-time intrusion detection in the Internet of Things." Ad hoc networks, vol. 11, no. 8, 2013, pp. 2661-2674.

[13] A. P. Athreya, B. DeBruhl, and P. Tague, "Designing for Self-Configuration and Self-Adaptation in the Internet of of Things", Carnegie Mellon University, 2013, pp. 585-592.

[14] S. Lessmann, B. Baesens, C. Mues, and S. Pietsch, "Benchmarking Classification Models for Software Defect Prediction: A Proposed Framework and Novel Findings", IEEE Trans. Software Eng., vol. 34, no. 4, pp. 485-496, July/Aug. 2008, (Paper=97, Status=F, Phase=2, Data=N).

[15] E. Arisholm, L.C. Briand, and E.B. Johannessen, "A Systematic and Comprehensive Investigation of Methods to Build and Evaluate Fault Prediction Models", J. Systems and Software, vol. 83, no. 1, 2010, pp. 2-17. (Paper=9, Status=P)

[16] T. Hall, S. Beecham, D. Bowes, D. Gray, and S. Counsell, "A Systematic Literature Review on Fault Prediction Performance in Software Engineering", IEEE Transactions On Software Engineerıng, 2012, Vol. 38, No. 6.

[17] S. Shivaji, E.J. Whitehead, R. Akella, and K. Sunghun, "Reducing Features to Improve Bug Prediction", Proc. IEEE/ACM 24th Int'l Conf. Automated Software Eng., 2009, pp. 600-604. (Paper=164, Status=P).

[18] C. Bird, N. Nagappan, H. Gall, B. Murphy, and P. Devanbu, "Putting it All Together: Using Socio-Technical Networks to Predict Failures", Proc. 20th Int'l Symp. Software Reliability Eng., 2009, pp. 109-119. (Paper=18, Status=P).

[19] PROV-DM: The PROV Data Model. [online] Available at: http://www.w3.org/TR/prov-dm/[Accessed 14 Nov. 2015].

[20] M. Aktas, B. Plale, D. Leake, and N. Mukhi, "Unmanaged Workflows: Their Provenance and Use", Data Provenance and Data Management in eScience, Berlin Heidelberg: Springer-Verlag, 2013, pp. 59-81.

[21] P. Chen, B. Plale, and M. S. Aktas, "Temporal representation for mining scientific data provenance", Future Generation Computer Systems-The International Journal Of Grid Computing And Escience, 2014, 36, pp. 363-378.

[22] M. Rabinovich, I. Rabinovich, R. Rajaraman, and A. Aggarwal, " A Dynamic Object Replication and Migration Protocol for an Internet Hosting Servic in Proc.", 19th Int'l Conf. Distributed Computing Systems, 1998, pp. 101-113.

[23] M.S. Aktas and M. Pierce, "High-performance hybrid information service architecture", 2010, Concurr. 22(15), pp. 2095-2123.

A Filtered-Page Ranking
An Approach for Previously Filtered HTML Documents Ranking

Jose Henrique Calenzo Costa and Carina F. Dorneles

Federal University of Santa Catarina
Technological Center
Informatics and Statistics Department
Florianpolis - SC, Brazil
Email: henriquecalenzo@gmail.com, dorneles@inf.ufsc.br

Abstract—**This paper describes a ranking approach applied over previously filtered documents, which relies on a segmentation process. The ranking method, called Filtered-Page Ranking, has two main steps: (i) page segmentation and irrelevant blocks removal; and (ii) document ranking. The focus of the first step is to eliminate irrelevant content from the document, which has no relevance to user query, by means of the Query-Based Blocks Mining algorithm, creating a filtered document that is evaluated in the ranking process. During the ranking step, the focus is to calculate the relevance of each filtered document for a given query, using criterias that prioritizes specific parts of the document and to the highlighted features of some HTML elements. As shown in our experiments, our approach outperforms the base line Lucene implementation of vector space model. In addition, the results demonstrate that our irrelevant content removal algorithm improves the results and our relevance criterias make difference to the process.**

Keywords–Page segmentation; HTML Ranking; Web content automatic extraction; Irrelevant content removal.

I. INTRODUCTION

The process of `ranking` documents is part of many applications, such as search engines [1][2][3], recommendation systems [4][5][6][7], document classification [8][9], among others [10][11][12]. The focus of approaches varies and usually defines different relevant parameters for the ranking. In general, the ranking process of documents has been treated traditionally as a matching problem between a query and a set of documents. In this context, a common challenge is to find a way to select representative documents to a specific query and to explore new ranking models that produce accurate results.

HTML documents ranking algorithms can be built by taking into account several aspects. Selvan et.al [13] propose three categories of ranking algorithms: (i) based on links analysis, which focus on links analysis of a document set to define the ranking; (ii) based on custom search, which considers the users' query or the feedback aspects provided by them; and (iii) based on page segmentation, which consists of algorithms that divide the page into blocks. We propose an approach that uses features from the three categories since considers the users' query on a fragmented document analysing the links on it. Beside that, the ranking function uses some parameters that consider most relevant those documents that have the query terms in key blocks such as main title, first sentence of paragraphs, highlighted sentences, etc. In the literature ranking algorithms, the existing approaches use the whole document in the process [1][2][3]. The problem is that, usually, we are interested only in the content regions that contain the query.

This paper describes an approach to rank previously filtered HTML documents, which is user query-based, called Filtered-Page Ranking (FPR). The ranking process has two main steps: (i) irrelevant content removal using page fragmentation; and (ii) documents raking using the filtered (fragmented) page. The intuition behind the process is to rank an HTML page using just its relevant and useful content. For "relevant and useful content" we mean content that is related to the user's query terms. The purpose of the first step is to generate a filtered document containing only user query content, which is evaluated in the ranking stage, through an algorithm called Query-Based Blocks Mining (QBM), which generates a filtered document that is evaluated in the ranking stage. The segmentation is performed based on the terms of user query, on important criteria that consider different documents components, and on some highlighted HTML elements. In order to do that, the documents are segmented into relevant, highlighted and disposal blocks, excluding those one considered irrelevant. During the ranking step, relevance criteria are used to indicate how close the content of a page is to the query terms. The ranking focuses on defining the relevance of filtered HTML pages for a given query. This paper presents the following contributions:

- an algorithm to remove irrelevant content: a user-query based method, that eliminates from the document those blocks that are considered irrelevant since they are not related to the user's query;
- an algorithm to rank segmented and filtered pages: a method that evaluates specific aspects of a document, with different weights, for ranking calculation, such as terms in bold, term occurrences in the title, highlighted terms (section III-A) and so on.

To evaluate our proposal, experiments have been performed on a document repository and the results are compared with the following existing proposals: the vector model, as the ranking algorithm [14], through the implementation of Lucene [15], and the irrelevant content removal algorithm called Content Extraction via Tag Ratios (CETR) [16]. The experiments show that our irrelevant content removal algorithm improves the results, and that the criteria used to calculate the relevance of HTML pages are meaningful in the ranking process.

This paper is organized as follows. In Section II, we present some works related to our proposal. The proposed `ranking` method is described in detail in Section III, where we show the irrelevant content removal phase and the ranking process itself. The experiments are presented in Section IV, showing the methodology we used and the results achieved. In Section V, the conclusions and the future work are described.

II. RELATED WORK

In this section, we present some related work of ranking methods for HTML pages classified into three different categories [13], which can be built by taking into account several aspects.

Proposals that are based on the links analysis focus on the links analysis of a document set to define the ranking. The classic PageRanking algorithm is an example that uses a ranking technique based on the relationship between several web pages [17] and Hypertext Induced Topic Search (HITS) [18], which was developed to quantify the `authority` and the `hub` values of a page. A page has a high authority value when it is pointed by many other pages (hubs) and a high hub value when it points to several other pages `(authorities)`. In this group, the algorithms are often fully automated and very useful for setting the initial ranking of a large set of web pages without a user interaction.

The second category, based on custom search, considers the users' query or the feedback aspects provided by them. In this category, Duhan et al. [19] uses the term Web Usage Mining (WUM) to identify these studies. In this technique, with the user being recognized by the system through information gathering (researches done, pages accessed), pages that may be more important for a particular search than others are found. The proposal of Joachims [20] is to use clickthrough data that specifically uses the information of links accessed (clicked) by the user to make these visited pages the priority. The method called Page Content Ranking (PCR) [21] evaluates the proximity of the web page with the query terms made. It is based on characteristics such as the frequency of terms, the number of pages containing the term and the occurrence of synonyms, comparing PCR with PageRank. The PCR applies a neural network to detect the importance of a page for a particular search, which requires network training and consequently user interaction. Another example of this category is the ranking algorithm of Lucene [22], which uses the Vector Space Model (VSM) or the Boolean model to determine the relevance of a given document in relation to a specific query from a user.

Finally, proposals that are based on page segmentation consist of algorithms that divide the page into blocks. Some works, such as FixedPS [23], Block-Based Web Search [24] and Computing Block Importance for Searching on Web Sites [25], use this approach. The main idea is to divide the document into homogeneous zones, where each one has the same type of content. Considering each block individually can be useful to separate the different kind of content, meanly to increase the ranking process performance.

The method proposed in this paper performs a segmentation process and at the same time considers the users query to improve the ranking and uses link analysis to calculate the page relevance, having similar aspects from all categories. Table I contains some features we use to compare the proposals, considering HTML/WEB specific aspects, personalized ranking and the use of user query for ranking document, user's navigation and the use of artificial intelligence.

font=footnotesize,sc,justification=centering,labelsep=period

TABLE I. WEB RANKING ALGORITHMS.

Algorithms	Particular HTML aspects (links, tags, styles...)	User's query based	User's Navigation	A.I
Page Ranking	Yes	No	No	No
PCR	No	Yes	No	Yes
VSM	No	Yes	No	No
FixedPS	No	Yes	No	No
ClickThrough Data	Yes	No	Yes	Yes
Block-Based Web Search	Yes	Yes	No	No
Block Importance on WebSites	No	Yes	No	No
FPR (our proposal)	Yes	Yes	No	No

Regarding the Block-Based Web Search method, PCR, VSM and Block Importance for Searching on WebSites, these take into consideration general aspects of ranking documents as frequency of terms and reverse frequency of terms, not taking into account the use of html tags for use criteria as highlighted terms, the tag <title> or <meta> (despite the Block-based Web Search perform the ranking of the content contained in the <title> tag only). Block Importance for Searching on Website also does not consider aspects like highlighted terms, if terms appear on the tags <title> and <meta> and this requires many pages using a similar template. The Page Rank does not check the proximity of the document consultation and ClickThrough Data uses machine learning that increases the complexity of the algorithm.

III. FILTERED-PAGE RANKING

In this section, we describe our proposed ranking method, called Filtered-Page Ranking (FPR). Before going into the details of the process, we first describe our notion of HTML page relevance and give a brief overview of the idea.

A. *HTML page relevance*

Some relevance criteria are based on a study of essential criteria for automatic indexing of text documents [26], where authors claim that to understand a document content the ideal is its full reading, although it is impractical. In that work, document segments and criteria that should be considered most important for indexing documents in digital media are defined. Considering some criteria defined in that work, in our proposal we believe that some criteria are more important to define the relevance of a HTML page: (i) the `document title`; (ii) the `introduction` and `the first sentences of chapters/paragraphs`; (iii) `tables` and `lists`; (iv) `highlighted words`; (v) the `frequency of terms`; (vi) `stop words`; and (vii) `sentence-term`. In addition to the criteria based on that study, since links are prominent elements of HTML pages, playing an important role in the design of web pages we also consider (viii) the `number of links with all query terms used as a description of links`. Intuitively, we can consider these components can represent very well a document without the need to consider the content as a whole.

As we are working with HTML document, we have made some adjustments in order to define the criteria: (i) `title`:

we consider the content in `title` and `meta` elements; (ii) `introduction and the first sentences of chapters and paragraphs`: our algorithm considers relevant the content that is close to the query terms in the document; (iii) `tables and lists`: all its contents is taken into account, being possibly represented, for example, by elements like `table`, `ul/ol`, `tr` and `li`; (iv) `highlighted terms`: they are emphasized in the text using specific HTML tags and can be underlined, bold or highlighted with different sizes or sources; these terms are taken into account on scoring an HTML document, increasing its relevance; (v) `frequency of terms`: the more a term of the user query appears in the document, the greater the relevance of the document.

Regarding `sentence-term`, the terms in a query tend to appear together. For example, when a user searches "recovery information", these two words tend not to be isolated (with no connection), they tend to appear near by, being terms of a sentence. The FPR penalizes web pages whose terms are far apart, as we can see in the correlation function in definition 6. `stop words` are irrelevant terms, without meaning that are not considered query keywords, usually represented by articles and prepositions.

B. *Overview*

The full process is executed over a DOM tree representation, which means the algorithm handles with nodes. There are two main and independent steps: (i) `page fragmentation and irrelevant content removal`: to eliminate those DOM nodes that have non-related information to the user query; and (ii) `document ranking`: to sort the relevant pages from a given query, making use of certain criteria indicating how close the document is to the query terms. The result generated from these steps is called `filtered DOM tree`.

For helping the process, the document metadata, containing information of the original document tree, are stored in the document repository. In general, the metadata comprise the document terms and their related nodes, as well as their properties (such as the HTML tag and the term occurrence in a node). Based on the terms used in the user query, the metadata presented on the filtered DOM tree are analyzed and used later to indicate the relevance of the this tree by calculating how close its content is to the query. Finally, the results are displayed in a ranking. If the filtered DOM tree does not have all mandatory terms, specified in the user query, it is not returned in the ranking. The way in which the metadata are stored in the repository depends on indexing methods and mapping structures, and it is not the focus of the work presented in this paper.

C. *Query-Based Blocks Mining*

The query-based blocks mining is the step of page segmentation and irrelevant content removal, in which the DOM tree is segmented into blocks. The blocks delimit the regions and the type of treatment performed over the DOM nodes. The objective of this phase is to extract a filtered tree that has only segmented blocks directly connected to the user query, discarding blocks with irrelevant contents.

1) Categorization of blocks: In this task, the DOM tree nodes are categorized into three groups: (i) `segmented blocks`; (ii) `disposal blocks`; and (iii) `highlighted blocks`. During the process, a categorized DOM tree is generated, whose categories are used to eliminate content, to extract useful content or to be used during the ranking phase.

Definition 1: `(Categorized DOM tree)`:

Let $N = \{n_1, ..., n_i\}$ be a set of nodes and $E = \{e_1, ..., e_i\}$ be the set of edges connecting the nodes in N. A categorized DOM tree DT is defined as a pair $DT = (N, E)$, where N is the set of nodes in which n_j is any node in A and can represent `segmented blocks`, `highlighted blocks` or `disposal blocks`.

A categorized DOM tree has both important nodes for the ranking process and nodes that must be eliminated. Those nodes can represent segmented blocks, highlighted blocks or disposal blocks, which can be treated as defined below.

Definition 2: `(Segmented Block)`: Let DT be a categorized DOM tree and n_j any node in DT. A block $Bsg = n_j$ is a sub-tree of DT called `segmented block`, such that n_j is any continuous region of the text, $Bsg \subset DT$.

Segmented blocks are sub-trees of the categorized DOM tree that are able to delimit regions, i.e., we consider segmented blocks to be elements that are capable of delimiting context (grouping HTML elements or sets of words that precede or follow the query keywords); a segmented block can be contained in others segmented blocks, generating nested segmented blocks. These regions may indicate blocks that contain the query terms and must be kept, as well as irrelevant content that must be eliminated. Generally, they delimit continuous regions of text or regions inserted within a context that groups them, such as, for example, tags `form` or `div`, which defines a set of data from a Web form or a given style and format, respectively. The HTML tags that can represent segmented blocks can be, for example, {`html, body, form, div, table, tr, iframe, article, section, ul, li, title, meta`}

Definition 3: `(Highlighted Block)`: Let n_j be any node in DT that can contain an HTML tag of character formatting. A block $Bhl = n_j$ is a sub-tree of DT called `highlighted block`, such that $Bhl \subset Bsg$ and Bhl is represented by a node that contains an element of character formatting.

Highlighted blocks are special blocks of a categorized DOM tree and are contained in a segmented block, representing HTML elements of character formatting. These elements format or highlight certain pieces of text, for example, they can underline text, mark bold or italic, and change the font size. A highlighted block is always contained in a segmented block and does not delimit regions considered text segment, it only highlights parts of continuous regions of text. It is not considered in the irrelevant content removal step, being preserved if its closest ascendant segmented block is also preserved. The highlighted blocks are important during the ranking step since they determine how close the text of the document content is to the query terms. They may be represented, for example, by the tags {`strong, b, i, u, span, a, h1, h2, h3, h4, h5, h6`}.

Definition 4: `(Disposal Block)`: Let n_j be any node in DT that can contain an empty, invisible or hidden element. A block $Bdp = n_j$ is a sub-tree of DT, called `disposal block`, such that $Bdp \subset DT$ and Bdp is an empty (it does not contain text nor sub-trees) or invisible or hidden element.

Disposal blocks are automatically deleted since they represent the irrelevant content of the page and do not have visible text content. The entire sub-tree of a disposal block is deleted automatically when: `(i)` the node represents an empty element, i.e., it has no text itself; `(ii)` the node is a hidden or invisible element, not appearing in the presentation of the HTML page; containing, for example, attributes like `"style" = "display: none"`, (`"visibility" = "hidden"` and `"visibility" = "collapse"`.

2) Filtered tree generation: In the categorized DOM tree, the main node is the main segmented block, which may be composed of many others segmented blocks. The segmented blocks having user query terms compose the filtered DOM tree.

Definition 5: `(Filtered DOM tree)`: Let DT be a categorized DOM tree, $C = \{t_1, ..., t_i\}$ a user query, $BDP = \{Bdp_1, ..., Bdp_m\}$ the set of all disposal blocks of DT, and $BSG_\phi = \{Bsg_1, ..., Bsg_n\}$ the set of segmented block of DT such that $BSG_\phi \not\subset C$. A filtered DOM tree Af is a tree such that $Af = DT - BSG_\phi - BDP$.

A filtered DOM tree consists only of segmented blocks that contain the user query terms, without the disposal blocks. The segmented blocks that do not have any of the query terms are discarded. In nested segmented blocks, the children blocks that do not have any query terms are excluded, preserving the ascendant segmented blocks if it, or at least one child segmented block, has at least one query term.

D. The ranking function

Before to introduce the ranking function, it is important to define the terms correlation function. For classic information retrieval models, the terms in a document are assumed to be mutually independent, which means a given term t_i tells us nothing about t_{i+1}. However, the terms occurrences are not uncorrelated. For example, the terms `'information'` and `'retrieval'` tend to appear together in a document about information retrieval systems [27]. In that document, the appearance of one of these terms attracts the appearance of the other. Thus, they are correlated and we must reflect this correlation. In this paper, this correlation is measured by means of the distance between terms, according to Definition 6 and Equation 1.

Definition 6: `(Correlation Function)`: Let $C = \{t_1, ..., t_n\}$ be a query and DT a categorized DOM tree. The correlation between terms in C and terms in DT is measured by the following function:

$$D(C, DT) = \begin{cases} 1, & \text{if } d(t_i, t_j) < th \\ \alpha, & \text{otherwise} \end{cases} \quad (1)$$

where th is the threshold that indicates a minimum distance between terms, inside the categorized DOM tree, and α is a value in the interval [0..1] used to penalize a given page when the distance between terms is bigger than th. The distance function $d(t_i, t_j)$ assigns a character distance value to each pair of term t_i and t_j (this distance can be calculated by any character distance function [28]).

In order to be in a top position in the ranking, the DOM tree has to have a minimum content related to the query, which can be in the text flow or in the links (typical case of e-commerce pages). This intuition is computed as defined in Equation 2.

Definition 7: `(Page-relevance Function)`: Let $C = \{t_1, ..., t_n\}$ be a query, DT a categorized DOM tree, $f_tt(DT)$ a function that returns the total number of terms in DT and $L = \{l_1, ..., l_k\}$ the set of k links in DT that have all terms of C. The Page-relevance is given by the following function:

$$CP(C, DT) = \begin{cases} 1 & \text{if } f_{tt}(DT) > x \vee k > y \\ \beta & \text{otherwise} \end{cases} \quad (2)$$

where x indicates the minimum amount of terms a page must have, y represents the minimum amount of links with all query terms the page must have and β is a value in the interval [0...1] used to penalize the page position.

The ranking function is defined taking into account the relevance criteria described in Section III-A, considering the importance of certain parts of the document (title, tables, highlights, for example), and the number of occurrences of query terms in certain parts of the document.

Definition 8: `(Ranking function)`: Let $C = \{t_1, ..., t_n\}$ be a query, DT a categorized DOM tree and $L = \{l_1, ..., l_k\}$ the set of k links in DT that have all terms of C. The ranking function $R(C, DT)$, which returns a score between C and DT, is:

$$\begin{aligned} R(C, DT) = {} & D(C, DT).CP(C, DT).(W_1.\sum_{i=1}^{n}(f_o(t_i, DT))) + \\ & (W_2.\sum_{i=1}^{n}(f_{hb}(t_i, DT))) + (W_3.k) + \\ & (W_4.\sum_{i=1}^{n}(f_{tm}(t_i, DT))) + (W_5.f_t(DT)) \end{aligned} \quad (3)$$

where
$D(C, DT)$ is the correlation function;
$CP(C, DT)$ is the page-relevance function;
$f_o(t_i, DT)$ is a function that returns the number of occurrences of a term t_i in DT;
$f_{hb}(t_i, DT)$ is a function that returns the number of occurrences of the term t_i in highlighted blocks of DT;
$f_{tm}(t_i, DT)$ is a function that returns the number of occurrences of a term t_i in the main title or in metadata of DT;
$f_t(DT)$ is a function that returns the total terms of DT;
W_i: the weight of each criterion.

The intention behind the ranking function $R(C, DT)$ is to calculate the proximity of a categorized DOM tree A with terms in C, using the relevance criteria presented in Section III-A, given a weight to each one. Furthermore, those pages, in which the distance between query terms are bigger than a threshold, or that do not have a minimum content related to the query, are penalized, respectively by means of the functions $D(C, DT)$ and $CP(C, DT)$.

font=footnotesize,sc,justification=centering,labelsep=period

TABLE II. RECALL X QUERY-BASED BLOCKS MINING AND CETR PRECISION.

Page	Total of Terms	tRel-A	t-Af		tRel-Afilt		Recall		Precision		F-Value	
			QBM	CETR	QBM	CETR	QBM	CETR	QBM	CETR	QBM	CETR
1	2223	1964	1759	1631	1759	1538	0.896	0.783	1.000	0.943	0.948	0.856
2	618	163	464	442	160	145	0.982	0.890	0.345	0.328	0.510	0.479
3	1078	738	811	28	733	0	0.993	0	0.904	0	0.946	0
4	5879	5108	3339	1912	3291	1841	0.644	0.360	0.986	0.963	0.815	0.525
5	2816	1855	1826	1836	1793	1821	0.967	0.982	0.982	0.992	0.975	0.987
6	623	328	328	322	328	322	1.000	0.982	1.000	1.000	1.000	0.991
7	1207	389	288	703	288	348	0.740	0.895	1.000	0.495	0.87	0.637
8	1311	0	868	1023	0	0	0	0	0	0	0	0
9	703	348	314	374	293	328	0.842	0.943	0.933	0.877	0.885	0.909
10	1722	1308	1271	1229	1270	1189	0.971	0.909	0.999	0.967	0.985	0.937
-	-	-	-	-	Average		0.803	0.674	0.815	0.657	0.787	0.632

IV. EXPERIMENTAL EVALUATION

In this section, we describe the experiments we performed to demonstrate the effectiveness of our proposal. The experiments have the following main goals: (i) to analyse the query-based blocks mining, aiming at evaluating its effectiveness in segmenting an HTML page and removing irrelevant content from the page; (ii) to perform a comparative analysis among different combination of removal algorithm and ranking algorithm; and (iii) analyse the FPR process itself.

A. Methodology and Evaluation Metrics

The total set of documents used in the experiments consists of 1,530 Web pages, collected from different news and entertainment websites. The queries were associated with five different domains: history, law, diseases, electronics and politicians. The different domains have been chosen in order to identify if any of them would behave differently from others. As our ranking function uses different weights, we have set them as follow. The number of occurrences of a term t_i in A: $W_1 = 9.98$; the number of occurrences of the term t_i in highlighted blocks of A: $W_2 = 15$; the number of links in A that have all terms of C: $W_3 = 15$; the number of occurrences of a term t_i in the main title or in metadata of A: $W_4 = 60$; the total terms of A: $W_5 = 0.02$. The values used to penalize the page position: $\alpha = 0.08$, $\beta = 0.1$.

The weights were manually calibrated based on observations of the database metadata. For the manual calibration, the weights were given initial values and adjusted for more or for less to best suit the improvement of the precision and recall of FPR ranking under original web pages (without filter). It is common to find Web pages with more than 10,000 or 20,000 words. Therefore, an apparently unimpressive weight of 0.02 found for the number of words becomes as significant as the other criteria used in the final ranking process.
Web pages that satisfy 30 queries in these 5 different areas were collected from google and classified by 5 different users to determine their relevance. Each page were scored from 1 to 4 in the following scale: insignificant (1), low significance (2), significant (3) and very significant (4). The pages with an average score higher than or equal to 3 were classified as being 'relevant' and the pages with an average score lower than 3 were classified as being 'irrelevant'. For each query the number of irrelevant pages is greater than or equal to the number of relevant pages and there are at least 10 relevant pages for each query.

Lucene was used as the baseline, because it is widely used in tools for local search with implementation (VSM) available and it is based on the performed query like FPR. It does not have the limitations as requiring recognition of users (ClickThrough Data), the use of A.I (PCR, ClickThrough Data) and the needs that many pages share the same template (Computing Block Importance for Searching on Web Sites). Block-Based Web Search have improvements compared to FixedPS and uses Web Pages. In section V it is mentioned that comparisons can be made between FPR/QBM and Block-Based Web Search, with the improvement of collecting the text content from tag <body> instead of <title> on method Block-Based Web Search.
As the baseline irrelevant content removal algorithm, we choose the CETR algorithm. The tests have been conducted with the following configurations: (i) Lucene: ranking algorithm of the classic vector model; (ii) FPR: our proposed ranking algorithm; (iii) FPR + CETR: our proposed ranking algorithm, on the basis of filtered documents through CETR algorithm; and (iv) FPR + QBM: our proposed ranking algorithm, on the basis of filtered documents through our irrelevant content removal algorithm.

The metrics we have used for evaluation were that from classical information retrieval community [27]: recall, precision and F-measure. As usual, the recall value was obtained by the ratio of relevant documents by each query, which in fact were recovered. The precision was calculated by the proportion of recovered material that were relevant, and F-measure is the harmonic mean of recall and precision.

font=footnotesize,sc,justification=centering,labelsep=period

TABLE III. PRECISION.

Ranking	P@10	P@15	P@20	P@10	P@15	P@20
	History			Law		
FPR+QBM	0.76	0.64	0.53	0.78	0.62	0.49
FPR(-)	0.78	0.60	0.49	0.73	0.55	0.40
FPR+CETR	0.64	0.53	0.45	0.70	0.617	0.51
Lucene	0.46	0.45	0.44	0.55	0.55	0.51
	Diseases			Electronics		
FPR+QBM	0.85	0.77	0.66	0.83	0.76	0.70
FPR(-)	0.82	0.72	0.59	0.70	0.67	0.59
FPR+CETR	0.78	0.67	0.58	0.73	0.62	0.53
Lucene	0.70	0.63	0.61	0.60	0.58	0.55
	Politicians			All		
FPR+QBM	0.87	0.69	0.53	0.81	0.69	0.58
FPR(-)	0.80	0.64	0.53	0.77	0.63	0.52
FPR+CETR	0.77	0.64	0.50	0.72	0.61	0.51
Lucene	0.83	0.644	0.54	0.61	0.56	0.53

B. Results

We now describe the experiments used to evaluate our proposed algorithms. We first present the QBM effectiveness in eliminating irrelevant content, and then provide a comprehensive evaluation of the ranking proposal.

1) Analysis of QBM: The QBM algorithm was analyzed in order to evaluate its effectiveness in removing irrelevant content from HTML pages, comparing it with a baseline, the CERT algorithm [16]. For this purpose, the following evaluation parameters were considered: (i) `tRel-Af`: total of relevant terms of the filtered DOM; (ii) `t-Af`: total of terms of the filtered DOM; (iii) `tRel-DT`: total of relevant terms of the original DOM. Using these parameters, it was possible to assess the precision and the recall as follows: $recall = (tRel-Af)/(tRel-DT)$; $precision = (tRel-Af)/(t-Af)$.

In general, the QBM results reached 80% to 85% of precision, being able to eliminate almost all the irrelevant content of the pages in many cases. As we can observe in Table II, our proposal has surpassed the baseline. The page listed as number 8 had 0% of precision and recall. This happens due to the fact that QBM and CETR does not consider semantic. For example, in a query "ceara history", in which the user's interest is related to the Ceara State history, the query can match it with a page of the history of Ceara Sporting Club. The same happens with the page indicated by number 2, which does not match the query "public service definition" with a relevant page because it brings a page about the definition of "public servant", in which, within the same segmented block, there is a text about "public service definition", i.e., only a small part of the document relates directly to the subject "public service definition". In page 3, CETR extracts the document main region, but having only irrelevant nodes to the query.

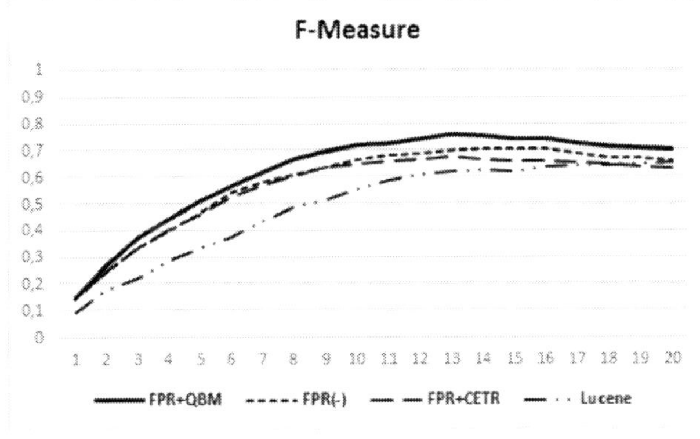

Figure 1. Results with f-measure.

2) Comparative Analysis: The results obtained in the comparative analysis were performed in two ways: (i) each domain result was individually analyzed in order to identify if any of them would behave differently from the general rule; and (ii) the overall results was analyzed, considering average values over the entire set of documents (1.530 documents), independent of domain, in order to obtain a general idea of its behavior.

In Table III, we present the precision results from experiments on three different rankings: P@10, P@15 and P@20. Analyzing the table, we can see that in the first 10 positions the combination of our two proposals, FPR+QBM, has the best ranking. This shows that our FPR ranking algorithm works well when used together with a good irrelevant content removal algorithm.

The results of the F-Measure values evaluation in the first 20 positions are shown in Figure 1. Figure 2 shows the curves of recall/precision values. Considering that FPR+QBM has, in the first twenty positions, average values of Precision and F-Measure better than Lucene, FPR+CETR and FPR (without filter), the effectiveness of our proposal is reached.

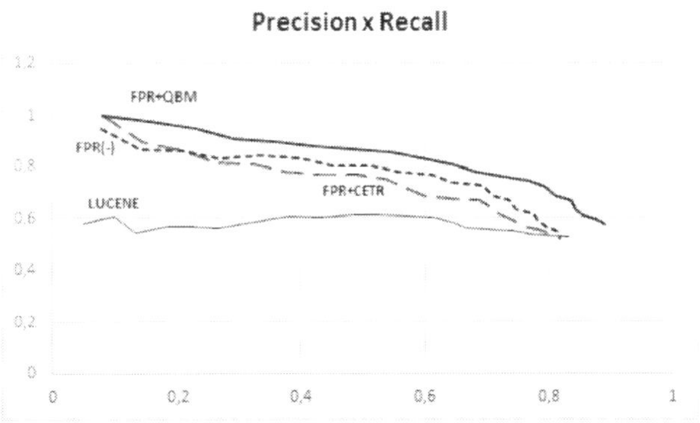

Figure 2. Precision x recall curve.

Analyzing the results, it is clear that the average recall, precision and F-measure on the first 10 positions are higher with the application of the proposed method than with the use of Lucene, which uses the vector model to define how close a document is to the query.

V. CONCLUSIONS AND FUTURE WORK

This paper presented a filtered-page ranking process based on the user query terms, relevance criteria involving the importance of certain parts of the document and highlighted aspects of certain components. The process involves segmentation of HTML pages and irrelevant content removal. The documents are segmented into blocks and those considered as irrelevant are deleted. Our proposed ranking method called Filtered-Page Ranking (FPR) works with prior elimination of irrelevant content, which is a satisfactory process when compared to some literature methods, and that can be used to define the relevant HTML pages in relation to a given query. As future work, we intend to find an optimum weight method of the important criteria for defining the ranking, and provide new relevant criteria for defining ranking and compare FPR/QBM with anothers methods specific of Web Pages like Block-Based Web Search (with the improvement of collecting the text content from tag `body` instead of tag `title`).

This paper presents a filtered-page ranking process based on the user query terms, relevance criteria involving the importance of certain parts of the document and highlighted aspects of certain components. The process involves segmentation of HTML pages and removal irrelevant content. The documents are segmented into blocks and those considered as irrelevant are deleted. Our proposed ranking method called Filtered-Page Ranking (FPR) works with prior elimination of irrelevant content, which is a satisfactory process when compared to some literature methods, and that can be used to define the relevant HTML pages in relation to a given query. As future work, we intend to find an optimum weight method of the important criteria for defining the ranking, and provide new relevant criteria for defining ranking and compare with other methods specific of Webpages like Block-Based Web Search (with the improvement of collecting the text content from tag body instead of tag title).

References

[1] A. N. Langville and C. D. Meye, Google's PageRank and Beyond: The Science of Search Engine Rankings. Princeton Ed., 2011.

[2] S. Brin and L. Page, "Reprint of: The anatomy of a large-scale hypertextual web search engine." Computer Networks, vol. 56, no. 18, 2012, pp. 3825–3833.

[3] A.-J. Su, Y. C. Hu, A. Kuzmanovic, and C.-K. Koh, "How to improve your search engine ranking: Myths and reality," ACM Trans. Web, vol. 8, no. 2, Mar. 2014, pp. 8:1–8:25.

[4] A. Karatzoglou, L. Baltrunas, and Y. Shi, "Learning to rank for recommender systems," in Proc. 7th ACM RecSys, 2013, pp. 493–494.

[5] L. Lerche and D. Jannach, "Using graded implicit feedback for bayesian personalized ranking," in Proc. 8th ACM RecSys, 2014, pp. 353–356.

[6] Y. Song, L. Zhang, and C. L. Giles, "Automatic tag recommendation algorithms for social recommender systems," ACM Trans. Web, vol. 5, no. 1, Feb. 2011, pp. 4:1–4:31.

[7] K. Balog and H. Ramampiaro, "Cumulative citation recommendation: Classification vs. ranking," in Proc. 36th ACM SIGIR, 2013, pp. 941–944.

[8] G. Berardi, A. Esuli, and F. Sebastiani, "Utility-theoretic ranking for semiautomated text classification," ACM Trans. Knowl. Discov. Data, vol. 10, no. 1, Jul. 2015, pp. 6:1–6:32.

[9] J. Fang, L. Guo, X. Wang, and N. Yang, "Ontology-based automatic classification and ranking for web documents," in Proc. 4th IEEE FSKD. IEEE Computer Society, 2007, pp. 627–631.

[10] J. Li, B. Saha, and A. Deshpande, "A unified approach to ranking in probabilistic databases," The VLDB Journal, vol. 20, no. 2, Apr. 2011, pp. 249–275.

[11] Y. Chen, X. Li, A. Dick, and R. Hill, "Ranking consistency for image matching and object retrieval," Pattern Recogn., vol. 47, no. 3, Mar. 2014, pp. 1349–1360.

[12] H. Zhu, H. Xiong, Y. Ge, and E. Chen, "Ranking fraud detection for mobile apps: A holistic view," in Proc. 22nd ACM CIKM, 2013, pp. 619–628.

[13] M. P. Selvan, A. C. Sekar, and A. P. Dharshini, "Survey on web page ranking algorithms," International Journal of Computer Applications, vol. 41, no. 19, 2012, pp. 1–7.

[14] G. Salton and C. Buckley, "Term-weighting approaches in automatic text retrieval," Inf. Process. Manage., vol. 24, no. 5, Aug. 1988, pp. 513–523.

[15] "Lucene," https://lucene.apache.org/core, accessed: 2016-04-12.

[16] T. Weninger, W. H. Hsu, and J. Han, "Cetr: content extraction via tag ratios," in Proc. 19th WWW. ACM, 2010, pp. 971–980.

[17] "The pagerank citation ranking: bringing order to the web," http://ilpubs.stanford.edu:8090/422/1/1999-66.pdf, accessed: 2016-04-11.

[18] J. M. Kleinberg, "Authoritative sources in a hyperlinked environment," Journal of the ACM (JACM), vol. 46, no. 5, 1999, pp. 604–632.

[19] N. Duhan, A. Sharma, and K. K. Bhatia, "Page ranking algorithms: a survey," in IEEE IACC, 2009, pp. 1530–1537.

[20] T. Joachims, "Optimizing search engines using clickthrough data," in Proc. 8th ACM SIGKDD, 2002, pp. 133–142.

[21] J. Pokorny and J. Smizansky, "Page content rank: an approach to the web content mining," in Proc. IADIS Conf. On Applied Computing, vol. 1, 2005, pp. 289–296.

[22] E. Hatcher, O. Gospodnetic, and M. McCandless, Lucene in action. Manning Publications Greenwich, CT, 2004.

[23] J. P. Callan, "Passage-level evidence in document retrieval," in Proc. of the 17th ACM SIGIR conference on Research and development in information retrieval, 1994, pp. 302–310.

[24] D. Cai, S. Yu, J.-R. Wen, and W.-Y. Ma, "Block-based web search," in Proc. 27th ACM SIGIR, 2004, pp. 456–463. [Online]. Available: http://doi.acm.org/10.1145/1008992.1009070

[25] D. Fernandes, E. S. de Moura, B. Ribeiro-Neto, A. S. da Silva, and M. A. Gonçalves, "Computing block importance for searching on web sites," in Proc. 16th ACM CIKM, 2007, pp. 165–174.

[26] G. Borges, G.; Lima, "Automatic indexing of text documents: Essential criteria proposal," Journal of Information Research, vol. 3, no. 1, 2014, pp. 360–370.

[27] R. A. Baeza-Yates and B. A. Ribeiro-Neto, Modern Information Retrieval. ACM Press / Addison-Wesley, 1999.

[28] "Simetrics," http://sourceforge.net/projects/simmetrics/, accessed: 2016-04-11.

Development of a Quality Metrics Definition, Evaluation and Quantification Framework for EUD Web Components

David Lizcano
School of Computer Science
UDIMA
Madrid, Spain
david.lizcano@udima.es

Andrés Leonardo Martínez
Google Software Department
Madrid, Spain
aleonar@gmail.com

Sandra Gómez, Ana Isabel Lopera, Miguel Ortega, Luis Ruiz, Juan Francisco Salamanca, Genoveva López
Conwet Lab
UPM
Madrid, Spain
{sgomez, alopera, mortega, lruiz, jfsalamanca, glopez}@conwet.com

Abstract—**Web components technology improves Internet applications development. Although still at the experimental stage, there is a growing interest in its quality metrics. We aim to define a reference and evaluation framework for measuring the quality of web components and mashups. This paper presents the pilot phase of a real experimentation environment for comparing reference metrics built from existing software quality metrics with curated metrics based on user-perceived quality. The preliminary results of the evaluation of the alpha version conducted by the developers who participated in platform design and development speak for the suitability of the selected approach.**

Keywords-quality metrics; web components; end-user programming.

I. Introduction

Web components are programmable HTML tags built using a compendium of open technologies. Web components are elements independent of external libraries that are built into web browsers and are able to encapsulate HTML, JavaScript and CSS in reusable functional modules. They improve web development componentization, improving quality and productivity. Although still at the experimental stage, they are being implemented using technologies like Polymer or Bosonic. Alongside technology development, there is a growing interest in quality metrics. This is not currently a hot topic, however, as highlighted by the articles related to web components [1].

We aim to define a reference and evaluation framework for measuring the quality of web components and mashups composed by interconnecting several components. This paper presents the pilot phase of a real experimentation environment for comparing reference metrics built from existing software quality metrics with mature metrics based on user-perceived quality.

The absence of a universally accepted formal framework that can be applied to determine the quality of web components has led to the adaptation of traditional standards. However, some trial standards have been launched. For example, there is the Gold Standard Checklist [2], which is modeled on the W3C checklist for Web Content Accessibility Guidelines (WCAG) [3], or the idea of establishing quality control as the main point for quality in web components [4]. Neither standard provided a sound groundwork for our approach. Therefore, we decided to devise a new framework.

This approach has resulted in the definition of a set of metrics for assessing quality based on real user experiences. For this purpose, we developed an online platform which provides a social network hub. This platform displays different versions of components for experimental groups composed of real users and gauges perceived quality for comparison against the traditional models.

The user platform operates like a testbench where end users interact with the web components under evaluation in order to gather the key events associated with the use of these elements. This provides a black-box view of the component, and the analysis focuses on the functions evaluated by an end user when he or she uses the user platform.

The main functions implemented in the experimentation platform enable users to log in with OpenID, define groups, aggregate information from different social networks and follow the posts by other members as a group. The components considered in this study consume data from several social networks, including Twitter, Facebook and LinkedIn.

From the conducted evaluation (of the illustrated in Figure 1 and Figure 2 or similar components), we found that most users had problems moving components. On this ground, this is one of the aspects to be improved.

Section 2 describes the state of the art of web components. Section 3 includes the technical details for developing the evaluation platform. Section 4 explains how the metrics elicited from users will be validated. Section 5 reports the preliminary evaluation of the platform, followed by the conclusions of the paper.

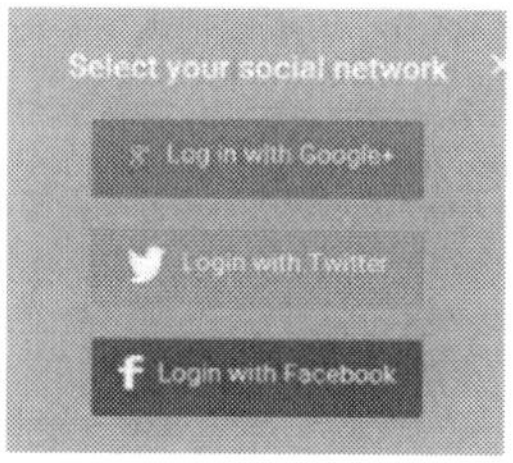

Figure 1. List of login components

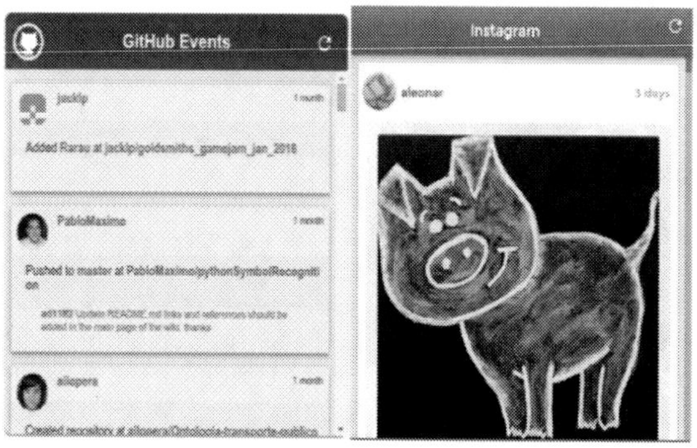

Figure 2. Examples of timeline components (Github and Instagram).

II. THEORETICAL FRAMEWORK

Web components refer to technologies for creating new HTML tags or components using conventional web development languages (HTML, Javascript and CSS) [5]. These new elements are easy to reuse and can embed all the component implementation details, which renders them transparent to the document in which they are used. Web components are a way of modularizing web elements, creating more complex tags to extend the tools available for building web applications or mashups.

There are four key enabling technologies, based on new standards defined by W3C [6]:

- Shadow DOM: enables the definition of a new subtree of document object model (DOM) elements separate from document rendering.
- Template: enables inert elements, which can be later activated, to be inserted into the document.
- Custom elements: establishes how the user can create new tags and new interfaces.
- HTML imports: defines how to insert templates and custom elements into the document.

There are no codes of good practice or standards related to web component development. As a result, end users may have to deal with a very large unstructured catalogue of components, including many elements designed to serve the same purpose. In other cases, there may be components that constitute a potential source of security vulnerabilities or data loss. This is a problem for end users because they do not know a priori how to tell which component is the best for the job that they are doing and are unable to detect vulnerabilities. On this ground, there is a need for a system capable of establishing and quantifying the quality of a component.

Formal metrics are used to establish software quality. These metrics define which aspects measure the quality perceived by the users that consume the software. There are several rules defining software quality, which, however, all have two clearly distinct concepts in common: software structure quality and software functionality quality. Functional quality stresses software conformance with a design based on defined software specifications. On the other hand, structural quality addresses the analysis of the internal structure and non-functional requirements of the software, such as security and maintainability.

There are several quality assessment models. Most are based on the ISO 9126 quality standard. For many years, this was the international software quality assessment standard. ISO 9126 defines software quality as the combination of a number of characteristics that represent attributes whose quality can be measured and evaluated. Some of these attributes are functional adequacy (satisfaction of stated or implied needs), performance efficiency (level of performance of the software and the amount of resources used under stated conditions), compatibility (capability of two or more components to perform their functions when they share the same hardware or software environment), usability (component understandability, learnability, ease of use and attractiveness for users), reliability (capability of software to maintain its level of performance under stated conditions for a stated period of time), security (capability of data protection so that unauthorized people or systems cannot read or modify data), maintainability (capability of the component to be effectively and efficiently modified) and portability (capability of a component to be effectively and efficiently transferred from one hardware, software, operating or application environment to another) [7]. This standard has been replaced by ISO 25010 [8], including a reworked software product quality model.

This new ISO standard covers two more aspects than its predecessor: security and compatibility. Additionally, some subcharacteristics have been renamed or added. The ultimate aim of ISO 25010 is to highlight the importance of software quality of use for users.

Although these formal models describe software quality, they do not cover all the facets of web component quality, as they neglect the user. The usability quality attribute does indicate that user needs to understand the component, but makes no mention of the fact that the target user's opinion is equally important, because component quality depends on whether or not it is used. There are not many web component and mashup quality model proposals that focus on web usability research. These models attribute the quality of the mashups and their respective components to their functional characteristics and their usability, such as service quality [9]. Although other models define metrics for establishing quality like SOA-based quality assessment [10], they address code aspects or in-development assessments, but do not take into account the user. There is also a mashup-specific model [11]. In no case, however, do they take into account external component attributes such as the availability of documentation about operation, social impact or data quality.

On this ground, the ConWet Laboratory DEUS work group, based at the School of Computer Engineering, Technical University of Madrid, has set up a portal in which the users can interact freely with social network web components. We have created different component versions, each with different characteristics. Users will interact with these versions at random to assess and rate the quality of the components. We will also collect user interaction data in order to discover how users interact with components and thus adapt the components to their way of thinking.

However, the focus of the approach is not entirely new, as there have been solutions that have focused on user-driven component interconnection. Two such approaches are Yahoo! Pipes [12] and Wirecloud [13]. Yahoo! Pipes is a solution for filtering the content of one or more queries in order to translate their content or answer the question. The deployed interface is rather complex for end users (which are the target audience of this platform). On this ground, we believe that ours is a better approach. On the other hand, WireCloud resembles our approach more closely, insofar as this solution also operates on individual elements that can be connected with each other. It has an easier to use interface than the Yahoo! Pipes. Even so, it has several buttons that do not clearly specify the functionality that they represent. However, element interconnection is highly automatic, as this platform does not work with web components like the ones used in this solution.

Additionally, there were other solutions aimed at creating web pages by interconnecting components (no web pages were created in the above examples). These solutions were based on end-user web site development. Some of these solutions were: Marmite [14], QED Wiki [15], PopFly [16] and JackBe Presto [17]. Marmite is a tool operating on the Firefox browser enabling users to gather information by searching the Internet. To do this, users had several operators (sources, filters, processors and sink) that they could use to gather the above information. On the other hand, QED Wiki is a mashup builder developed by IBM that was based on the Wiki concept. This solution simplified much of the technology side, like editing, commenting or publishing. Apart from web pages, users were able to quickly develop prototypes using this tool. On the other hand, PopFly was a solution developed by Microsoft whose main goal was to enable users to create their own web portal by adding content (like images or text), as well as adding a title and page profile. Content could be added to other spaces, like Facebook, or blogs, like WordPress. Finally, the Jackbe Presto tool provides users with a choice of filters and connections in order to visualize the collected data and build custom applications. Note that some of these solutions are no longer in use, as only the tools that achieve some level of maturity have managed to survive and remain active.

III. Development

In this section, we explain the underlying architecture of the platform, detailing the technologies used on each side (client and server) and the implementation of the formal metrics considered in the early phase of the development.

A. User *environment architecture*

The user environment is organized as a client-server architecture, with separate technologies for each side. The languages used on the client side, which is divided into different modules, are JavaScript, HTML and CSS, accompanied by technologies like AngularJS or Polymer. Polymer is used exclusively to create web components, whereas AngularJS is used, among other things, to integrate the components into the portal.

As shown in Figure 3, the client and server side are split into different modules. The client side is divided into four modules, each of which pursues different goals to the others. The first is the client interface, which takes care of defining what users see and how they interact with the portal. The second is responsible for connecting with the server side in order to send and receive data, which also offers components depending on the data that it receives. The third module is responsible for interconnecting components that are part of a user profile. Using this module we can take measurements illustrating how a user interacts with the components. Finally, the fourth module collects the measurements gathered from user interaction with the dashboard.

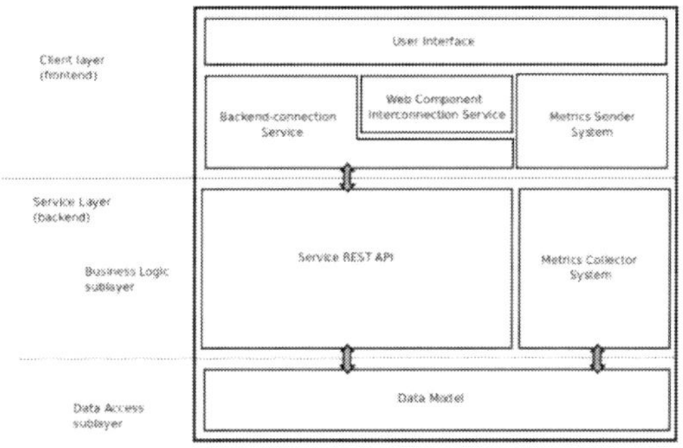

Figure 3. User environment architecture (Picbit)

The server side, on the other hand, is divided into two layers. One layer addresses the application logic and the other is responsible for data persistence and storage. The first layer is divided into two modules, one of which defines a REST API to enable the client to access defined resources of different types, including user type, component or credential. We have defined a different API (application programming interface) for each resource, and another to support auxiliary operations. The other module is responsible for processing the metrics of the different components: it fetches the events generated on the client side, calculates the metric values and assigns the respective value to each component.

On the other hand, the data sublayer is composed of a single module that takes care of the persistence of the generated data. To do this, we used the NDB (non-relational database) Python API to define the entities required to store this information. We opted for a non-relational model, defining different entities to store information related to the data managed by the application.

We chose a non-relational model in preference to a relational model because of the way in which the data were to be generated. Relational models are perfectly well-suited to applications storing ordered data. For example, this model is ideal for projects where user data are to be stored. However, a non-relational model which is better at processing continuous query reception and should be used if the information is generated more continuously and it is not so important whether or not the information is ordered. Although we need to store user information in this case too, the priority is to store all the information received as a result of user interaction with the portal. Therefore we opted for a non-relational model.

B. Technology selected for the *user environment*

Figure 4 and Figure 5 show the distribution of these technologies on the client and server sides, respectively. Although some of these technologies are used to connect modules, they are not illustrated below as we are concerned with the module technologies.

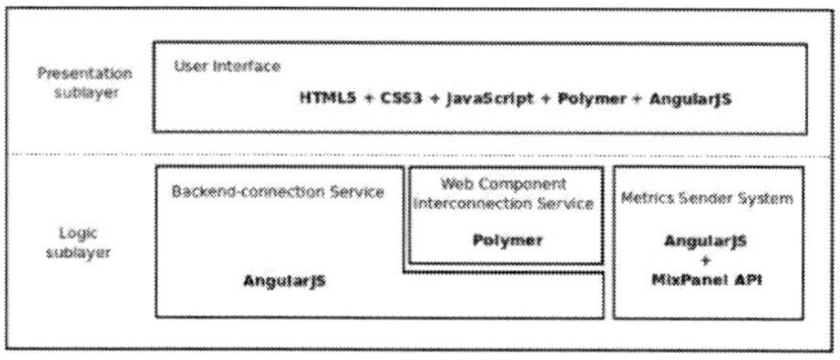

Figure 4. Client-side technology diagram

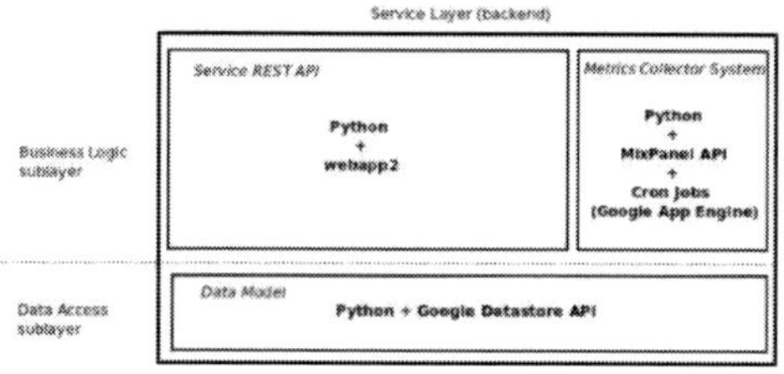

Figure 5. Server-side technology diagram

There are now a wide range of technologies available for creating a user interaction portal. On this ground, we had to select the ones best suited to the target objectives. The selected technologies are detailed in the following.

1) Polymer

Web component development framework promoted by Google which implements W3C-defined standards. This technology is used as a library capable of managing the implementation, reuse and injection of web components. Web components are inserted into a new HTML document as if they were a new tag that is defined in the respective language.

Polymer is capable of implementing simple components, like a button, and even creating elements that may constitute a proper application.

2) Angular JS

Framework implementing the model-view-controller pattern (MVC), which is capable of creating dynamic web applications, aimed at increasing the availability of frontend development tools, and simplifies and eliminates the web application code. In our case, it is used to integrate different web components into the portal.

3) App Engine

The Google App Engine is used as the platform as a service (PaaS) to deploy the portal, exploiting its manageability and maintenance features. Some specialized services built into the platform, like NDB for information management and storage and Memcache for temporary data storage in cache memory, are also used. NDB is just a storage service offering an API for operating on the Google App Engine Datastore, whereas Memcache is a service that operates like a cache memory for storing some data that need to be saved during the user session.

4) Mixpanel

MixPanel satisfies the need for a service capable of monitoring user-portal interaction behaviour and collecting component interaction data. MixPanel stores these data for later retrieval using an API.

The collected data are used to see if changes to the latency, completeness and usability metrics affect user-perceived component quality. To do this, different sentences (mixpanel.track (name_event, [properties_event])) [18] are included on the client side that sends the data to the service (the module has to be have been loaded as specified in the reference).

5) Bower

The user platform is responsible for managing which dashboard version is served to the user. The Bower framework is used to manage the dependencies of a particular dashboard. The components belonging to a dashboard version are contained in a specified bower file, loaded from the client side. The platform server side is responsible for specifying the components that are part of the dashboard for the client side.

C. Determination of end user-based metrics

User-application interaction data are useful for calculating quality metrics for the components that they are using. The first thing to do in order to assess component quality is to look at which metrics are best suited for the stated goals and which user actions the platform will offer.

Firstly, we decided to use a small number of metrics to get a rough idea of the quality of the components. These metrics are calculated internally by the component and do not require user interaction.

We had to decide which of the set of metrics studied for the SOA architecture and mashup to include in the first version of platform. Due to the complexity of the metrics presented in Section VII, we decided to look for metrics that were easier to define, leaving the adoption of the metrics specified in the related work section for a more advanced stage.

The metrics considered under these circumstances are as follows:

- **Completeness**: aims to measure the accuracy of the output component data. It takes into account a set number of messages, gathered first from the social network server and then from the component, and checks that the messages received from both sources are equal.

$$GeneratedOutputData \div SearchedOutputData$$

The metric value is generated by assigning values to the different accuracy levels shared by both sources. Assignment is nonlinear, that is, 70% completeness is not equivalent to a metric value of 7, that is, a reasonable weighting system has to be defined to try to understand how missing data affect component quality.

- **Latency**: is defined as the time that it takes to execute the component from the time when the query is sent to the server until the component displays the data on screen.
- **Data refresh time**: aims to determine the time that it takes the component to refresh the information when there is system data input. For example, how long does it take for a component to visualize the new information from a tweet published at a specified time? Different automatic refresh times are tested to find out which is the best accepted by the users. The refresh time is set by measuring the difference between the time at which the message is displayed by the component and the time at which the message is received by the server.
- **Usability**: evaluates user interaction aspects, covering most aspects of usage. As this is such a broad dimension, theoretical usability is first evaluated based on the checklist published and approved by W3C. The procedure is to rate the component against the checklist items to assign the first rating. This aspect will later be rated more directly through site rating. In this manner, the theoretical usability can be compared against real usability.

The assumption is that the metrics are established by comparing data output by the social network server and by our components. Accordingly, a series of conditions should be agreed with the social network provider by means of service level agreements (SLA), specifying a service between the above service provider and service users.

At this stage of the research we have analysed mature web components developed by our work group. Mature components are subject to continuous development, as feedback is received from the values recorded for the dimensions measured during the research (completeness, latency and usability).

The analysed components play the role of specific social network consumers. We developed several versions of each individual component including slight variations (as shown in Figure 6). Each version introduces a change that will have an impact on one of the dimensions to be measured in order to determine the impact of this variation on the overall quality of the component. Accordingly, there are four versions of each component:

- Stable version of the component, with high metric values.
- Version including changes to latency dimension.
- Version including changes to data completeness dimension.
- Version including changes to usability dimension.

The different versions described above are used to compose different dashboards for one and the same user and evaluate the user experience in each case. For each user, there are four different dashboard variations, and each variation includes components from a specified version.

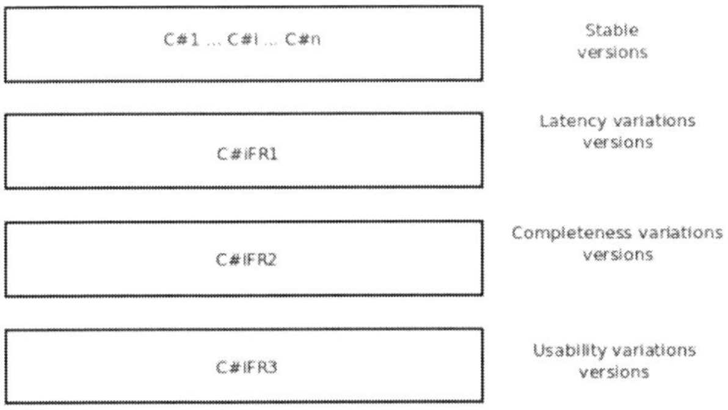

C#: Version of a given component
FR: Final Release
Figure 6. List of component versions

As a result of user interaction with the components in their dashboard, MixPanel fetches the events generated on the client side, acting as an analytical platform. Each event is associated with a particular dimension.

A distinction is made with respect to the dashboard from which this event is fetched in order to calculate the metrics for each dashboard. Each event type is included in the calculation of one of the four defined metrics, which are also divided into two different groups of metrics:

- **Inter-user metrics.** Measured on the interaction events between all the platform users.
- **Intra-user metrics.** Measured on the interaction events associated with a particular user.

IV. VALIDATION

Once the platform has been tested internally, users can start to interact with the components in order to collect data from real users. The aim of this process of validation is to find out what impression the components make on real users who are given the chance to rate these components. This will output metric values assigned by users and the internally output values will be able to be compared with the ratings based on end-user interaction with the platform.

A. *Data collection on user interaction and metric calculation*

User interaction is monitored to ascertain how users perform with the different components built into the portal.

TABLE I: CHARACTERIZATION OF USERS

Characterization	*Group 1*
Gender	
Male	15
Female	0
Age	
20-30 years	13
Over 30 years	2
Educational attainment	
Secondary School	5
Vocational Training	1
Bachelor's Degree	5
Master's Degree	4
Employment	
Student	5
Employee	2
Both	8
Experience and previous knowledge	
Python	15
JavaScript	14
HTML	12
CSS	14

Users interact with mature components. The users of the beta versions advise on which aspects of the components could be improved. New component versions will then be created that behave differently with respect to different aspects. Only one characteristic of each component will be changed, such as refresh time or an intentional data input error to alter a metric. These components are assigned a default rating greater than they warrant based on their real quality.

When users log in to the portal, they are presented with a random version of the components, and their interaction is monitored. They will then be able to rate their user experience. The user ratings should gradually correct the component quality rating until it stabilizes at a more realistic value.

During user interaction with the portal, data, such as the time spent using each component, portal tab closure or how long the user was logged in to the portal for, are sent to MixPanel. These data are later collected in order to calculate the respective metrics. The main purpose of these data is to validate user outcomes, for example, by not storing a rating by a user that has only interacted with the component for one second, as it would be unreliable.

Data is collected by means of a daily server task which fetches and stores the data from MixPanel. When these data are available, another task is launched to recalculate the metrics and update the respective values.

B. Analysing data normality (normal use conditions)

Normal data refers to data that are repeated over a long period of time. For example, the collection of training data can take up to a week. The data collected over this time are useful for establishing a baseline that we will take to be the normal behavior. By establishing this baseline of normality, we can assure that the use conditions of both the modified and standard component versions are as similar as possible. Accordingly, it is more feasible to draw conclusions about the behavior of the components from the user viewpoint.

V. EVALUATION

The first component evaluation was conducted in a very controlled environment with a very definite user profile. This profile matches users aged from 20 to 30 years with programming experience. The evaluation was held on the development work group premises. A total of 15 users were assembled for 10 minutes (the profile of the users can be viewed in Table I). They were given some brief instructions and asked to interact with the platform and components to complete a number of tasks. This test was conducted as a litmus test. However, we intend to run tests with other user profiles before releasing a stable version, as we believe that this platform has the potential to be a real solution for users and not just a mere test box.

The purpose of this study is to establish a correlation between the defined target metrics (completeness, latency, data refresh time and usability) and user opinion in order to determine the success of the metrics and measure web component quality from two perspectives. The metrics are a formalization of aspects that are considered to have an impact on component quality and have to be compared with user-perceived quality. This determines how sensitive users are to a deviation from the metric baseline values.

The experiment lasted no more than 15 minutes and was divided into several parts. During the first part, users were given a brief description of the purpose of the survey and of the platform, as well as some very basic instructions to follow. During the second part, the user performed the tasks and a team member made observations. During the third part, the users completed the survey addressing their opinion of platform use and some personal and professional data in order to put together a profile of the users that participated in the experiment. Two members of the development team were with the user at all times. One team member answered any questions that the user had about interacting with the interface and the other took notes on the actions that the user performed to complete the set tasks.

Below, in Figure 7, is a photo of the interaction process.

Figure 7. Interaction process.

After receiving instructions, the user started to interact with the platform and completed a series of tasks (log into the system using the network of choice, add two components to the work environment, move one of the added components, delete the unchanged component, log out and log in again using the network of choice). This did not take them longer than five minutes. As they performed these operations, some users made comments that were taken down by the experiment observer. These comments will be discussed later along with the results and opinions of the users that took the survey. After interaction, the users completed a survey on their user experience. This survey is available at [19]. Based on the above interaction and survey, we were able to infer a number of quantitative and qualitative findings, as well as gather the impressions that the platform made on users.

The results of the survey and the values selected during the user interaction will be analyzed by the work group in order to change the aspects that users found hardest to use. The main goal of this study is to improve the platform for alpha testing involving a larger number of people in order to prevent misunderstandings of its features. User comments after platform use are very important for this purpose.

In order to assure that user characteristics did not bias the study, we conducted an ANCOVA. The analysis showed that user characteristics had no impact on the analysed features. Thus, there is no statistical evidence of the results being biased by the users who took part in the evaluation. In any case, more studies will be executed with a higher and more heterogeneous population in order to completely rule out the possibility of the results being biased.

First, let us detail how the users expressed their opinion. We were able to gather user opinions in different ways. First we analysed the comments that the users made while interacting with the platform. These are usually comments suggesting improvements or pinpointing aspects of the platform that are not absolutely intuitive. These comments were taken down by the experiment observer. Second we analysed the opinions that the users expressed in the surveys taken after interaction with the platform. These opinions were mostly consistent with what users had mentioned as they performed the tasks. All these comments and opinions are discussed below.

The observer took note of the users' first impressions of platform use, possible improvements or any aspects that they did not find altogether intuitive. Additionally, we recorded whether or not the user performed the task. We found that actions related to user dashboard modification are the hardest for the users to complete. The dashboard-related tasks with the highest error rate on the part of the users were add and modify dashboard components with an error rate of 60% and 80%, respectively. Exceptionally, we had to help some users out, in one case to add and in two cases to modify components. The interaction of these actions needs to be redesigned in future platform versions for the purpose of improving interface usability. After observing user behaviour, our conclusion is that the best option in this case is to enable users to move components around the workspace using the drag and drop feature. The dashboard management tool also requires simplification.

The users did not have much difficulty with the system login and logout actions, and 60% used the same social network in the first and second logins that they were asked to perform in the experiment. Thus, we conclude that users understand the concept of creating a platform profile using one of their social networks.

The opinions reported by users in the surveys often matched what they had said while completing the tasks. The survey was composed of short-response and multiple-choice questions. The question statements were neutral in order to prevent response bias. Short-response questions were used to elicit user ratings of particular aspects of the user experience or check whether they remembered the steps required to complete a particular task. The multiple-choice questions ascertain the level of agreement/disagreement with different items on a scale from 1 (strongly disagree) to 5 (strongly agree). The survey results are shown in Figure 8.

The subjective ratings of users with respect to the platform and the components were positive. Of the comments received, it is noteworthy that around 53% of users positively rated the workspace simplicity in terms of interaction and design, and none of the users rejected the idea of using the platform daily.

As regards improvement suggestions, all users recommended a change in component management and suggested associating contextual menus with components or redesigning their associated gestures. They also advised increasing the salience the platform's help section in order to assist any users that have trouble performing any of the possible actions.

Generally, the components made a good impression on users. They highlighted the fact that they were well designed and covered an acceptable range of social networks. However, as the study primarily targeted platform management, further studies will be required to gather more conclusive results in this respect.

On the whole, the study revealed aspects of the interaction that would need to be redesigned and provided a preliminary picture of what users think about the concept and target functionality of the platform. Based on the ratings, we can say that the idea of linking the publications of several social networks on a single page will be grounds enough to attract users to our platform and thus be able to gather information from the designed metrics. Nevertheless, some of its features needed to be improved to make it more intuitive and easier to use.

Figure 9 and Figure 10 show snapshots of platform screens used in the testing, and some screens that were displayed to users. Generally speaking, the results of the survey shown in Figure 8 encourage us to forge ahead with platform development, taking into consideration the survey findings and increasing the platform functionality.

VI. RELATED WORK

For decision making on which aspects were to be measured for the usability metric, we searched the literature for papers on quality assessment for similar applications and

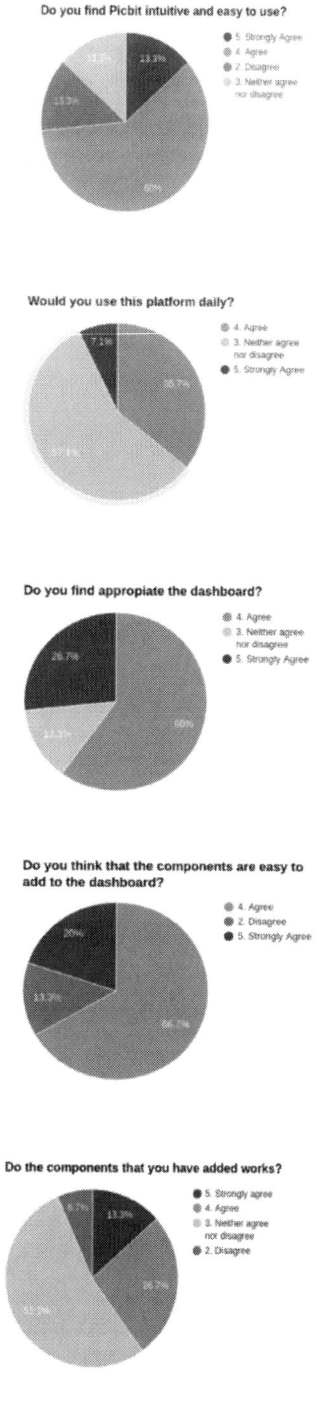

Figure 8. Results of the usability survey

specifically references related to service oriented architecture (SOA) [10] and mashups [11].

After reviewing these papers [10] [11], the only proposal that matched what we were looking for was an article that designed a quality model for a SOA application. As we were unable to extract results from these papers, we found it very hard to compare our approach with the solutions presented in the referenced papers [10] [11]. The tables below show how their authors measured the metrics for this model.

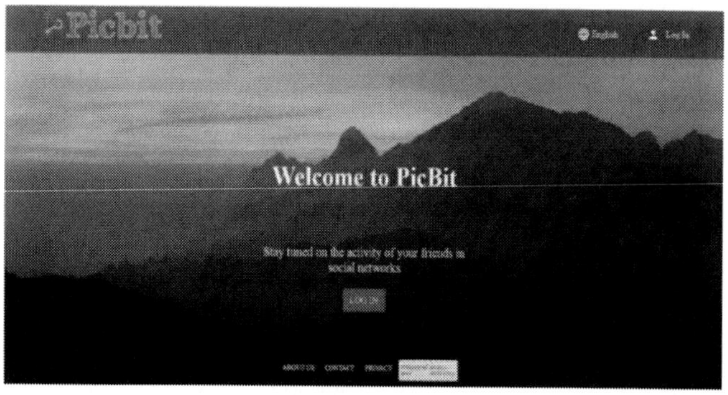

Figure 9. PicBit Landscape

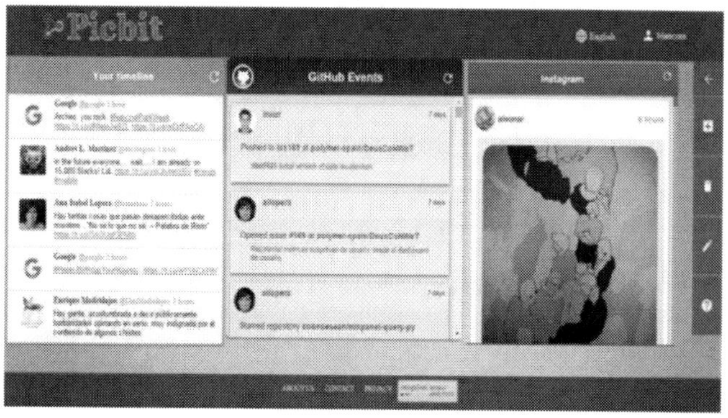

Figure 10. PicBit with some added components.

TABLE II: INTERNAL METRICS

Description	*Internal metric*
Number of Operations	SIM_NO
Number of Fine-Grained Parameter Operations	SIM_NFPO
Number of Message Used	SIM_NMU
Number of Asynchronous Operations	SIM_NAO
Number of Synchronous Operations	SIM_NSO
Number of Inadequately Named Operations	SIM_NINO

TABLE III. EXTERNAL METRICS

Description	*External metric*
Number of Consumers in Same Level	SEM_NCSL
Number of Directly Connected Producer Services	SEM_NDPS
Number of Directly Connected Consumer Services	SEM_NDCS
Total Number of Producer Services	SEM_NTPS
Total Number of Consumer Services	SEM_NTCS

TABLE IV. SYSTEM METRICS.

Description	*System metric*
System Size in Number of Services	SM_SSNS
Number of Inadequately Named Services	SM_NINS
Number of Inadequately Named Operations	SM_NINO
Total Number of Messages Used	SM_TMU
Number of Asynchronous Operations	SM_NAO
Number of Synchronous Operations	SM_NSO
Number of Fine-Grained Parameter Operations	SM_NFPO
Number of Process Services	SM_NPS
Number of Intermediary Services	SM_NIS
Number of Basic Services	SM_NBS

The tables (Table II, Table III, Table IV, Table V and Table VI) below show the proposed metrics for analyzing the quality of a service oriented architecture (SOA).

Table II shows internal service metrics, which can be defined in the service code. These metrics can be calculated by means of static code review.

Table III addresses data that depend on user execution, as well as the number of simultaneous consumers.

Table IV refers to all the data that can be gathered from the system as a whole, taking into account defined operations, interactions and services.

Table V shows how the values of the metrics defined to assess the quality of the application are calculated. They use internal, external and system metrics to determine the values for these aspects.

TABLE V. DERIVED METRICS

Derived Metric	*Description*
Average Number of Directly Connected Services (DM_ADCS)	(SEM_NDPS + SEM_NDCS) / SM_SSNS
Inverse of Average Number of Used Messages (SM_IAUM)	SM_SSNS / SM_TMU
Number of Operations (DM_NO)	SM_NSO + SM_NAO * 1.5
Number of Services (DM_NS)	SM_SSNS
Squared Avg. Number of Operations to Squared Avg. Number of Messages (DM_AOMR)	(SM_NAO + SM_NSO / SM_SSNS)^2 / (SM_TMU / SM_SSNS)^2
Coarse-Grained Parameter Ratio (DM_CPR)	(SM_NSO + SM_NAO - SM_NFPO) / (SM_NSO + SM_NAO)
Adequately Named Service and Operation Ratio (DM_ANSOR)	((SM_SSNS - SM_NINS) / SM_SSNS * 2) + (SM_NSO + SM_NAO - SM_NINO) / (SM_NSO + SM_NAO) * 2

TABLE VI. DESIGN PROPERTIES – METRICS RELATIONSHIPS

Derived metric	*Design Property*
Average Number of Directly Connected Services (DM_ADCS)	Coupling
Inverse Average Number of Used Messages (DM_IAUM)	Cohesion
Number of Operations (DM_NO)	Complexity
Number of Services (DM_NS)	Design size
Squared Avg. Number of Operations to Squared Avg. Number of Messages (DM_AOMR)	Service granularity
Coarse-Grained Parameter Ratio (DM_CPR)	Parameter granularity
Adequately Named Service and Operation Ratio (DM_ANSOR)	Consumability

Finally, Table VI shows how the calculated values are related to the defined properties to assess the quality of the application.

None of the above metrics were included in the first version of the framework, but we believe that they all potentially have a role to play in our service. They are to be included later, as they require more complicated calculations than the metrics that we have adopted.

VII. Conclusions

Formal standards do not adequately cover web component quality as they focus on different software architectures and exclude user interaction as a basis of measurements. Standards like ISO 25010 include a wide range of metrics, which are far from easy to apply to web components.

After reviewing the state of the art, we have found that developed best practice guidelines or recommendations with respect to quality web components and web component mashups are still preliminary. Research by both more formal organizations like W3C and developer communities that have emerged around technologies like Polymer or Bosonic has focused to date on concept formalization and supporting technologies.

A platform that focuses on the interaction of user groups within social networks represents a real evaluation environment that reduces biases associated with artificial experimentation environments. The metrics of completeness, latency, data refresh time and usability are easily modified functionally, enabling the creation of multiple versions of the same web component.

Controlled exposure to real users yields user satisfaction metrics based on simple web analytics which can be analyzed through correlational studies. The preliminary results of the evaluation of the alpha version conducted by the developers who participated in platform design and development speak for the suitability of the selected approach.

In coming platform iterations, the platform will be released in an open Internet environment in order to corroborate the results reported in this paper in a broader context. This should test the hypothesis that formal component quality and user interaction metrics are correlated.

References

[1] Articles. Web Components.org (Retrieved May 12th, 2016). Available at http://webcomponents.org/articles/

[2] The Gold Standard Checklist for Web Components. GitHub, Inc. (Retrieved May 12th, 2016). Available at https://github.com/webcomponents/gold-standard/wiki

[3] Web Content Accessibility Guidelines (WCAG) 2.0. W3C. (Retrieved May 12th, 2016). Available at https://www.w3.org/TR/WCAG20/

[4] Basic Quality Control Concepts. Philosophe. (Retrieved May 12th, 2016). Available at http://philosophe.com/testing/qc/

[5] Overson, J. & Strimpel, J. (2015). Developing web components. Sebastopol: O'Reilly.

[6] Main page. Web Components.org. (Retrieved April 4th, 2016). Available at http://webcomponents.org/

[7] Norma de Calidad ISO/IEC 25010. Iso25000.org (Retrieved April 4th, 2016). Available at http://iso25000.com/index.php/normas-iso-25000/iso-25010

[8] International Organization for Standarization. Systems and software engineering – Systems and software Quality Requirements and Evaluation (SQuaRE) -- System and software quality models. ISO 25010:2011 Ginebra: ISO, 2001, 25 p.

[9] A Model for Web Services Discovery with QoS. S. Ran. ACM SIGecom Exchanges. Volume 4, Issue 1. Spring 2003. Pages 1 - 10.

[10] A Design Quality Model for Service-Oriented Architecture. B. Shim, S. Choue, S. Kim, S. Park. Software Engineering Conference, 2008. APSEC '08. 15th Asia - Pacific. Pages 403 - 410.

[11] A Quality Model for Mashups. C. Cappiello, F. Daniel, A. Koschmider, M. Matera, M. Picozzi. Web Engineering. 11th International Conference, ICWE 2011. Pages 137 - 151.

[12] Yahoo! Inc. About pipes (Retrieved April 12th, 2016). Available at http://real.pipes.yahoo.com/pipes/

[13] ConNWeT Lab (UPM). Welcome to WireCloud! (Retrieved April 12th, 2016). Available at http://conwet.fi.upm.es/wirecloud/

[14] Marmite: Towards End-User Programming for the Web. J. Wong. 2007 IEEE Symposium on Visual Languages and Human-Centric Computing. Pages 270 - 271.

[15] Service Oriented Architecture - SOA. QEDWiki: Putting a Web 2.0 face on SOA. IBM, Inc (Retrieved April 19th, 2016). Available at http://www-01.ibm.com/software/solutions/soa/newsletter/jan07/article_QEDwiki.html

[16] A. Bradley, D. Gootzit. Who's Who in Enterprise 'Mashup' Technologies. In Gartner Research, ID G00151351, 7th September 2007 (Retrieved April 20th, 2016). Available at: http://liquidbriefing.com/pub/Harmonia/IndustryAnalysts/whos_who_in_enterprise_mashu_151351.pdf

[17] JackBe's Presto: A Self-Service, On-DemandData Integration, Mashup Based, Dashboard-Oriented, Business Intelligence Tool. Beye NETWORK, a TechTarget company (Retrieved April 19th, 2016). Available at http://www.b-eye-network.com/view/15018

[18] Tutorial: Tracking your first event. Mixpanel (Retrieved April 5th, 2016). Available at https://mixpanel.com/help/reference/tracking-an-event

[19] Google, Inc. Encuestas Usabilidad (Retrieved April 4th, 2016). Available at https://docs.google.com/forms/d/1s0js0h3KoxcWNamlWQr9Wzblw-BIT1gCraI_e_g3Rdc/viewform

A Logical Design Process for Columnar Databases

João Paulo Poffo* and Ronaldo dos Santos Mello†
Informatics and Statistics Department
Federal University of Santa Catarina
Florianópolis/SC, Brazil 88040-90
Email: jopapo@gmail.com* and r.mello@ufsc.br†

***Abstract*—Emerging technologies often break paradigms. NoSQL is one of them and is gaining space with the raising of Big Data, where the data volume exceeded the petabyte frontier and the information within these data can be of great importance to strategic decisions. In this case, legacy relational databases show themselves inadequate to efficiently manage these data and, consequently, their traditional project methodologies should must be reviewed to be suitable to new data models, such as the NoSQL columnar model. Regarding columnar database design, the literature lacks of methodologies for logical design, i.e., processes that convert a conceptual schema to a logical schema that optimize access and storage. Thus, this work proposes an approach for logical design of columnar databases that contributes to fill the void between classic project methodologies and the technological forefront with the NoSQL movement, in particular, columnar databases. Preliminary experiments had demonstrated that the methodology is promising, if compared with a baseline.**

Keywords–database design; logical design; nosql; columnar database.

I. Introduction

With the advent of the cloud computing paradigm, the opportunity to provide DataBase Management Systems (DBMS) as services is strengthened, as witnessed by Amazon RDS and Microsoft SQL Azure [1]. NoSQL is one of these movements which is standing out by providing DBs with high availability and scalability. These characteristics are essential to social media, profile repositories, content providers, among other applications [2].

NoSQL is a commonly known term that covers several non relational DBs which can manage high amounts of data. They are categorized by key/value, column, document and graph DBs [3][4]. In *DB-Engines* [5], there is a ranking of DB products and in the top ten, seven of them are relational. However, what draws the attention are the three others: MongoDB (a document DB), Cassandra (a columnar DB) and Redis (a key/value DB).

A DB is called columnar when the smallest information unit to be manipulated is a column. The best way to imagine it is like a two-level data aggregation structure [6]. As in key/value DBs, the first level is a key that identifies an aggregation of interest. The difference with respect to columnar DBs is that the second level contains several columns that can hold simple or complex values, and these columns can be accessed all at once or one at a time.

The traditional DB design methodology has three main phases: conceptual, logical and physical design [7]. In contrast, this sequence seems to have been suppressed for columnar DBs. It neglects the conceptual design phase, starting with the column sets design and how they will be accessed [8].

Based on this motivation, this work proposes a reconciliation between the classical DB design approach and columnar DBs, contributing with a logical design process that considers the semantics of the application domain (a conceptual schema) and aims to achieve an optimized conversion from a conceptual schema to a logical columnar schema. A conceptual model must be expressive, simple, minimal and formal [9] and there are several models that respect these standards. In this work, the Extended Entity-Relationship (EER) conceptual model is considered. We also propose several conversion rules from an EER conceptual schema to a logical notation suitable to the columnar data model. This logical data model is another contribution of this work, which can also be applied to represent a reverse engineered schema of a columnar DB. The most adherent usage of our approach is in long-term running high-growth applications that needs to scale, like never-ending games and social network, among others. All these features are demonstrated through an experimental evaluation.

Preliminary related work are [10], where the conceptual model are mapped into hierarchical model (XML), and [11], who proposes to do the same, but targeting object-oriented DBs. However, they do not focus on NoSQL DB design. We just borrow from them some ideas for the proposed conversion rules. In [12], it is presented a *NoSQL Abstract Model (NoAM)* which aims to embrace the data model of any existing NoSQL DB, and [13] focuses on Cassandra columnar DBMS. Sharp et al. [14] and Schram et al. [15] suggest limited orientations for the logical and physical design with columnar DBs. However, all of them lack information about how to provide logical design based on a conceptual schema. Other works [4][8][15] deal with logical design using columnar DBs, but do not present detailed conversion rules as well as an evaluation of their proposals. Distinctly, Meijer and Bierman [16] present a mathematical model to NoSQL DBs and demonstrates their correlation with the relational model. However, it does not make reference to columnar DBs nor deals with conceptual design or conversion process. In short, the literature still lacks a comprehensive approach to this problem.

The rest of this paper is organized as follows. Next section analyzes related work, exposing their strengths and weakness, as well as the gap filled with this work. In Section III, fundamentals about DB design and NoSQL, with emphasis in columnar DBs, are presented. Section IV is dedicated to our proposal for logical design of columnar DBs, including its formalization. Some experiments are designed and evaluated in Section V, followed by our conclusions in Section VI.

II. Related Work

Besides the classical methodology for relational DB design [7], some conceptual to logical conversion for non-relational DBs proposals are found, such as XML DBs [10], object-oriented DBs [11] and NoSQL DBs [12][13]. Still, there are several guidelines for how to directly convert some logical structures in columnar DBs [4][8][14][15][17]. What is evident in this current literature is the lack of a clear and comprehensive approach that transforms a conceptual schema, such as an EER schema, into a logical schema for columnar DBs.

Schroeder and Mello [10] proposes a mapping approach from a conceptual model (EER) to an equivalent XML logical model. Its process comprises conversion rules for all EER concepts and it is improved by considering workload information. Despite its different focus, its methodology is well-suited to convert complex objects as our work. The same applies to [11], whose target is an object-oriented DBs. Both have a comprehensive EER-to-logical conversion approach into their specific outputs, but they do not explore NoSQL DBs.

The proposal [12] stands for a NoSQL DB design solution to any kind of NoSQL data model. The basis of their approach is what they call an abstract data model using aggregates called NoAM. Their process considers a conceptual data model, a design of aggregated objects in NoAM, a high level NoSQL DB design and its implementation. Although the proposal acts in the three design phases, it does not focus on columnar DBs, and does not consider all the conceptual constructs, such as composite attributes and N:M relationships, nor formalizes conversion rules between a conceptual modeling and logical representations in the NoAM model. The approach in [13] is similar but more complete, as it covers all concepts from an ER conceptual model (without extensions introduced by EER) for a logical design. A logical columnar DB schema for Cassandra is also proposed. The proposed conversion is query-oriented and enforces redundancy, which is consistent with three followed assumptions: *know your data, know your queries, aggregate and duplicate your data.* Our approach differs from this one by not considering aggregates and being validated experimentally.

Taking a look now at industry efforts, Microsoft presents detailed instructions to the creation of columnar DBs optimized for writing and reading [14]. These guidelines are enriched by considering the *Wide-Column* concept, which is similar to a matrix transposition, i.e., the focus is on the columns instead of the rows. They determine what must be done to maximize scalability, availability and consistency, but they lack the conceptual data modeling related to the domain.

The case study in [15] presents a system whose relational access and data volume grows very fast (*Twitter* data). So, the authors propose the usage of a columnar DBMS (Cassandra). All of the study, challenges and system construction are discussed. They explain how to perform the transition to the columnar DB and their results. They manually use workload information to optimize the design by applying denormalization. They also presents a practical case and its challenges, but they lack a formalization and validation of the process. Besides, they also suppress the conceptual design phase.

Similarly, only to contrast relational and non-relational approaches, Wang and Tang [8] show simple principles of conceptual design using UML and the straightforward conversion to Cassandra. However, their proposal considers a very restrict set of conceptual structures, and does not formalizes its process. In [4], the conceptual design (based on the ER model) of a case study for an application related to *blog posts* is converted to MongoDB (a document DB) and Neo4j (a graph DB). Their focus is not on the conversion itself, but the access

TABLE I. RELATED WORK COMPARISON.

Feature / **Work**	Schroeder & Mello 2008 [10]	Fong 1995 [11]	Sharp et al. 2013 [14]	Schram & Anderson 2012 [15]	Wang & Tang 2012 [8]	Kaur & Rani 2013 [4]	Meijer & Bierman 2011 [16]	Bugiotti et al. 2014 [12]	Chebotko, Kashlev & Lu 2015 [13]	This work 2016
Conceptual design	●	●	○	○	◐	◐	◐	●	◐	●
Logical design	●	●	●	●	◐	◐	◐	●	●	●
Conversion rules	●	●	○	○	○	◐	○	●	●	●
Columnar DB	○	○	●	●	●	○	○	◐	●	●
Validation	●	●	○	○	○	◐	●	●	◐	●

optimization, enriching our process with their troubleshooting. Differently, the approach in [16], named *CoSQL*, presents a mathematical model to key/value DBs and demonstrates its correlation with the relational model. It also defines a common query language to relational and non-relational DBs based on the relational algebra. Its proposal to defined a logical layer had inspired our conversion process by proving a conceptual-to-logical correlation for NoSQL DBs. However, this approach does not formalize a conversion process nor validate it.

Table I shows a comparison of related work. It highlights five features: *Conceptual design* indicates that there is at least one kind of conceptual model considered by the work; *Logical design* indicates that the related work considers logical design; *Conversion rules* indicate if the work clearly defines rules to transform a conceptual schema into a logical schema; *Columnar DB* focuses on this kind of DB and, lastly, if the approach reports some kind of *Validation*. To each feature is assigned one of three signs: the work fully supports the feature ●, the feature is not mentioned ○ or the feature is partially treated ◐.

As shown in Table I, only our proposal fully covers all the considered features. The formalization of the conceptual-to-logical conversion rules, the definition of the conversion process and its validation are the main contributions of this work. These points are detailed in Section IV.

III. FUNDAMENTALS

This section presents the fundamentals related to the classical DB design, NoSQL DBs and columnar DBs.

A. DB Design

The DB design aims to rightly define real world facts and their relationships, as well as their modeling in a target DB, aiming at maximizing storage and access requirements. The classical phases of DB design are: data requirements gathering, conceptual, logical and physical design [7].

Several conceptual models are available for DB design, like Unified Modeling Language (UML), Object with Roles Model (ORM), and the most representative one, the EER [7][9]. The three main EER concepts are: *(i)* entity (an abstraction of a set of similar real world objects), *(ii)* relationship (a semantic connection between entities), and *(iii)* attribute (a property associated with an entity or relationship).

Figure 1 shows an example of an EER schema. In this example we can identify abstract constructs such as classification (entities and their attributes), aggregation (composite attributes or association relationships) and generalization (subset and superset behavior) with associated constraints. In traditional

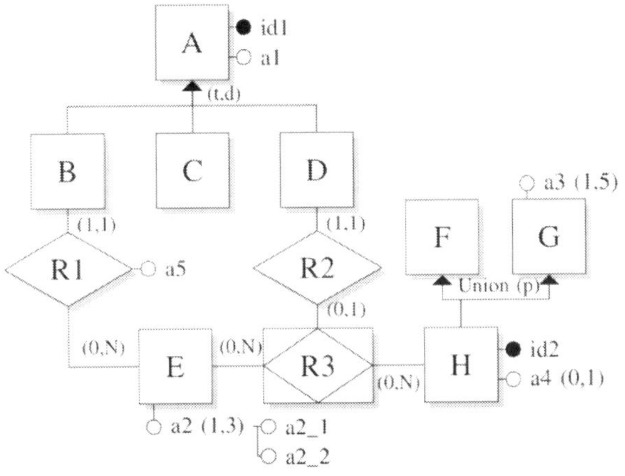

Figure 1. An example of EER schema [10].

DB design methodologies, this conceptual schema is the basis for generating a logical and then a physical schema in the target DB model. In the first case, this mapping is supported by a conversion process that offer alternatives to generate an optimized DB schema.

B. NoSQL

A DB is based on a data model and a set of operations that allow data definition and manipulation. Data manipulation, in particular, respects the classical Atomicity, Consistency, Isolation and Durability (ACID) properties [6]. Until recently, this fundamental and untouchable acronym ruled sovereign.

However, digital data show today a fast growth in Volume, Variety and Velocity (VVV). Such a phenomena is called *Big Data*, which typically corresponds to massive data collections that cannot be suitable handled by traditional DBMSs that respect to the ACID properties. In order to address Big Data management, movements like *NoSQL* and *NewSQL* had emerged [3].

NoSQL, in particular, covers a wide range of technologies, architectures and data models. NoSQL DBs usually do not ensure ACID properties in order to avoid the overhead to guarantee them and provide better scalability and availability [18]. Instead, they are Basically Available, hold a Soft state and are Eventually consistent (BASE), i.e., availability and partitioning are prioritized to the detriment of consistency.

NoSQL DBs comprises the following data models [3]: *(i)* **key/value** DBs store data items identified by a key and indexed by hash tables. Values can contain both simple and complex data, but are accessed as a single unit. Queries are usually only directly by key; *(ii)* **columnar** DBs store heterogeneous sets of columns for each data item. Each column holds a simple value or, in some cases, a set of nested columns; *(iii)* **document** DBs store data items that are called documents, which are usually stored in XML, JSON or BSON formats. Unlike key/value DB, values can be semistructured and one document usually hold a set of attributes; *(iv)* **graph** DBs maintain nodes and edges, and both can hold attributes. It is the only one that support explicit relationships.

The focus of this paper is on columnar DBs, which is detailed in the following.

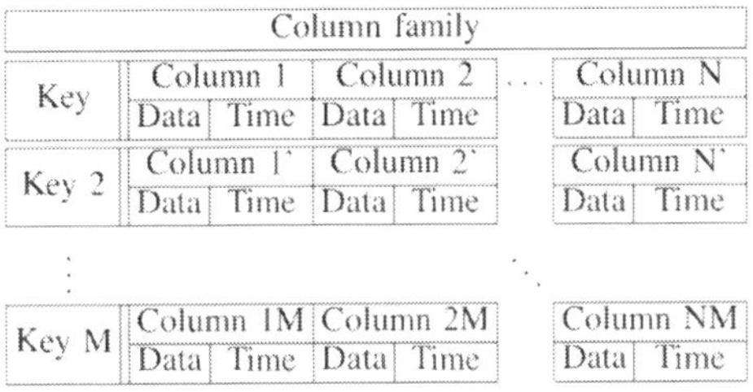

Figure 2. Columnar DB data model representation.

C. Columnar DBs

Columnar DBs (also known as extensible records, wide-column, column-family, column-oriented or BigTable-implementations) are so named because the smallest portion of information increment is a column. Each column has basically a name and a value, and a column value can hold a simple value or a set of columns, as stated before. A column also contains a timestamp which is used to manage mutual exclusion regarding concurrency problems.

A column family is a container of lexical ordered columns [19]. Thus, columns that are read together must be kept in the same column family. It is possible to add undeclared columns to a column family. Its flexible structure allows it. So, it is frequently sparse. A key uniquely identifies each line in a column family. This key can define, according to its partitioning strategy, in which cluster server the data are stored. The same key can be used in different column families. Figure 2 shows a basic representation of this data model.

Cassandra is a popular columnar DBs, originally created by Facebook and now maintained by Apache [20]. It has some special features like super column and composite keys. The former works like a nested column family. The latter is a way to add one dimension to the key into a column family.

It is important to empathize that there is not a global rule or standard with respect to the columnar DB data model. This is highlighted by Table II, that shows which concepts are supported by the main columnar DBMS. It indicates three kinds of information regarding each DB product: it supports the concept ●, it does not support it ○, or it's possible to workaround the concept or it exists in a limited way ◐.

TABLE II. DATA MODEL CONCEPTS FOR COLUMNAR DATABASES.

Feature / DB	Cassandra	Riak	HBase	DynamoDB	Accumulo	Teradata	SybaseIQ
Collection data type	●	●	●	●	◐	●	●
Flexible structure	●	●	●	●	●	●	○
Composite keys	●	○	○	●	○	●	●
Super columns	●	○	○	○	○	○	○

Columnar DBs can be horizontally and vertically partitioned. Some of the good candidates to use this kind of DB are logs, content providers, personal pages, blogs, among others [6][21]. On the other hand, columnar DBs are not a good choice when the scope of a system is not clear, because of the high cost on deep structural changes. Despite flexible, changes almost always must be adjusted in the application and may deteriorate its performance. This is not the case of classical relational approach because of its rigid structure. Therefore, columnar DBs are more sensitive to query pattern changes than

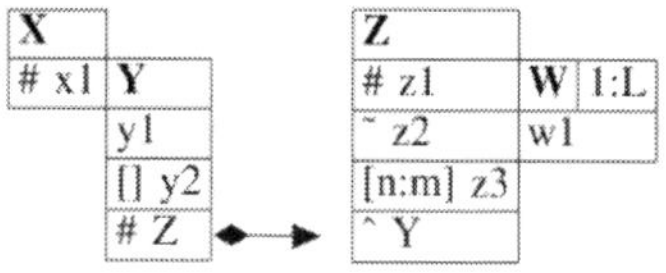

Figure 3. Overview of the diagrammatic notation of a columnar DB schema.

in the schema, other than relational DBs. This fact strengthens the need for a well-defined conceptual and logical design.

IV. Proposal

This section details our approach for logical design of columnar DBs. First, it introduces a logical design notation for columnar DBs. In the following, the overall conversion process of an EER conceptual schema to a logical columnar DB schema is defined in terms of high level algorithms, inspired by [9].

The general reasoning of our conversion process is to offer a logical schema with data sets that support nested column families and bidirectional relations. The first strategy is achieved by the use of *shared keys*, which provides access efficiency as close related data are stored near each other. The second strategy is used when the first strategy is not applied, being achieved through *artificial relations*. Both concepts are detailed in the following. We decided not to consider the traditional aggregate approach for logical modeling of NoSQL databases, followed by most of the related work, because it can generate deep nested data relationships which cannot be efficient, in terms of accessing, for some application domains, as illustrated in our experimental evaluation (see Section V).

A. Logical Notation for Columnar DBs

The conceptual modeling represents relevant data but not how they are persisted in the DB [7]. So, it is necessary to provide some abstraction level of the DB to the user. The generation of this abstraction level is called logical design, and it comprises the transformation of a conceptual schema into a logical schema suitable to the DB data representation.

The conceptual-to-logical conversion is a transformation between data models in different abstraction levels. As there is no a standard for the columnar DB data model, we define a logical notation for this data model. The concepts of our logical notation are defined in the following.

Definition 1 (Column): A column c is a tuple $c = \{(n, v, t) | n = \text{name}, v = \text{value}, t = \text{timestamp}\}$.

Definition 2 (Column family): A column family is a map $f : A \mapsto B$ where $\mathtt{A} = \{\text{key}\}$ is a set of unique keys, and $\mathtt{B} = \{\mathtt{c}\}$ is a set of columns such that, for every $\alpha \in \mathtt{A}$, there is a unique object $f(\alpha) \in \mathtt{B}$.

Definition 3 (Shared key): Given a logical columnar DB schema S so that $F \in S$ is a column family and $F' \in S$ is another column family, a key is shared if $key(F) = key(F')$, i.e., a key is a shared key if the same value is used the identifier of two or more column families.

Definition 4 (Artificial relation): Given a logical columnar DB schema S so that $F \in S$ is a column family and $F' \in S$ is another column family, there is an artificial relation if $c_i \in F = key(F')$, i.e., if any column in a family match the key of a column family.

Figure 3 shows the notation for the logical representation of a columnar DB schema proposed in this paper. A column family is represented by a rectangle with the name on top and an optional cardinality constraint in its side. This cardinality constraint allows the definition of repeatable columns within a family when a column family is nested into another one (W, for example). Each internal line in a column family represents a column where the hash symbol (#) means the key, tilde (˜) means a mandatory column, caret (ˆ) means an artificial relation and brackets ([]) define unrestricted internal collections. Brackets with values ([n:m]) mean an explicit cardinality constraint. No column data types are described in this version of the logical notation as NoSQL DBs supports virtually anything.

A shared key is the reuse of the key of another column family. It is represented by the coupling of two or more column families in a way that its hierarchy is visible. In other words, a column family that intends to share the key of another one is welded with the column family that holds the original key, like X to Y, and Z to W. The artificial relation is represented by a line that connects column families whose tips are arrows or diamonds, like Z to Y. The arrow means the existence of a column with the caret (that stores the key of the other family) and the diamond means an aggregation on the column. Finally, the 1:L relationship (also introduced in this work) represents a not known superior limit, like 1:N relationships, but this limit is not high. Usually the "L" side is associated to weak entities (employee dependents, for example). It allows the use of shared keys, which cannot be used in 1:N relationships.

B. Conversion Process

It is important to notice that, due to the flexible nature of columnar DBs, it does not enforce several restrictions. The application must be responsible for it. It is argued in [22] that the absence of a DB schema is a fallacy. A schema always exists, but instead of being enforced by the DB, the application assumes the control of data integrity constraints. In this context, the concept of shared key, as introduced before, was defined to deal with the absence of referential integrity in columnar DBs. This strategy avoids the number of physical references between column families, and, as a consequence, the overhead to manage the referential integrity.

The high level algorithms for mapping EER constructs to the columnar DB logical representation are presented in the next Sections. These algorithms are based on the notion of entity paternity, which is defined as follows.

Definition 5 (Entity Paternity): Given two entities E_P and E_C, we say that E_P is parent of E_C (or, in other words, E_C is child of E_P), if: (a) E_C is a specialized entity and E_P is the generic entity in a specialization relationship; (b) E_P is the entity that unifies two or more entities in an union relationship, being E_C one of the unified entities; (c) E_P is a mandatory entity that has 1 as maximum cardinality *on its side* in a 1:1, 1:N or N-ary relationship.

In short, our process traverses all entities and, for each entity, it checks if there is a relationship where this entity is a child. If it exists, the parent entity in the relationship is prioritized, i.e., it is converted first. This checking and prioritization is repeated until there is no more parent entities.

When all column families are generated from entities (in a recursive way that takes into account paternity relationships), column family keys are defined and entity attributes are converted. The process ends with the conversion of the relationships, which can generate new columns and column families to represent adequately its dependencies. All of this conversion reasoning is detailed in the following.

C. General Conceptual to Logical Schema Conversion

The algorithm in Figure 4 is the main conversion process. Its input is an EER schema. All the entities of the EER schema are traversed[:2 (line 2)] and, for each one, the algorithm in Figure 6 is triggered[:3]. Its output is added to the set of column families that compose the columnar DB logical schema and then returned[:5].

```
  Input: EER schema (α)
  Output: Columnar DB logical schema (α′)
1 α′ ← ∅
2 foreach ϵ ∈ α|ϵ is an entity do
3 |  α′ ← α′ ∪ createFamily(ϵ)
4 end
5 return α′
```

Figure 4. Conceptual to logical schema conversion

Example 1 (Schema conversion): The conversion of the EER schema of Figure 1 generates the columnar DB logical schema in Figure 5 according to algorithm in Figure 4.

When an entity is visited by the loop, its parent entity is converted before it, in a recursive way, if it exists (see algorithm in Figure 6). Each converted entity is marked to avoid its repeated conversion. The loop in this algorithm aims to reach all EER schema entities, even the ones that are part of disjoint groups of related entities. A general example is given in the following, and details about the conversion of each EER construct are further exemplified.

D. Column Family Generation

The input of algorithm in Figure 6 can be an entity or a relationship and it outputs a set of column families. For each analyzed entity, this algorithm provides the conversion of all other conceptual constructs related to it (relationship types and attributes). The same holds if a relationship is being treated. First, it initializes the set of output column families[:1]. If the entity or relationship was not visited yet[:2], then a list of EER concepts is created with generalizations, unions and association relationships where the input entity is child[:3]. If the input is a relationship, it is assumed that it does not have relationships, so the list is empty.

Then, for each concept[:4], the same algorithm is triggered recursively with its parent as input[:5]. Next, a new column family is created[:7] with a name[:8] and a key (see algorithm in Figure 7). In the following, for each attribute of the input[:10], algorithm in Figure 9 is called[:11] to define a suitable column (or even an aggregated column family) to the new column family. The new column family is added to the result set[:13],

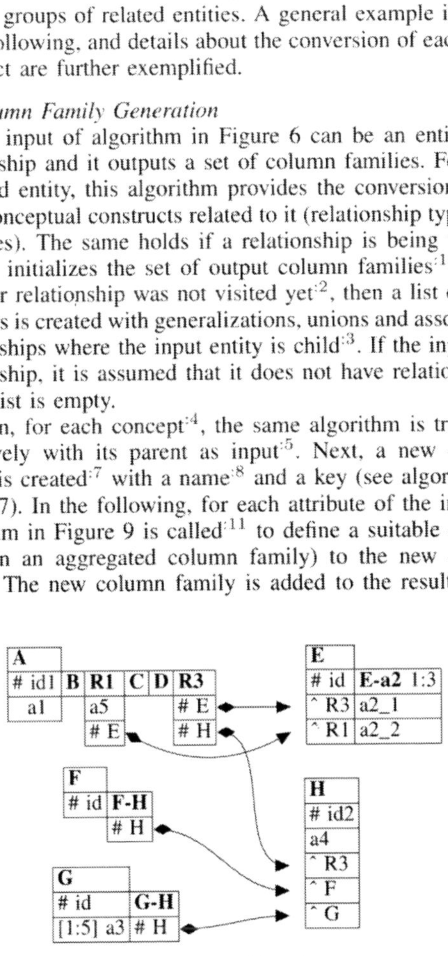

Figure 5. Example of output columnar DB logical schema generated from the EER schema of Figure 1.

followed by the traversing of the list created before, as well as reflexive or N:M relationships of the input entity[:14]. Thus, for each relationship, algorithm in Figure 10 is triggered with the relationship and the new column family. Finally, its output is added to the result set[:15] and the result set is returned[:18].

```
   Input: Entity or relationship (ϵ)
   Output: Column family set (ω)
1  ω ← Preexistent column family referring to ϵ or empty set
2  if checkAndMarkIfIsFirstVisitTo(ϵ) then
3  |   π_P ← generalizations, unions, n-ary and binary parent
   |     relationships of ϵ, in this order.
4  |   foreach π ∈ π_P do
5  |   |  ω ← ω ∪ createFamily(Parent entity in π)
6  |   end
7  |   ϵ′ ← New empty column family
8  |   ϵ′.Name ← ϵ.Name
9  |   ϵ′.Key ← defineKey(ϵ)
10 |   foreach δ ∈ ϵ|δ is an attribute do
11 |   |  ω ← ω ∪ convertAttribute(ϵ′, δ)
12 |   end
13 |   ω ← ω ∪ ϵ′
14 |   foreach π ∈ ϵ|π ∈ π_P ∨ π.Type ∈ {reflexive, N : M} do
15 |   |  ω ← ω ∪ convertRelationship(π, ϵ′)
16 |   end
17 end
18 return ω
```

Figure 6. Algorithm for entity or relationship to column family conversion (`createFamily`)

Example 2 (Column family generation): The conversion of the entity `A` occurs seamlessly creating the homonym column family and its attributes. Next, when converting `B`, it searches for parent relationships and finds a total disjoint generalization. As the parent entity `A` is already converted, it creates the column family `B` and decides for a shared key. The same occurs for `C` and `D`.

E. Shared Key Generation

The algorithm in Figure 7 is responsible to generate a shared key. It receives as input an entity or relationship and returns the set of attributes that compose its key. Initially, the result set receives the key of the input[:1]. If such a key does not exist[:2], then if the input is an entity[:3], it builds a list of generalization or mandatory `1:L` or `1:1` relationships, respectively[:4], so the result set receives the first item on the list[:5]. We chose the first item in order to get the parent relationship with the most potential cardinality, so the shared key concept can be better exploited. If the input is a relationship[:6], the key is the side of the relationship with maximum and minimum cardinalities as 1[:7]. Finally, if the result set is still empty[:9], a customized key is defined as a new column ID[:10].

```
   Input: Entity or relationship (ϵ)
   Output: Attributes which compose the key (ω)
1  ω ← ϵ.Key
2  if ω = ∅ then
3  |   if ϵ is entity then
4  |   |  π ← Parent generalizations, 1:L and 1:1 parent mandatory
   |   |    relationships of ϵ, in this order
5  |   |  ω ← π_1.Key
6  |   else
7  |   |  ω ← key of the (1,1) side of ϵ, if exists
8  |   end
9  |   if ω = ∅ then
10 |   |  ω ← {ID}
11 |   end
12 end
13 return ω
```

Figure 7. Algorithm for key definition (`defineKey`)

Example 3 (Shared key generation): Consider the initial conversion of entity `A` of Figure 1. As it has an identifier attribute (`id1`), it is defined as the key of its corresponding column family. As `A` is a parent entity of `B`, `C`, `D`, `R1` and `R3`, they all share its key, as shown in Figure 5.

F. Artificial Relation Generation

When a shared key is not possible, e.g., for the conversion of `N:M` relationships and partial generalizations, an artificial relation is defined. The term artificial stands for the fact that it is a relation whose integrity must be managed by the application, not the DBMS. The algorithm in Figure 8 is invoked by the algorithm in Figure 10, but we present it close to the definition of shared keys for sake of better understanding. The algorithm in Figure 8 is responsible to define artificial relationships in a columnar DB logical schema through the generation of additional column families for them. These additional column families are categorized as *auxiliary* (when it shares the key with its parent) or *intermediary* (when it is an independent family referenced by an auxiliary one).

```
Input: Two column familes (ϵ1; ϵ2) and the relationship (π)
Output: Additional column families (ω)
1  ω ← ∅
2  if ϵ1 was created for a relationship then
3  |    ϵ' ← ϵ1
4  else
5  |    ϵ' ← Preexistent column family between ϵ1 and ϵ2
6  end
7  if ϵ' = ∅ then
8  |    ϵT ← Temporary entity whose name is composed by the names
   |      of the input associated with ϵ1 through a 1 : 1 relationship
9  |    ϵ' ← createFamily(ϵT)
10 |    ω ← ϵ'
11 end
12 δ1 ← New key column
13 δ1.Name ← ϵ2.Name
14 ϵ' ← ϵ' ∪ δ1
15 if π.Type ≠ (N : M) ∨ π promoted to associative entity then
16 |    δ2 ← New column that represent an artificial relation
17 |    δ2.Name ← ϵ2.Name
18 |    ϵ2 ← ϵ2 ∪ δ2
19 end
20 return ω
```

Figure 8. Algorithm for artificial relation creation (`createArtificialRelation`)

The input of this algorithm are two column families (first and second ones), and the relationship. It outputs additional column families necessary to the definition of the artificial relation. The algorithm is divided in two parts: *(i)* the definition of the source column family, and *(ii)* the definition of the artificial relation.

In order to define the source column family, it checks if the first column family was created from a relationship$^{:2}$. If yes, it means that it can behave as an auxiliary family that can receive additional columns (Example 4), so it is set as the source column family$^{:3}$. If not$^{:4}$, the algorithm searches for a column family that was created to associate the two input column families (Example 9), and sets it as the source family$^{:5}$. After that, if no source family was defined$^{:7}$, a temporary entity is created$^{:8}$ with a `1:1` relationship with the entity referring the first column family (to allow the definition of a shared key), and the result of the conversion of the temporary entity is set as the source column family (Example 5).

After the source column family is defined, the artificial relation is established by creating a new key column$^{:12}$, naming it$^{:13}$ and adding it to the source column family$^{:14}$. Only if the relationship is not `N:M` or it is promoted to an associative entity$^{:15}$, the other side of the artificial relation is defined as a column$^{:16}$. It is named$^{:17}$ and added to the second column family$^{:18}$. At the end, the generated column family set is returned.

Example 4 (Artificial relation for N-ary relationship): A `N:M` relationship promoted to an associative entity is handled exactly like a N-ary relationship. When the entity `E` of Figure 1 is going to be converted, it is detected that it has a `N:M` relationship (`R3`) with `H` that was promoted to an associative entity. So, it creates the column family `R3`. The definition of the key detects that there is a parent `1:1` relationship with `D` through `R2` and shares its key. Then, an artificial relation is defined from `E` to `H` through `R3` (column `E`). When `H` is further converted, the artificial relation for the other direction is created (column `H` in `R3` - see Figure 5).

Example 5 (Artificial relation for 1:N relationship): When the conversion process analyzes entity `E`, it detects that it has one parent entity `B` through `R1`. So, `B` is converted first. After, the column family `E` is created and its relationships are converted, in this case, `R1`. During `R1` conversion (Algorithm in Figure 10), it detects that it is a binary `1:N` relationship with attributes. Therefore, a column family is created for the relationship. When it happens, the algorithm detects that it can share a key with its mandatory side. So, the column family `R1` is created and it receives the key of `E` as a secondary key. In this way, `B` can reach any `E`. Finally, `E` receives a column referencing `R1` and the association becomes bidirectional.

G. Column Generation

The algorithm in Figure 9 is responsible to convert an attribute of an entity or relationship. It receives as input the target column family and the attribute to be converted. The output is a set of additional column families. The first part verifies if the attribute is composite$^{:2}$. If yes, it creates a new column family$^{:3}$, names it$^{:4}$, gets the key of the input column family$^{:5}$ (shared key), sets the same cardinality from the conceptual attribute$^{:6}$ and then, for each child attribute of the composite attribute$^{:7}$, it calls itself recursively$^{:8}$ to convert it, and the output is added to the result set. Next, the created column family is added to the result set$^{:10}$. If the attribute is not composite$^{:11}$, a new column is created$^{:12}$, named$^{:13}$, the cardinality of the attribute is copied$^{:14}$ and the column is added to the input column family$^{:15}$. At the end, the result set with the possible created column families is returned$^{:17}$.

Based on the algorithm in Figure 9, we can summarize the attribute conversion cases as follows: *(i)* a **key attribute** generates a column family key, i.e., a mandatory and unique information within a column family; *(ii)* a **mandatory and optional attribute** generates a column in a column family; *(iii)* a **multivalued attribute** generates a collection column in a column family; *(iv)* a **composite attribute**, as it is not a native feature of columnar DBs, it is represented as a new column family with a shared key; *(v)* a **multivalued composite attribute** is converted in the same way of a composite attribute with the additional definition of a cardinality constraint for the generated column family.

Example 6 (Column generation): The attribute `a1` of the entity `A` is an example of a monovalued mandatory attribute. It generates a simple column in `A`. The column family `E-a2` is an example of how a composite attribute is converted. The composite attribute itself turns into a column family and their attributes become columns.

H. Relationship Conversion

This section details the conversion of EER relationships to a columnar DB logical schema. In traditional relational DB design, the conversion of `1:1` relationships usually merges the involved entities into an unique component in the logical schema [10][11]. Instead, our approach creates at least two

```
Input: Column family (ε') and attribute (δ) to convert
Output: Additional column families (ω)
ω ← ∅
if δ is composite then
    ε'' ← New empty column family
    ε''.Name ← ε'.Name + δ.Name
    ε''.Key ← ε'.Key
    ε''.Cardinality ← δ.Cardinality
    foreach δ' ∈ δ|δ' is a child attribute do
        ω ← ω ∪ convertAttribute(ε'', δ')
    end
    ω ← ω ∪ ε''
else
    δ' ← New column
    δ'.Name ← δ.Name
    δ'.Cardinality ← δ.Cardinality
    ε' ← ε' ∪ δ'
end
return ω
```

Figure 9. Algorithm for attribute to column conversion (`convertAttribute`)

column families (a third one is additionally created if the relationship has attributes) and typically a shared key is used to nest it. The advantage of this approach is that the shared key puts data together through sharding. The merging of entities can leverage underutilization as all the columns of a key are loaded to memory.

Different from `1:1`, `1:N` relationships always generate artificial relations. It is also defined an auxiliary column family associated with the parent side through a shared key to handle relationship information. This separation allows the auxiliary entity to concentrate reads because it knows the exact keys of related data and the application can conveniently decide which information is important to acquire.

For `N:M` relationships, two difficulties arise: *(i)* how to access the data of the related entity through the relationship, and *(ii)* how to do it efficiently. For a better adherence to columnar DBs, it is necessary to both column families to know each other keys. Thus, instead of including the relationship in a particular column family, it is created an auxiliary one on each column family that refers each other in order to maintain bidirectional navigability, separation of concerns and keeping related data near.This strategy is expanded to N-ary relationships, where the main difference is that it has more dimensions associated to it and the creation of the relationship column family is mandatory to hold all the references and its different cardinalities.

Example 7 (Binary relationship conversion): The relationship `R1` is `1:N`. In this case, an artificial relation is created. We have a parent column family `B` and a child `E`. The parent receives an auxiliary column family `R1` with a shared key that points to the child and the attributes of the relationship. The child receives a column referring the parent. So, it is possible to navigate to `B` children through `R1`, and `E` can access its parent through the new column.

The conversion of relationships is supported by the algorithm in Figure 10. It deals with all existing EER relationship types. Its input is a relationship and the source entity, and its output is a column family set. In the first part of the algorithm, we initialize the result set to empty[:1] and proceed the analysis and treatment of each type of relationship[:2]:

- **Binary or reflexive** relationship does not consider a promoted associative entity or `N:M` relationship[:3]. If the relationship has attributes[:4], it creates a column family[:5] and makes it the parent of the relationship[:6]. Then, if the parent and the source column family do not share the key or the relationship is reflexive[:8], the creation of an artificial relation is triggered[:9] and the output is added to the result set;
- **N-ary** relationship considers a promoted associative entity or `N:M` relationship[:12]. It creates a column family to the relationship[:13] and a temporary binary relationship (with the same cardinality on the source entity, and maximum cardinality 1 on the output column family[:14]) that is converted recursively. Its output is added the result set[:15];
- **Generalization or union** relationship initially checks if it is partial or the entity do not share a key with its parent[:18]. If so, an inverted artificial relation between them is created, using the source as parent and the parent entity in the relationship as child[:19]. The generated output is added to the result set.

Temporary relationships are transient and its lifetime ends within its scope. So, it ceases to exist after its use. Its objective is to break the input relationship into smaller binary ones that can be handled by the available structures in our notation for columnar DBs.

```
    Input: Relationship (π) and source column family (ε)
    Output: Column family set (ω)
 1  ω ← ∅
 2  switch π.Type do
 3      case (Binary ∨ Reflexive) ∧ not (N:M ∧ promoted to associative
          entity) do
 4          if π.Attributes ≠ ∅ then
 5              ω ← createFamily(π)
 6              π.Parent ← ω
 7          end
 8          if ε.Key ≠ π.Parent.Key ∨ π.Type = Reflexive then
 9              ω ← ω ∪ createArtificialRelation(π.Parent, ε, π)
10          end
11      end
12      case N-ary ∨ (N:M ∧ promoted to associative entity) do
13          ε_R ← createFamily(π)
14          π_T ← Temporary binary relationship with the same
              cardinality on ε and maximum equals 1 on ε_R
15          ω ← ω ∪ ε_R ∪ convertRelationship(π_T, ε)
16      end
17      case Generalization ∨ Union do
18          if π is partial or any entity in π cannot share key among
              them then
19              ω ← ω ∪ createArtificialRelation(ε, π.Parent, π)
20          end
21      end
22  end
23  return ω
```

Figure 10. Algorithm for relationship convertion (`convertRelationship`)

Example 8 (Generalization conversion): Entity `A` is the parent entity in the generalization relationship and it is converted before its specializations. For entity `B`, the algorithm verifies that the parent entity (`A`) is already converted and then proceeds its own conversion. So, the family `B` is created and, as it is a specialized entity in a total generalization, it shares its parent key. In this case, no new column family is created as the relationship is represented by the shared key. The same reasoning is applied to the entities `C` and `D`.

Total unions are similar to total and disjoint generalizations (t,d) because all instances have a single inheritance. Thus, the same reasoning to convert generalizations applies. Partial unions are more complex because of the possibility of multiple inheritance, as well as none at all. Thus, the conversion process treats this kind of relation as a N-ary relation.

Example 9 (Union conversion): The entity `H` is a partial union of `F` and `G`. Considering that the first entity to be converted is `F`, the conversion process initially checks if `F` parents were already converted, as explained before. In this

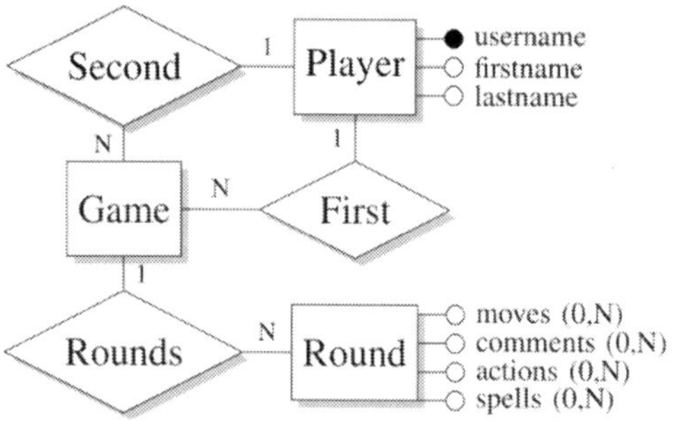

Figure 11. EER schema obtained through a reverse engineering process from the logical modeling for a game domain presented in [12]

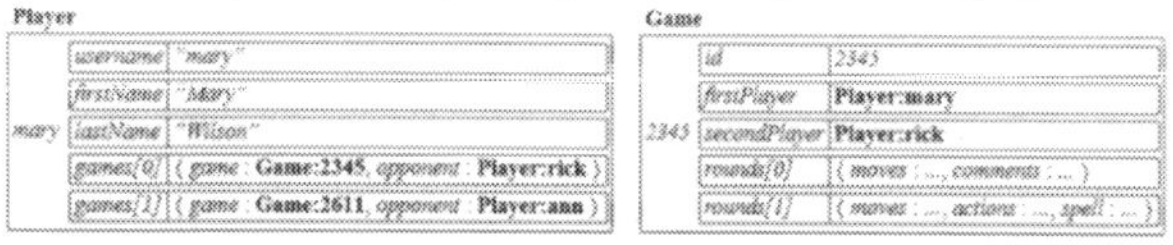

Figure 12. A sample in the NoAM abstract model [12].

case, H was not treated yet, and then H is converted first. The H column family is created and, as it does not have any parent relation, the processing returns to F, which is then converted. At this time, it is verified that the union is partial and an intermediary column family to hold the artificial relation is created (F-H). The same holds to G.

V. Experimental Evaluation

The aggregation strategy for logical modeling prioritizes data accessing, avoiding read and write operations on different nodes. This is the reasoning behind *NoAM* [12], a close related work that also deals with NoSQL logical design. Such a strategy considers that is most efficient to gather all related data in a single operation. However, some problems arise from this strategy, like transporting irrelevant data for query operations or the need to persist the whole aggregate for update operations. This experiment intends to explore these limitations and to highlight our approach as a more efficient solution. The case study proposed by *NoAM* is a game application, and we compare it with our approach by adapting their experiments to a scenario which game data grows to a deterrent size. This scenario is suitable to modern game applications that, in many cases, simply never end.

To evaluate our approach, the EER schema in Figure 11 was generated through a reverse engineering process from the NoAM logical modeling (Figure 12), composed by two aggregates: `Player` (with game references) and `Game` (with

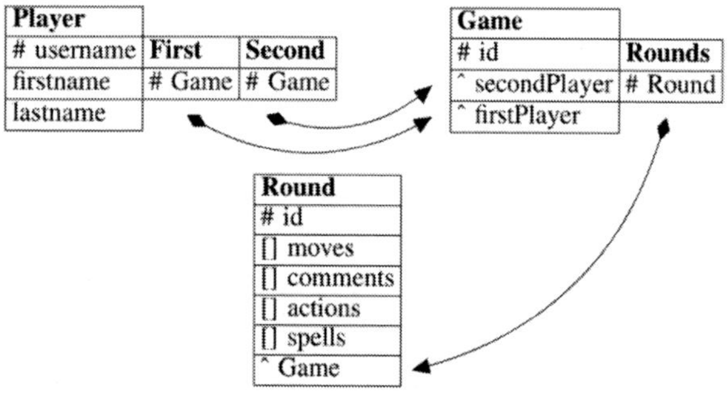

Figure 13. Logical modeling for a columnar DB in the game domain generated by our proposal.

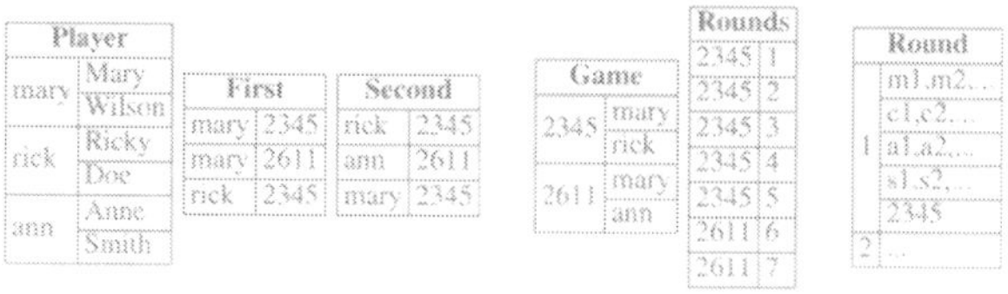

Figure 14. Physical modeling sample for in the game domain generated by our proposal.

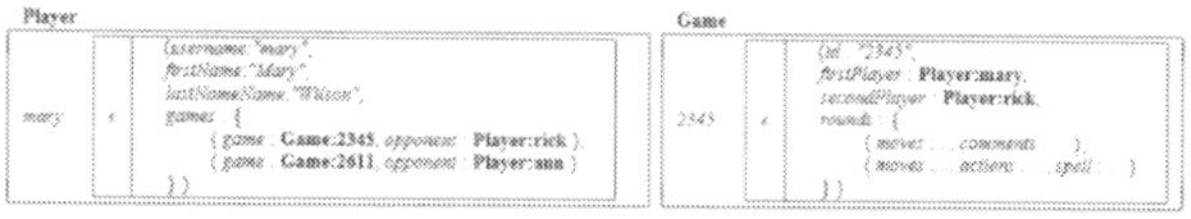

Figure 15. Physical modeling sample for in the game domain in NoAM [12].

its rounds).

The EER schema is then converted by our approach into the columnar logical schema presented in Figure 13. A sample of persisted data generated by our approach is shown in Figure 14, and part of this same sample represented by the NoAM approach is shown in Figure 15. The main difference between both proposals is that ours expands the number of column families from two to six. However, three of them are referenced by shared keys (`First`, `Second` and `Rounds`), so the data is near and easily referenced. Three artificial relations exist and the same number of references are made by the NoAM proposal (`firstPlayer`, `secondPlayer` and `Game`). Besides, all the attributes in both modelings are similar, except for `opponent`, that it is assumed to be the opposite player.

In order to evaluate our proposal, we have implemented both logical schemata in the Cassandra columnar DB, and we compare read/write operation timespan according to a scenario which we believe that the NoAM approach cannot handle well. For running our experiments, a remote Cassandra cluster with three nodes was deployed. Its overall performance is not the focus of this work nor the latency with data transport.

An algorithm to rule the experiment was defined and consists of two parts: *(i)* creating a game and; *(ii)* playing the game. In short, for each created game, a hundred rounds multiplied by the game count were created. Each game has two players and both are updated to maintain a list of games they are playing. A game creation is a single write operation. To update the list of games of both players, 2 reads and 2 writes are necessary. To add a round to a game, it is needed 1 read and 1 write operation. Thus, at the end of the fourth game, 2.020 reads and writes were accomplished.

The presented charts are comparisons between NoAM (solid line) and our proposal (dotted line). The X axis represents the iterations of the algorithm, and the Y axis is the average spent time in seconds. Figure 16 shows the spent time with write operations for the four games and its rounds, and Figure 17 shows the spent time with read operations. The deep drops in these charts (near iterations 100, 300, 600 and 1000) denotes the start of new games (with empty rounds).

The experiment shows that, as the data blocks (or aggregates) grows, in NoAM approach, the timespan also raises. For small sized aggregates, the timing is similar for both approaches. However, when a single game reaches 70 rounds, they have a drop of 50% in terms of performance comparing to our approach. With a hundred rounds, NoAM is 2.6 times slower. Therefore, the increasing size of the aggregate impacts

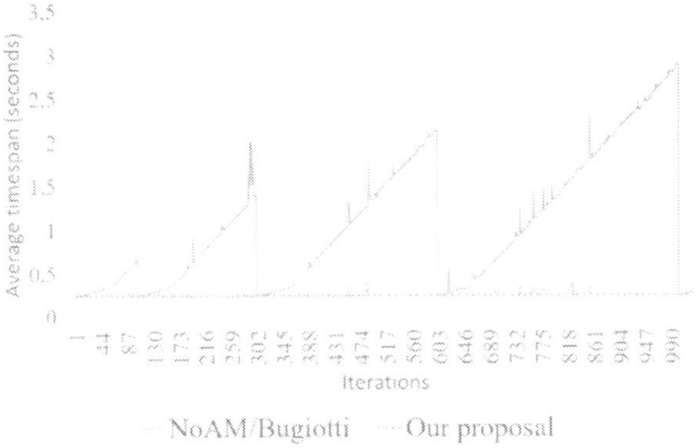

Figure 16. Average write time for a thousand iterations.

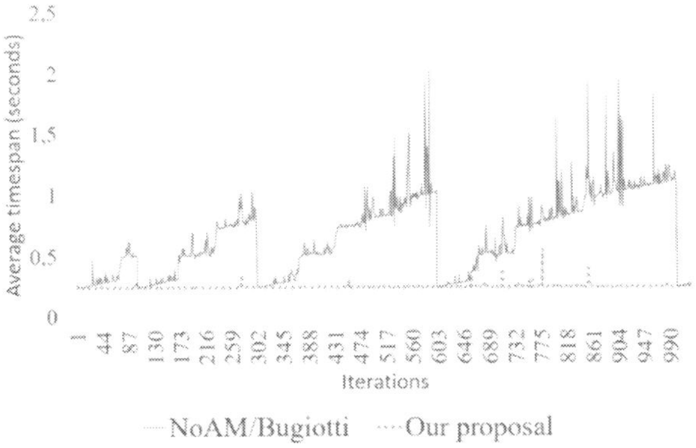

Figure 17. Average read time for a thousand iterations.

almost linearly to their performance decrease. This situation does not occur in our proposal because we make use of significantly smaller amount of data for each operation, and it happens independently of the hierarchical height on Y axis. Thus, our approach continues to be scalable as the number of game rounds grows.

The only inconvenient is that to gather all game data, our approach needs to pose several queries. However, these round-trips have a minimized impact on performance, as recent Application Programming Interfaces (API) can issue several queries in a single request to the server.

VI. CONCLUSION

This work represents a connection between classical DB design and columnar DBs, proposing an efficient approach for DB columnar logical design from an EER conceptual schema. Our contributions are a logical notation for columnar DBs, a set of conversion algorithms that generates a logical schema in that notation, as well as an experimental evaluation that compares our approach against a close related work (the *NoAM* approach), with very promising results. Our logical notation defines a minimal set of concepts needed to achieve a suitable structure to be implemented in a columnar DB.

The experimental evaluation shows a data modeling for columnar DB which reveals to be impracticable to NoAM [12], but viable to our approach.

We argue that scaled and massive data is not only for data mining. This work makes a progress in an area that urges to make NoSQL a reliable alternative to classical relational DB design. Domains where data that tends to grow very fast require efficient logical modeling strategies, as proposed in this paper.

Future work include experiments with existing benchmarks and other typical Big Data domains, like social networks, as well as the consideration of the application workload information in our logical design process. Workload information is important as a guide to define optimized logical structures for the most frequently accessed data by the application operations.

REFERENCES

[1] C. Curino et al., "Relational cloud: A database service for the cloud," in 5th Biennial Conference on Innovative Data Systems Research, Asilomar, CA, January 2011, pp. 235–240.

[2] T. Hoff, "What the heck are you actually using nosql for?" http://highscalability.com/blog/2010/12/6/what-the-heck-are-you-actually-using-nosql-for.html, 2010, retrieved: Apr. 2016.

[3] A. B. M. Moniruzzaman and S. A. Hossain, "Nosql database: New era of databases for big data analytics-classification, characteristics and comparison," International Journal of Database Theory and Application, vol. 6, no. 4, 2013, pp. 1–14.

[4] K. Kaur and R. Rani, "Modeling and querying data in nosql databases," in Big Data, 2013 IEEE International Conference on, Oct 2013, pp. 1–7.

[5] Solid IT, "Db–engines ranking," http://db-engines.com/en/ranking, 2016, retrieved: Apr. 2016.

[6] P. J. Sadalage and M. Fowler, NoSQL distilled: a brief guide to the emerging world of polyglot persistence. Pearson Education, 2012.

[7] S. B. Navathe, C. Batini, and S. Ceri, "Conceptual database design: an entity-relationship approach," Redwood City: Benjamin Cummings, 1992.

[8] G. Wang and J. Tang, "The nosql principles and basic application of cassandra model," in Computer Science Service System (CSSS), 2012 on International Conference, Aug 2012, pp. 1332–1335.

[9] R. Elmasri and S. B. Navathe, Database systems. Pearson, 2005.

[10] R. Schroeder and R. d. S. Mello, "Improving query performance on xml documents: a workload-driven design approach," in Proceedings of the eighth ACM symposium on Document engineering. ACM, 2008, pp. 177–186.

[11] J. Fong, "Mapping extended entity-relationship model to object modeling technique," vol. 24, 1995, pp. 18–22.

[12] F. Bugiotti, L. Cabibbo, P. Atzeni, and R. Torlone, "Database design for nosql systems," in Conceptual Modeling. Springer, 2014, pp. 223–231.

[13] A. Chebotko, A. Kashlev, and S. Lu, "A big data modeling methodology for apache cassandra," in Big Data (BigData Congress), 2015 IEEE International Congress on. IEEE, 2015, pp. 238–245.

[14] J. Sharp, D. McMurtry, A. Oakley, M. Subramanian, and H. Zhang, "Data access for highly-scalable solutions: Using sql, nosql, and polyglot persistence," Microsoft patterns & practices, 2013.

[15] A. Schram and K. M. Anderson, "Mysql to nosql: data modeling challenges in supporting scalability," in Proceedings of the 3rd annual conference on Systems, programming, and applications: software for humanity. ACM, 2012, pp. 191–202.

[16] E. Meijer and G. Bierman, "A co–relational model of data for large shared data banks," Communications of the ACM, vol. 54, no. 4, 2011, pp. 49–58.

[17] L. Cabibbo, "Ondm: An object-nosql datastore mapper," Faculty of Engineering, Roma Tre University. Retrieved June 15th, 2013.

[18] A. Milanović and M. Mijajlović, "A survey of post-relational data management and nosql movement," Faculty of Mathematics University of Belgrade, Serbia, 2012.

[19] R. Mathies, "Cassandra data model," http://wiki.apache.org/cassandra/DataModelv2, 2015, retrieved: Apr, 2016.

[20] Apache Foundation, "Cassandra wiki," http://wiki.apache.org/cassandra, 2009, retrieved: Feb, 2015.

[21] R. Cattell, "Scalable sql and nosql data stores," SIGMOD Record, vol. 39, no. 4, 2010, pp. 12–27.

[22] B. Schwartz, "Schemaless databases don't exist," https://vividcortex.com/blog/2015/02/24/schemaless-databases-dont-exist, 2015, retrieved: Apr, 2016.

SLA-constrained Feedback-based Software Load Distribution Algorithm that Minimizes Computing Resource Requirement

S. R. Venkatramanan
PayPal
San Jose, CA
e-mail: raven@paypal.com

R. Hariharan and A. S. Murthy
eBay
San Jose, CA
e-mail: rehariharan@ebay.com and asmurthy@ebay.com

***Abstract*—We describe a load distribution algorithm in this paper that uses the current transaction response time as feedback for dynamically routing traffic to a minimal number of machines that run a business function (pool), with the constraint to consistently meet the response time requirements. This enables us to dynamically vary the number of nodes as per traffic levels, traffic mixes, and varying node capacities - a typical scenario in cloud environments. First, we present details of the basic algorithm followed by an extended version. Both have been implemented and tested in the eBay private cloud. We include graphs that show how the number of active nodes vary with incoming traffic volume while preserving the response time requirements. Results of using the extended version illustrate how the performance of the mirror environment closely matches that of the real environment while running production traffic.**

Keywords-Software Load Balancer; feedback; SLA; load distribution; minimum nodes; energy optimization

I. INTRODUCTION

eBay's network sees varying amounts of traffic that show a diurnal variation, with traffic peaks during mid-day and evening hours. Early morning and midnight traffic varies from being half of the peak to even less, depending upon the business function served. Traffic handled by a typical node serving a typical business function on the network is shown in Fig 1.

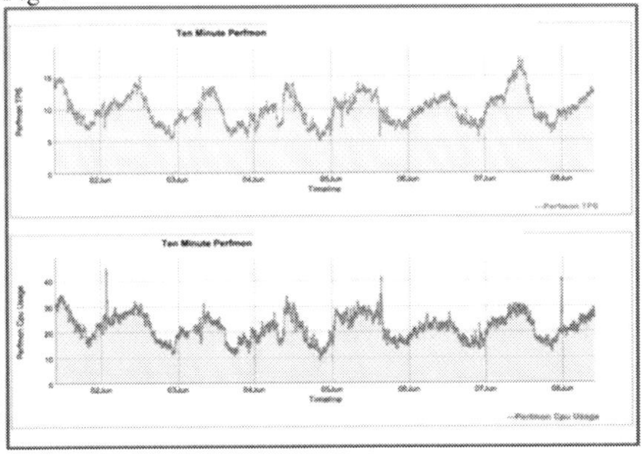

Figure 1. Traffic pattern seen in a typical node running a typical application

This means a number of nodes allocated to handle peak traffic of a given business function or application are idling for a significant part of the day. However, capacity managers are often uneasy about reducing the size of application pools during times of reduced need because any unexpected increase in traffic might result in the response time requirements not being met.

The above situation warrants two needs:

- An automatic way to detect the saturation state of nodes and augment the pool
- Ability to readily deploy and shutdown nodes as requirement dictates

Detection of the saturation state has to be dynamic and the system should be able to trigger the addition of new nodes in time, as needed, without affecting the application response time. It is possible to quickly add nodes capable of taking traffic in a responsive cloud setup using some of our earlier work, i.e., configure a node, deploy code, and bring it into traffic in a short amount of time.

In addition, if the right number of nodes in an application pool is dynamically managed, it can result in a significant reduction in energy consumption in the data center, in terms of power and cooling, while preserving the application response times through the course of the day, irrespective of traffic levels.

Nodes of the eBay cloud, about 185,000, come from various processor generations and systems technologies and thus, one Virtual Machine (VM) of a given size (CPU, memory, etc.) may vary significantly in capacity from another VM. Hence, using a round robin load dispatching will stress these nodes differently. In order to overcome the effect of varying technologies, weighted round robin is suggested. However, in a cloud environment, an application run by a guest VM does not have a dedicated environment on the host system and the background load on the host can vary considerably. This means the weights used would not only depend upon the technology used, but also vary with the other applications and their load on the host system. This performance variation is described in detail in [1]. Keeping the weights correctly defined becomes a complex task and does not guarantee the required transaction response time.

The main focus of this paper is to present a heuristic algorithm that minimizes the number of nodes needed to handle the traffic at any time with a constraint of preserving response time needs. This sets the stage to power machines up as needed and take down machines when not required for an extended period of time in the cloud environment.

The rest of the paper is organized as follows. In Section II, we present a summary of the types of routing algorithms used, stating how our algorithm differs from those algorithms. Section III has the description of the basic algorithm, where the requests and their response time distribution are more or less similar. Since the algorithm relies on routing requests to a minimal number of nodes, we also detail a heuristic method to route transient bursts in traffic in the case where the maximum number of nodes available is less than necessary for that traffic level (degraded operation). Section IV contains the changes needed to extend this procedure to heterogeneous traffic. We detail in Section V how we verified the performance of this algorithm. Section VI has the detailed results for both implementations and Section VII presents our conclusions.

II. CURRENT WORK IN CLOUD TRAFFIC ROUTING ALGORITHMS

Load balancing algorithms mainly fall into two categories- static algorithms and dynamic algorithms. According to recent survey papers [2][3], optimal routing algorithms to maximize throughput used in the cloud are based on shortest queueing with maximum weight scheduling at each server. The same policy is shown to be queue length optimal. These algorithms are also shown to be optimal for resource usage under heavy traffic conditions. Algorithms described in these surveys are all dynamic and are based on stochastic arrivals. In all the algorithms addressed in the literature, the number of servers traffic is routed to is given apriori. All optimization is done to either maximize throughput or to provide the best experience for the request, given the set of available servers.

Another survey paper by Katyal et al. [4] presents a thorough classification of routing requirements in the cloud and various algorithms that cater to these requirements. Static algorithms are based on routing to a given set of IP addresses or given machines that have the needed resources. Dynamic algorithms, presented in this paper, use the state of the system to route the request

There is a detailed comparison of various types of load balancing methods presented in a recent paper [5] that proposes the development of a new method for getting improved response times from servers. Active VM Load Balancer [5] comes close to what we propose, among the methods described in that paper. It takes into consideration the number of requests currently allocated to a server in deciding where to route the next incoming request. However, all available nodes are always open to receiving traffic and traffic is routed to nodes such that the quality of service is best. None of the algorithms described in [7] (Round Robin, Weighted Round Robin, Throttled Load Balancing, Dynamic Load Balancing using system utilization, and Active VM load balancer) vary the number of nodes to which traffic is routed.

None of these algorithms surveyed deal with routing to a minimal number of servers at any time. What makes our work unique is the fact that our algorithm routes the requests to a minimal number of nodes, freeing up unused nodes while maintaining the application response time requirement.

III. BASIC ALGORITHM DESCRIPTION

All commands or requests (embedded in the URL) come to the Software Load Balancer (SLB) and are forwarded to the node of choice. In the basic version of the algorithm, we only consider requests corresponding to similar response times. Subsequently, we extend this to more realistic environments with heterogeneous requests.

A. *Algorithm Principle*

Little's Law [6] describing the relationship between response time and number of requests in the system states

$$L = \lambda \times W \qquad (1)$$

where, 'L' is the number of requests in the system, λ is the arrival rate of requests, and 'W' is the expected response time. In other words, response time 'W' and the number of requests in the system 'L' are linearly related. So, by controlling the maximum number of requests (or *connections* to a node, and equivalent to L in the above formula), we can control the response time effectively. This is the main idea behind this algorithm.

In the eBay private cloud, Service Level Agreement (SLA) for various commands is typically governed by the distribution of the response times. Henceforth, we will refer to the response times as SLA in this paper. We use the *historical median* of the currently observed response time, with consideration to the time of day, for baseline (*SLA-med*), and the *2nd standard deviation* (*SLA-95*) for tolerance. We accumulate the deviation of observed transaction response time of a node from *SLA-med* for each of a predefined set of transactions. As the accumulated value exceeds a certain predefined threshold proportional to *SLA-95*, we adjust the value for the maximum allowed *connections* into that node. To illustrate this, consider the following example. Let the median response time for a given command equal 100ms (*SLA-med*=100ms) and the 95th percentile (~2nd

standard deviation or P95) equal 200ms (SLA-95=200ms). Now, if the next series of response times are 120ms, 90ms, and 150ms, then the differences accumulated would be 20ms, -10ms, and 50ms respectively, summing up to 60ms. When the sum of response times of transactions up to a given number exceeds a given threshold, we take action by reducing the maximum number of *connections* allocated to that node.

To understand the statistical basis of this, let each response time x_i be normally distributed with a mean μ and standard deviation σ. If $y_i = x_i - \mu$, then the sum of k such differences, $\Sigma_i\ y_i \sim N(0, \sqrt{k} * \sigma)$. So the difference will exceed $+/-3*\sqrt{k} * \sigma$, with a probability < 1%. When this happens, this either signifies a very rare occurrence or it shows a shift in distribution of the variable, implying that the response times are either systematically increasing or decreasing. If the response times are increasing, we could control it by decreasing the maximum connections we allow into the node and vice-versa. For normal distribution, mean should be equal to median; however, our empirical distribution is not normal and has outliers. Hence, in our method we choose median instead of mean as it is more stable and not influenced by outliers. Further, since the traffic volume and response times, influenced by the traffic, are not temporally constant, median is calculated over a moving window and SLA, taken from the historical data, is changed over time.

The Software Load Balancer (SLB) maintains an ordered list of nodes and attempts to send the requests to nodes in that order. If a node that occurs earlier in the ordered list has *connections* available, then the request is sent to that node. The requests will use a minimal number of nodes as a result of maintaining an ordered list and sending traffic to the earlier nodes, until they cannot serve the request within the required service time constraint, likely because of lack of resources on that node. We can tune this threshold to achieve the necessary SLA by controlling the maximum *connections* into a node. Note that the action to increase or decrease the *connections* is based only on the SLA target (median and P95 values), which are essentially surrogates used to represent resource utilization. It is to be noted that poor performing applications will also be exposed by this.

B. *Procedure*

Flow charts in Fig. 2 and Fig. 3 show how the load distribution algorithm works in the SLB. Fig. 2 shows how the maximum number of *connections* (*CMax*) is dynamically adjusted for any given node after each transaction (*N*) is completed by that specific node in the pool. Each node is initialized with its own *CMax* and they are based on historical observation of traffic handling capability of the overall pool, taking into consideration the time of day, the day of week, and the season. Its value is adjusted, as described in the flow chart, based on the value of an accumulator which essentially maintains the sum of differences between the actual observed response times seen at the node and the expected response time or SLA.

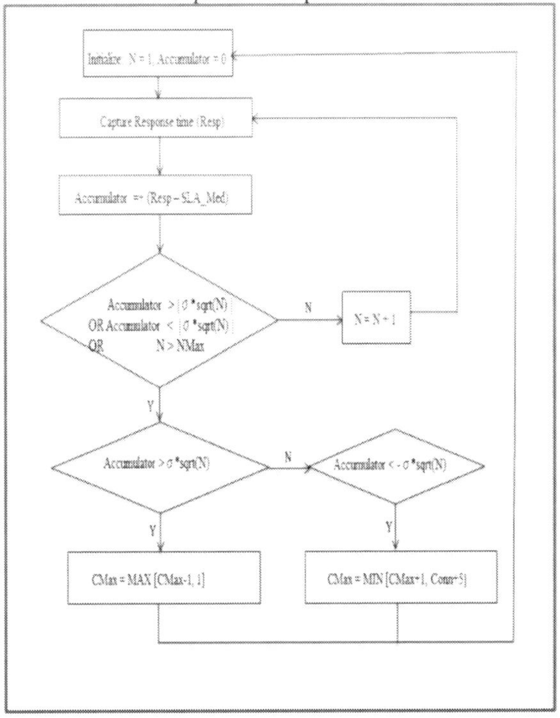

Figure 2. Basic Flow Chart to determine Max connection for each node

The accumulator is reset whenever either a predefined maximum number of transactions (*NMax*) have been completed by the node or when *CMax* is modified as a result of the accumulator exceeding certain thresholds. A buffer of 5 connection counts while decreasing, prevents the reduction of connections too soon and from being unable to accommodate any surge in traffic while idling. It also ensures traffic is not black-holed into one node when transactions complete too fast because of error returns or bugs in the application.

C. *Node choice and Degraded Operation*

Fig. 3 shows how a choice of the node to route the request to is made when a new request comes into the SLB. It is to be noted that when there is no node found fit to route the request to (a case when there should have been more nodes made available but not fulfilled for whatever reason), the load distribution procedure drops to a lower grade of service level. Degraded service level is applicable only in cases when the system does not provision additional nodes in time.

Routing can use the following in such cases.

- Simple Round Robin or random routing to the available nodes.

- Use of a relaxed SLA (gradually increasing the SLA by 10% at a time) to determine a new *CMax* for each node and routing the request to the first node with available connections. We will refer to this method as Relaxed SLA.

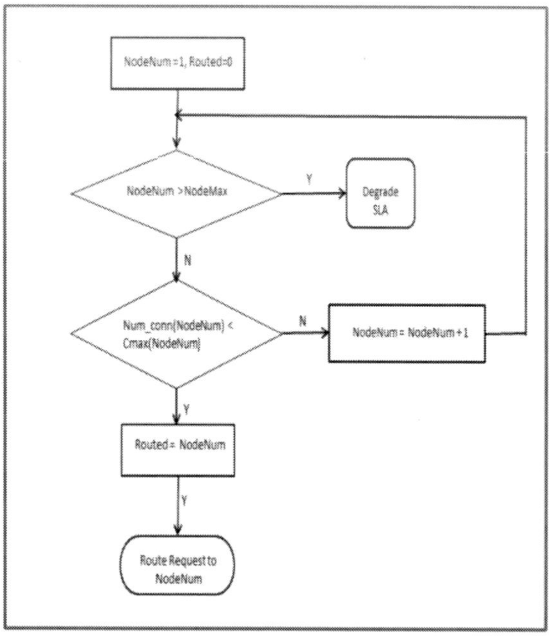

Figure 3. Basic Decision Flow Chart

Details of degraded operation will be beyond the scope of this paper though both of the following methods have been implemented and verified. We use the latter method, in the final implementation, by always maintaining a secondary *CMax* value corresponding to relaxed SLAs. In a situation where no node is considered available under the relaxed SLA, we repeatedly try from the first node, using the secondary *CMax* (that is 10% higher than the value at the previous level of relaxation) until a node, if any, that permits traffic to be routed is found. This process of relaxing SLA is done iteratively.

IV. HETEROGENOUS ENVIRONMENT

The preliminary version of the algorithm described above is only applicable to a homogeneous environment where all requests have a response time requirement of the same order. However, a single eBay application can handle requests of different types with varying response time needs, ranging from a few milliseconds to nearly a second. If incoming requests to such an application is handled as a single type with a large variation, this large variance makes it difficult to effectively adjust the *CMax* value.

We extend the basic version of the algorithm by grouping commands with similar response times. Using the historical median and standard deviation of the response time for a command as input variables, we use *KMeans* to classify the commands into a limited number of groups. The number of groups is determined by the number of peaks observed in the distribution of response times of all commands. For a distribution as shown in Fig. 4, the number of groups will equal to 2. In cases where multiple modes in the distribution come from the same command, due to multi-modal distribution of the response times of the same command, the number of groups to classify the commands should be appropriately reduced. Once the number of groups is chosen, *KMeans* classification is used to group the commands.

In a production environment, the behavior of commands and their respective response time distribution varies continuously, mainly due to variability in user behavior. Therefore, the grouping process is repeated each hour to ensure minimum variability within a group.

Once the commands are classified into multiple groups, we introduce SLB Group Modules as in Fig. 6, with each module handling only commands for a single group.

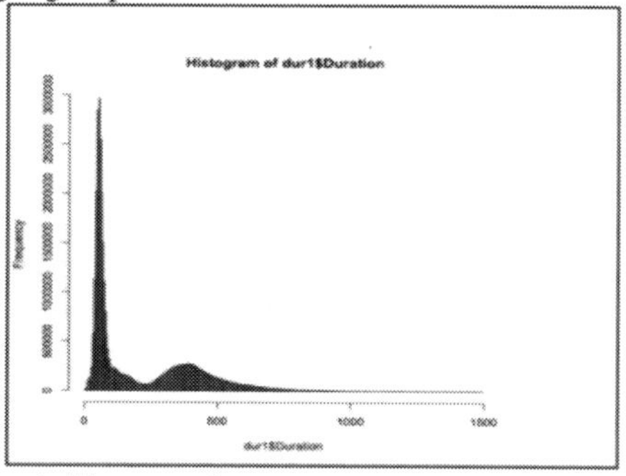

Figure 4 - Histogram of response distribution of all commands

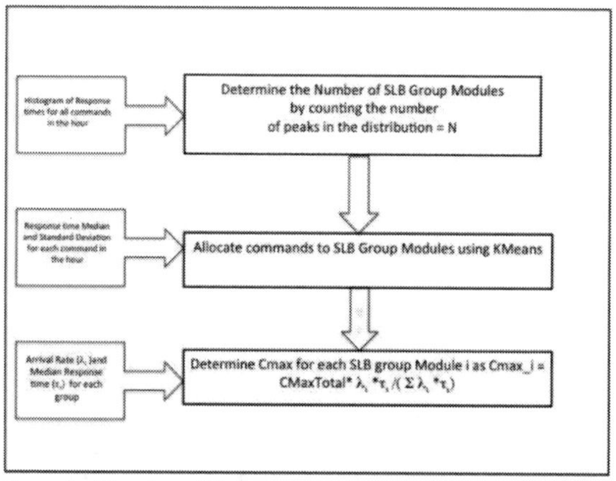

Figure 5: Allocation of Commands to groups and Seeding CMax for each group

The next step is to allocate a base number of connections for each group. This is done by weighting the total number of connections according to arrival rate * median response time for each group. Fig 5 summarizes this process.

Fig 6 shows how commands are routed to individual SLB Group Modules by the master router.

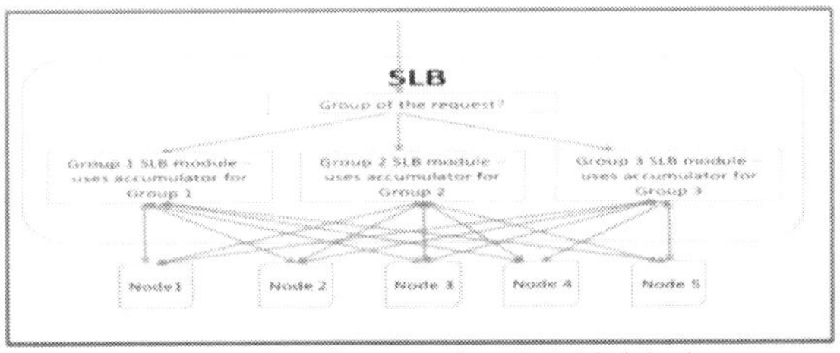

Figure 6. Routing of commands to SLB Modules in a Heterogeneous environment

V. VERIFICATION ENVIRONMENT

Algorithm verification was accomplished as follows. A typical eBay application (in Java) was deployed on 4 nodes each configured with 4 processors and adequate memory, and backed by necessary services and databases. Transactions executed by this application during a typical day were captured from the production application logs and they were grouped by similar measured response times. This provided a workload to be later played back by JMeter [7] instances and targeted to the SLB running various algorithms. In the first phase, we restrict the transactions to a single group with homogeneous response times; the later phase will include transactions with wider response times.

Multiple Jmeter instances were used to control traffic rate and patterns. Performance metrics were obtained through JMX interface built into the application as part of routine measurement infrastructure. This infrastructure provides measurements such as throughput (Transactions Per Second), CPU utilization, and Transaction Response Time, besides JVM heap related metrics, aggregated over a selected interval such as 1 minute, 10 minutes, or one hour. For short experiments of an hour or two durations, 1-minute aggregation is used. In the first set of experiments presented, we use round-robin routing to handle the degraded state of operation.

VI. RESULTS

Here we discuss the results of executing this algorithm showing the traffic arrival pattern as well as the corresponding performance trend of each of the nodes with respect to the elapsed time. Fig. 7 shows the intensity of the load in terms of active users on the system as time goes by. Fig. 8 shows the throughput achieved by each of the nodes, their corresponding CPU utilizations, and response time of the requests on corresponding nodes. Discontinuities in the later part of Fig 8 and Fig. 9 are because of the measurement infrastructure dropping measurement data.

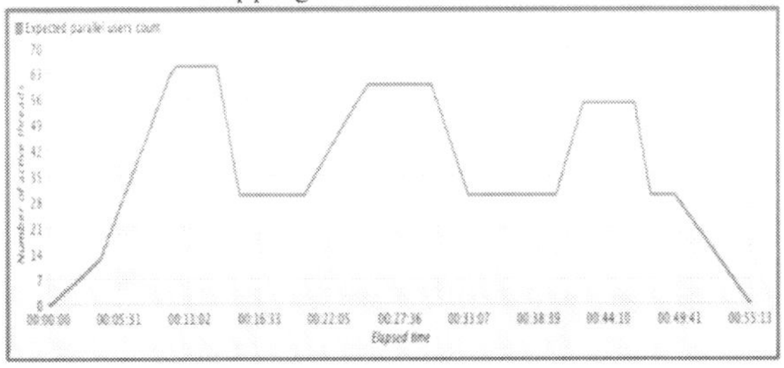

Figure 7. Arrival Pattern with multiple load variations

Fig. 8 demonstrates the recoverability of the system following this algorithm in a cyclical traffic pattern, including a small burst (from 9 to 12 minutes into the test) that was not compensated by an increase in the number of nodes resulting in a brief loss of response time SLA (800ms). However, as the load eases up after about 13 minutes into the run, CPU utilization starts to come down, also bringing the response time under SLA. Eventually, when the traffic slows down considerably, nodes start to drop off in LIFO fashion. As can be seen from the CPU utilization plot, Fig. 8b and Fig. 9b, this algorithm provides for completely removing a node from the pool between 15 and 20 minutes and, again, between 32 and 45 minutes of this abridged test.

The reader is encouraged to also note that one of the nodes shows 25% CPU utilization even before traffic begins in the graphs in Fig. 8b and Fig. 9b. Driving one of its 4 CPUs into an artificial loop and consuming 25% of the available resources purposefully degrades that node. This is to demonstrate the resilience of the algorithm when nodes of heterogeneous capabilities are presented, or during misbehavior of any of the nodes in the pool that may be unavoidable but not easy to extricate in time.

TABLE I. COMPARISON OF RESPONSE TIMES

	Median			P95			Count
Command	Target	Ref	T-R in %	Target	Ref	T-R in %	Ref
AdvS	123	109	12.84	262	238	10.08	3892
AllD	103	112	-8.04	208	218	-4.61	5540
ChsM	457	459	-0.44	1228	1028	19.44	8960
Cust	43	39	10.26	138	138	0.00	1206
FavS	19	222	-91.44	106	417	-74.47	1010
FndH	637	613	3.92	2236	2881	-22.37	43
FndM	90	96	-6.25	1098	5315	-79.34	593
GetC	76	75	1.33	76	75	1.33	1
JsDi	569	559	1.79	1054	1066	-1.11	11625
Prev	163	160	1.88	260	242	7.44	722
RecC	363	368	-1.36	517	544	-4.96	82951
SvSD	320	322	-0.62	549	558	-1.61	273873
SePr	477	477	0.00	682	686	-0.45	1631
SRPR	679	676	0.44	1400	1432	-2.23	1444307
SRSS	560	561	-0.18	1111	1170	-5.04	200592
SelO	585	579	1.04	1060	1059	0.09	62547
SimI	575	583	-1.37	915	985	-7.11	131498
V4Aj	244	104	134.62	323	196	64.96	4
Vero	832	750.5	10.86	2830	907	212.14	2
ZipP	44	42	4.76	96	71	35.21	426
TOTAL							2231423

Table I summarizes a test run where live traffic from multiple servers was mirrored into the SLB created to handle heterogeneous requests with 3 groups. The servers allocated to the SLB were part of the eBay cloud, thus representing the same environment as the current servers. The reader is drawn to the highlighted row that shows how response time requirement was met, both median as well as 95th percentile, for the most predominant type of request in a typical traffic composition of the peak day of the week by executing the algorithm.

Resource Consumption Ceiling

Brief loss of SLA, from 9 to 12 minutes into the test, (Fig. 6c) was mainly because CPU was driven to about 95% utilization leaving insufficient processing capacity even for basic bookkeeping functions of the system. Adherence to the set response time SLA can be controlled by introducing an additional constraint on maximum resource utilization, or running the application at a slightly lower priority that gives system processes an opportunity to do their functions necessary for the stability of the system.

An experiment was conducted to simulate this constraint by limiting the incoming traffic to use just under 90% CPU and the results given below in Fig. 9b are indeed encouraging in confirming that observation.

VII. CONCLUSION

We have presented in this paper an algorithm for efficient allocation of resources while adhering to response time requirements of applications under varying load conditions in cloud environments. The full potential of this algorithm can be realized with an adjunct system to flex up and flex down the nodes as needed.

Future work should include a mechanism for a trigger to add and remove nodes, and has built-in hysteresis to avoid frequent add/remove. The trigger mechanism should have complete knowledge of the cloud environment and should provide enough lead time based on provisioning time needed by the underlying cloud management system and the traffic intensity or rate of change in the traffic.

ACKNOWLEDGMENT

Authors would like to acknowledge Rami El-Charif, former Technical Fellow at eBay Inc., for his valuable contribution in discussions and guidance throughout this exploratory design and implementation of this algorithm and eBay management for its support.

REFERENCES

[1] Hariharan R, Murthy A.S., and Venkatramanan S. R., "How to handle noisy neighbors?", CMG Conference Proceedings, 2014, pp. 345-351.

[2] Kuppuswamy, K, and Mahalakshmi, J, "A survey on routing algorithms for cloud computing, IJCA Proceedings on International Conference on Computing and information Technology 2013 IC2IT (4), pp. 5-8, December 2013.

[3] Mohana, S. J, Saroja, M, and Venkatachalam, M, "Cloud balancing- A survey", International Journal of Engineering Research and Development, Volume 8, Issue 8 (September 2013), pp. 13-17

[4] Katyal, M, and Mishra, A, "A comparative study of static and dynamic load balancing algorithms", International Journal of Distributed and Cloud Computing, Volume 1 Issue 2 December 2013, pp. 5-14

[5] Zaouch, A. and Benabbou, F, "Load balancing for improved quality of service in a cloud", International Journal of Advanced Computer Science and Applications, Vol 6, No. 7 (2015), pp. 184-189.

[6] Little, J. D. C. (1961). "A proof for the queuing formula: L = λW", Operations Research 9 (3), pp. 383–387. JSTOR 167570

[7] Apache Foundation. "JMeter: Graphical server performance testing tool" Available for download at http://jmeter.apache.org/download_jmeter.cgi, Last Access Date: 21APR2016

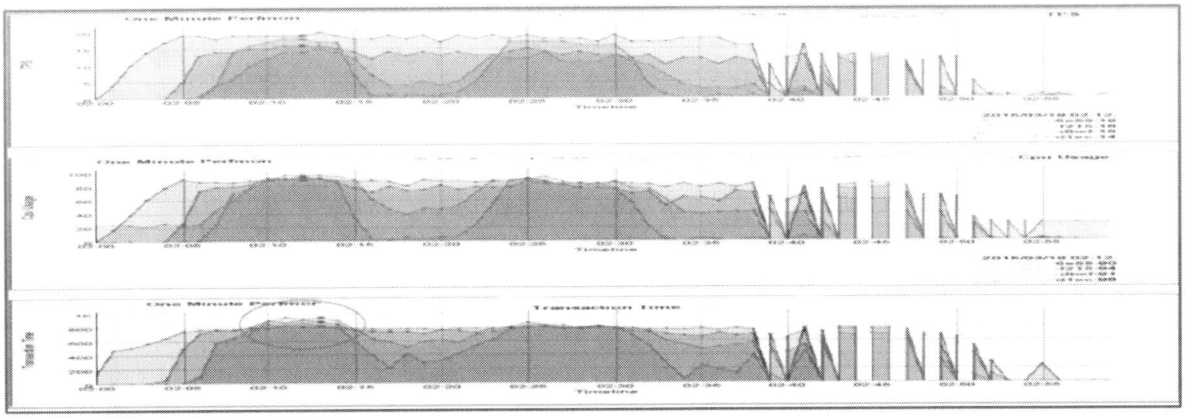

Figure 8. Under-provisioned System - SLA Violation at peak load. 8a – TPS, 8b – CPU, 8c – Transaction Time

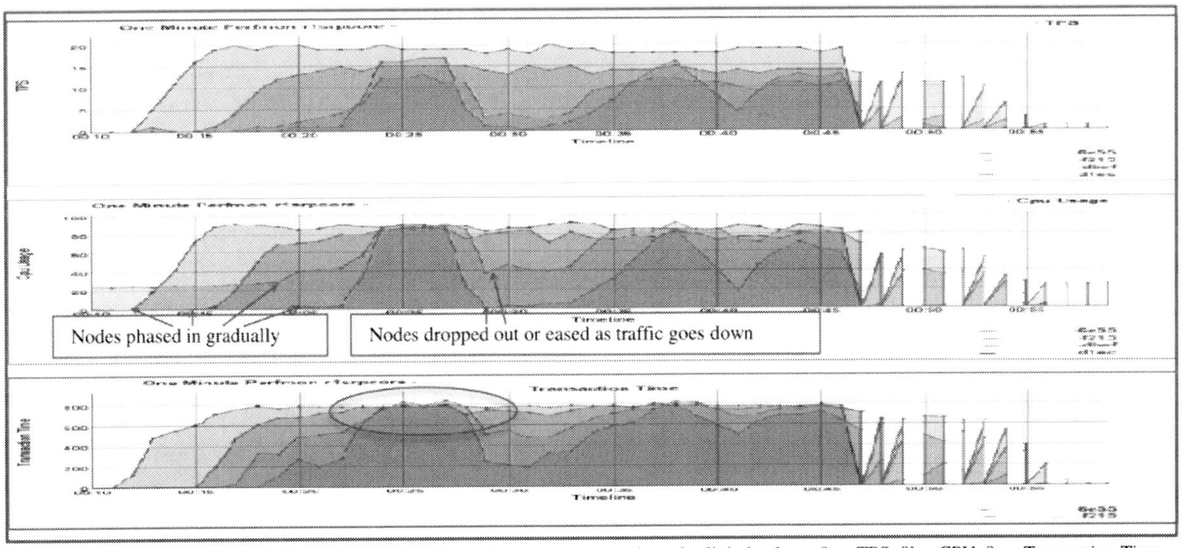

Figure 9. System Behavior under controlled load – Opportunity to remove a node under light load. 9a – TPS, 9b – CPU, 9c – Transaction Time

Semantic Service Management for Enabling Adaptive and Evolving Processes

Johannes Fähndrich, Tobias Küster, and Nils Masuch

DAI-Labor
Technische Universität Berlin
Berlin, Germany
e-mail: {firstname.lastname}@dai-labor.de

Abstract—**With the rise of new paradigms like the Internet of Things, where thousands of devices and services of different providers are to be connected to complex processes, service-oriented approaches come to the fore. However, current solutions still lack of comprehensive methodologies how to dynamically manage and combine services to fulfil the given goals. In this paper we present a semantic-based service management methodology that enables the semantic description of services and provides an automatic service discovery and composition solution at design- and runtime. Furthermore, we present development tools that support the usage of semantic web technologies and we describe an execution environment where the approach is embedded. We conclude with an evaluation scenario from an e-mobility research project.**

***Keywords*–Semantic Service Enhancement; Semantic Service Matching; Automated Service Composition; Model Transformation; BPMN Processes; OWL-S; Semantic Service Descriptions**

I. Introduction

The ever increasing digitalization of our societies leads to a vast amount of new possibilities, but also challenges. In the meantime, many companies, administrations and devices share their data or functionalities with others via application programming interfaces (APIs) or services respectively. Examples are the smart home or the transportation domain. In the first case, many different devices, such as smart meters and household appliances are addressable and can be regulated remotely. In the second case, the market is being extended by new services, such as car-sharing, bike-sharing and ride-sharing offers, which are provided digitally and where the user can find, reserve and unlock the most appropriate one via an API. Furthermore, the vehicles themselves can be configured via services and the environment is also becoming more digitized (charging-stations, parking spots, traffic analysis services, etc.). And even more sophisticated is the approach of the Internet of Things (IoT) which intends to connect services across domain borders.

However, in all cases there are some huge challenges that have to be overcome in order to exploit their potential. At first there is the requirement of finding a service. Different approaches like Universal Description, Discovery and Integration (UDDI) have been proposed, but none really has made it into the market. Second, there is the need for interoperability. Since a homogeneous data environment in open, extensible platforms is unrealistic, automated mapping solutions between models or ontologies respectively are one potential approach. And finally, due to the increasing amount of services, there is a strong requirement for automatic interpretation of services and their composition to value-added functionalities.

Especially for the last challenge, semantic technologies are an appropriate approach by providing structured data to machines. However, this does not come without a price. The management overhead can be immense especially for developers not familiar with semantic technologies. Therefore it was our goal to develop a semantic-based service management methodology that considers the whole life-cycle of semantic services including more sophisticated algorithms for automation. More concretely, we provide development tools for model transformation, for the semantic description of services and their deployment in order to set up a service. Furthermore, we propose how to find and match services at design-time and how to easily integrate them either to Java code or into a Business Process Model and Notation (BPMN) editor. Based upon that we developed comprehensive matching and service composition techniques that can be used both at design-time and at runtime.

This paper is structured as follows: In Section II, we present the different components that constitute our approach to semantic service engineering, and in Section III we show how those components are combined to form a holistic development method for semantic services and their composition. In Section IV, we demonstrate how the different components and the method have been applied in a research project in the e-mobility domain. Finally, we present some related approaches in Section V before we conclude in Section VI.

II. Components

First, we will describe the several components that make up our approach to semantic service engineering. We subdivided this section into three parts: First, we will have a look at the fundamental aspects, i.e., the semantic service matcher and planner, and describe their behaviour in detail. Then, we introduce different tools that help in the development of semantic services and in their aggregation and orchestration to complex, value added processes. Finally, we present the execution environment, making use of a multi-agent framework while at the same time being fully interoperable with existing Web Services Description Language (WSDL) and Representational State Transfer (REST) services.

A. Semantic Service Core

Since the beginning of research in semantic service matching, matchmakers have matured in precision and recall [1]. Thus, the focus of service matching has shifted to the integration of non-functional parameters and formal modelling of system properties. The development on the Service Matcher that had the best Normalised Discounted Cumulative Gain

(NDCG) value in the last S3 contest in 2012 [1], called $SeMa^2$, has been focused on formalising and distributing the architecture of $SeMa^2$ and enabling a learning mechanism to customise the matching results to a given domain. We start this section by describing how we modelled the architecture, the matching probability, its aggregation and which parameters for the learning can be extracted. For an even more detailed discussion about $SeMa^2$, we refer to [2].

1) Architecture of a modern Service Matcher: The service matching task can be broken down into subtasks like matching the inputs of the request and the advertisement, or comparing their textual descriptions. In the $SeMa^2$ architecture each of these subtasks has been explicitly encapsulated in a so called *expert* which can be distributed following the agent paradigm.

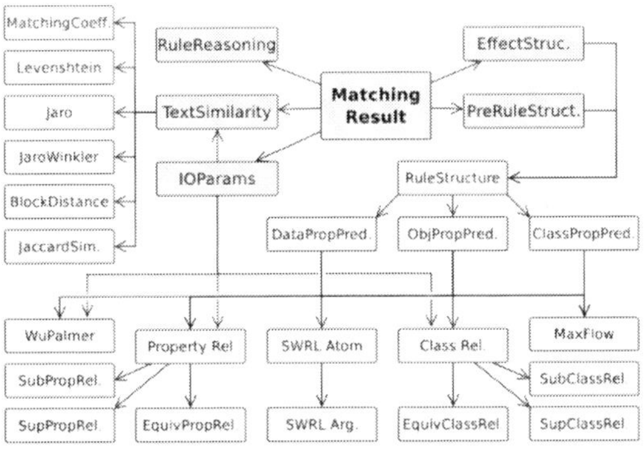

Figure 1. Expert System of the $SeMa^2$. High-level experts are composed of low-level experts, all contributing to the Matching Result.

As shown in Figure 1, the $SeMa^2$ consists of 28 different experts, which are dependent from each other (edges of the graph). The "Matching Result" represents the overall result of a matching request. It is also defined as an expert as it aggregates the results from the opinions of four types of experts: the text similarity expert, comparing the textual descriptions of a service, the in- and output parameter expert looking at the parameters and results of the services, the effect structure expert evaluating the similarity of effects, and the rule reasoning expert which evaluates whether the precondition and effect rules are satisfied with the same parameters. Each of those experts uses other experts to help forming its opinion, expressing the matching score of one aspect of a service. Thus, each expert encapsulates such a scoring method, which can be reused by multiple experts or extended with new scoring as the architecture evolves.

2) Probabilistic model of opinion: The different opinions of the experts are formalised by utilising the results of Morris [3], as probabilities $p_i(R, A)$. As an expert i observes aspects of a request R and advertisement A and calculates their distance. We can abstract this opinion as $p_i(\Theta|d)$ where Θ is the subject of interest and d are the observations. $p_i(\Theta|d)$ could be interpreted as a degree of belief of Θ observing data d. For more details see [2].

To aggregate the opinions of the different experts, an Opinion Pool is used. Here, a weighted mean of the opinions is created, for which we chose a weighted arithmetic mean called linear opinion pool [4] in a previous work [2]. This arithmetic mean has been generalised by Genest [5] to be able to use weights in the interval $[-1, 1]$ in a more general class of linear opinion pools. With this formalisation, the quality of the different aspects can be weighted during the aggregation. Choosing those weights is done during the learning phase.

3) Learning Semantic Service Matcher: Selecting weights for each experts instances ($SeMa^2$ for now has 128 experts instances), we do not only assess the performance of the expert, but also the quality of the description of the service, the ontologies of the domain and if present specific description aspects of a domain. These interdependencies are the reason why we are unable to learn the performance of an expert in general and reuse the weights for other matching domains.

For the learning, $SeMa^2$ implements different standard learning mechanisms, reaching from genetic algorithms implemented with the Watchmaker Framework [6] to simulated annealing [7]. For the statistical evaluation the Semantic Web Service Matchmaker Evaluation Environment (SME2) tool [8] is used, calculating the NDCG of each expert and adapting its weight according to the optimisation strategy used during the learning. As a drawback, this ability to adapt to the domain makes an offline learning phase necessary, where a test collection of example services needs to be defined, including a relevance rating for the training set of service to be used by the SME2 tool.

4) Semantic Services Planner: The ability to automatically compose services to reach a given goal is called service planning [2]. The service planner based on the $SeMa^2$ utilises the service matcher for three tasks: first, to reason about effects and preconditions to find applicable service. Second, to reason on parameter selection for grounding the services and third, to apply the execution of a service to reach a new state.

Name: ServicePlan
Input: S_{start}, S_{goal}, Services **Output:** Service Composition

$path \leftarrow []$
$Closed \leftarrow \emptyset$
$Open \leftarrow \{S_{start}\}$
while $s \leftarrow StateSearch.next(Open)$ **do**
  if $s \notin Closed$ **then**
    if $s = S_{goal}$ **then**
      return $reconstructPath(path + [s])$
    end if
    $grounded \leftarrow ServiceSearch.UsefulServices(s)$
    if $grounded \neq \emptyset$ **then**
      $succ \leftarrow \{execute(s, g) \mid g \in grounded\}$
      $Open \leftarrow Open \cup succ \setminus Closed$
      $path \leftarrow path + [s]$
    end if
    $Closed \leftarrow Closed \cup \{s\}$
  end if
end while
return failure

Figure 2. Service Planner algorithm

The algorithm in Figure 2 describes a standard planning approach applied to service planning. Here, the contribution is a planning in the service world without translating the service to the Planning Domain Description Language (PDDL) or similar to solve the planning problem.

The search used is defined in the function *StateSearch.next(Open)*. Depending on the implementation of the state search, the next state to be extended is selected. Here an A^* or equivalent algorithm can be used. In each state s that will be extended next, the selection of the services and their grounding is formalised in the function *ServiceSearch.UsefulServices(s)*. Here a set of grounded services is selected, which define the transition to the following open states. The state transition function is given by *execute(s, g)*, where the output and the effect of a service are integrated into the given state s. This is a theoretical execution, since the execution at runtime includes backtracking and a context sensing mechanism to sense the effect of a service. After extending a multitude of nodes during the search of the state space, the function *reconstructPath(path)* reduces the path from the goal to the start state to a minimal call of services.

The complexity of algorithm 2 depends on the implementation of the state search and state pruning mechanism, being the heuristic which selects useful services, including the complexity of the service matcher used. In general, the worst case complexity of such an algorithm is exponential [9, p.72].

By planning on services we accept a number of challenges:

- *Service Grounding* checks all parameters of services to be executed next and creates all combinations of individuals that fit those parameters. These combinations lead to multiple (possibly infinite) grounded services out of one service description. Here the challenge lies in the selection of continuous parameters.
- *Output Integration* into the state poses a challenge since it is not clear how a service without effect can influence the state. One example of such services are information providing services, which are not world altering services [10]. Thus, here we create an assertion of the class of the output, creating an appropriate individual, equivalent to the "AgentKnows" of Doherty et al. [11].
- *Semantic Web Rule Language built-ins (SWRLb)* are mathematical extensions like "greater than", string manipulations or description of time. Additionally, lists are modelled in SWRLb but are not supported by reasoners like Pellet [12].
- *Semantic Web Rule Language XML Concrete Syntax (SWRLx)* is an extension to the Semantic Web Rule Language (SWRL) allowing to model individual creation, creation of classes and properties. This is vital to the service planning, because service execution might create individuals or classes, which can not be modelled without SWRLx built-ins.

B. Development Tools

The method for semantic service management and development makes use of two development tools, which are both implemented as Eclipse plugins [13] and thus can seamlessly be integrated into the developer's usual workflow.

1) Semantic Service and Ontology Manager: In order to be able to integrate intelligent planning algorithms, the environment has to come up with the necessary infrastructure. One essential requirement in this respect is the semantic description of functionalities or services. Since current standards such as the Web Ontology Language for Web Services (OWL-S) [14] are not easy to describe from scratch, we developed a plug-in called Semantic Service Manager (SSM) [15], providing a set of features supporting a semi-automatic description of services. The core of SSM is an Ontology Manager, which enables the developer to include and utilize Web Ontology Language (OWL) ontologies for the application in semantic service descriptions. However, since many development approaches use other languages to specify the domain of concern, such as the Eclipse Modeling Framework (EMF), the Ontology Manager also provides a transformation process from EMF to OWL.

Based on the Ontology Manager the developer is then able to describe the service according to name, description, input and output parameters and finally preconditions and effects. The latter ones can be described via the Semantic Web Rule Language (SWRL) and for this purpose SSM comes with a syntax highlighting editor and structure parser. The description can then be utilized in different ways. Either it can be deployed to a semantic service repository (see Section II-C), it can be sent to a BPMN process (see next paragraph), or it can be linked to a service of the multi-agent framework JIAC V (Java-based Intelligent Agent Componentware, version 5) [16]. With these options at hand, the developer can easily connect semantic descriptions to services and is able to deploy them immediately.

The second purpose of the SSM is the search and utilization of existing and running services within a distributed environment. Therefore the SSM provides a *Service Discovery View* where the developer can define (incomplete) parameters of a service and search the platform directory using the $SeMa^2$ matcher. The developer can also adapt the weightings of the different matching techniques used. After selecting one of the services they can either be pushed to the *Visual Service Design Tool* (VSDT) to use it within a BPMN process, or a code inclusion function can be triggered that inserts the service call code into the open Java window.

2) Visual Service Design Tool: While basic services are usually implemented in the form of Java classes or equivalent, for service compositions business process modelling notations have proven useful. Using the VSDT, existing semantic services can be orchestrated to complex processes [17] using the BPMN notation [18].

The VSDT integrates with the Semantic Service Manager view in the way that services from the SSM can be imported into the VSDT. With a single click in the User Interface (UI), an according service description is added to the currently opened VSDT process, together with data types representing the different ontology concepts. That service can then be used in a service task and combined with other services to a complex process.

Next, those processes can be exported to executable languages such as BPEL (Business Process Execution Language) processes [17] or JIAC agent behaviours [19], being the execution environment used in this approach. In the case of JIAC agents, VSDT processes can either be compiled to JIAC beans, encapsulating an accordant behaviour, or they can be interpreted directly. In this work, we will focus on the interpreting approach, as further described in the following section.

C. Execution Environment

The services are executed as part of a JIAC multi-agent system. This way, each service is running on an individual agent, providing an adequate level of modularity and encapsulation. The environment also provides interfaces to other types of (web) services, such as SOAP (Simple Object Access Protocol) and REST, which can be integrated transparently with JIAC.

1) JIAC V Multi-agent Framework: The execution environment is based on *JIAC V*, a multi-agent framework also incorporating many aspects of service-oriented architectures [16]. The agents are situated on agent nodes (runtime containers). Each agent's behaviours and capabilities are defined in several agent beans, providing different general and application-specific functions (see Figure 3).

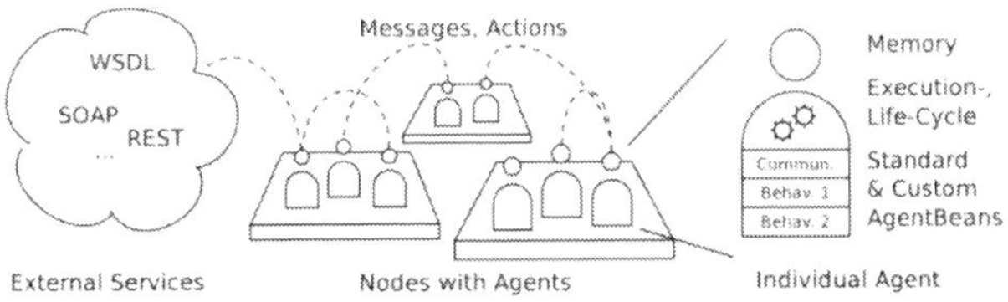

Figure 3. Components of a JIAC multi-agent system and individual agents (adapted from [20])

Complementary to message-based communication, one of the core mechanics of JIAC agents is to expose *actions*. Depending on its scope, an action can be found and used by other components of the same agent, by other agents on the same node, or by any agent on the network. Each JIAC agent node has a directory of known agents and actions, both on the same node as well as on other nodes, that can be used for querying and finding specific agents and actions using according templates. Given just the name, or the inputs and outputs of an action, the directory will find and return an action that matches that template (if such an action exists), which can then be used for creating an according intention.

For integration with other services, the WSDL- and REST-services integration beans can be used. Those components do both have two effects: First, all the JIAC actions accessible via the directory will be exposed to the outside world as according WSDL or REST services, respectively, and second, additional JIAC actions will be created and exposed, representing each of the WSDL and REST services known to those beans. Thus, JIAC agents can seamlessly and transparently be integrated with both, REST and WSDL services.

Integrating the semantic service matcher into JIAC was very natural and straightforward. Whenever a semantic service template (as opposed to a plain JIAC action template) is passed to the directory, the directory will delegate it to the semantic service matcher bean, which will return the best matching service. To the agent invoking the service, it is fully transparent whether it is a standard JIAC action or a semantic service.

In order to utilize the service matching and planning functionalities within the JIAC environment it was necessary to extend the existing action model for agents by means of a semantic service description model. The model is oriented towards the OWL-S standard dividing information into Profile, Process and Grounding parts. The latter can either reference JIAC action information but it can also define WSDL or REST attributes.

Loosely coupled to the JIAC environment is the Semantic Service Repository. Each platform can host multiple of these repositories, where the developer can deploy and manage its service descriptions. As this seems pretty static on first sight, we included a mechanism in which only in cases when a service is running and recognised by the directory, the linked service descriptions are considered for matching.

2) JIAC based BPMN Interpreter: One of several application-independent components for JIAC agents is the process interpreter bean, enabling the agent to interpret and execute BPMN processes created with the VSDT.

The process interpreter bean is composed of three layers: First, the *process interpreter bean* itself provides actions for adding processes to be interpreted and for managing already running processes. Also, it acts as an interface to the agents, providing functionality for sending and receiving messages and invoking other actions from within the BPMN processes. Finally, it exposes all the processes (that have an according start event) as actions so they can be used by other agents.

Whenever a process diagram is added to the process engine bean for interpretation, an *interpreter runtime* is created, which is responsible for each process spawned from this process diagram. It keeps track of events and creates a new instance of that process whenever an event corresponding to the respective start event occurs. Different volatile *process instances* are responsible for running the processes spawned by the runtime, executing the different activities and keeping track of the current state of the process, i.e., which activities are ready for execution, as well as the values of the different process variables.

Making use of JIAC's communication and service infrastructure, the interpreted processes can automatically make use of other JIAC actions, and – if the respective proxy beans are present – of WSDL and REST services. If the semantic service matcher is installed in the node, it is automatically used for finding services according to the templates used in the processes. The current state of the interpreter bean – the active runtimes, their respective process instances, and their internal states – can be monitored using a simple UI, also providing an interface for manually starting processes and for the processes to interact with the user, e.g., for BPMN user tasks, or for querying missing service parameters.

III. Methodology for Semantic Service Development

In the following, we will sketch a process of how the different components introduced in the last section are used together to form a methodology of semantic service engineering. At its base, the method is similar to other software- and service engineering methodologies, but combines those with requirements for and contributions of semantic services. An overview of the methodology is shown in Figure 4, using the BPMN notation, and highlighting how the different components are used in the stages of the process. In the following, we will describe the different steps in more detail.

A. Ontology Engineering

The first step in creating semantic services is to model the ontology that will be used for describing the service's inputs,

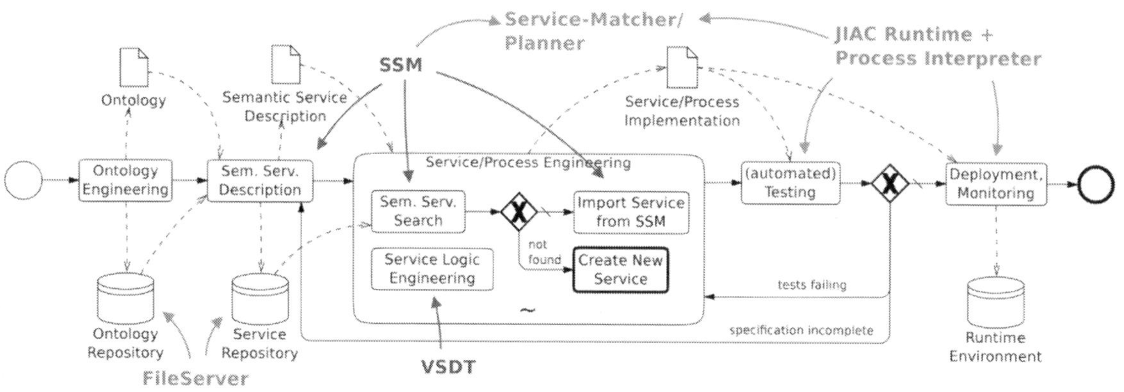

Figure 4. Semantic Service Management and Development Process, as a BPMN process, and associated components: Green: Semantic Service Core; Blue: Development Tools; Red: Execution Environment.

outputs, precondition and effect, if any. This is particularly important, since one of the main motivations for semantic services is for those services to be easily findable, reusable, and composable with other services; thus, whenever possible it should be the aim to reuse, or, if necessary, extend existing ontologies, instead of creating new ones. This step is also concerned with mapping the ontological concepts, for example described in OWL, to a representation that is closer to the service implementation, e.g., Java classes (or vice versa, starting with Java classes and generating according OWL ontologies).

The new or modified ontologies are then uploaded to a server hosting a repository of known ontologies, so they can be used in the next step, as well as in other services. There is no specific tool for this step in our method. Ontologies can be created, e.g., with Protégé,[21] or generated from existing Java classes or EMF models [22].

B. Creating Semantic Service Description

Next is the creation of the semantic service description itself, defining the "contract" of the service. Of course, this step is not particular for semantic services, but is a common practice for all of service- and software engineering. The major difference is that besides name, textual description, input and output parameter, also the preconditions and effects of a service can be defined. Especially the latter, which in our approach can be described with the semantic rule language SWRL, extend the attributes of a service in a way that matching or planning processes can deduce its purpose and its formal prerequisites. However, as describing semantic terms can be challenging, we paid attention to provide a user-friendly editor with syntax-highlighting, auto-completion and validation parser. Currently missing, but contemplated is the integration of several QoS attributes, making the selection of services also sensitive to non-functional aspects.

The new service description is uploaded to a service repository, adding it to the list of services usable by the semantic service matcher and planner. In our method, the SSM tool is used for creating the service descriptions using OWL-S. Existing ontologies can be browsed (but not edited) for selecting concepts for input and output, while preconditions and effects are specified using SWRL. The finalized service description can then be deployed to the repository and an accordant stub for the service implementation can be generated.

C. Service- and Process Engineering

The bulk of the service development process is occupied with engineering the service's implementation. While the service's method declaration can be generated from the semantic service description, its body has to be implemented by a developer. Here, we can differentiate two main activities: Identifying and integrating existing services, and developing the logic that combines those services to a new service, or process, with added value.

There are three ways how services can be searched, identified, and imported into the currently developed process, using the SSM tool:

- The service can be searched for, using a semantic service template, and the service best matching the template is integrated into the current service.
- In case no single service satisfies the template, the semantic service planner can be used to automatically find a service composition that, as a whole, matches the template; the individual services of that composition are then integrated into the current service in the appropriate sequence.
- Instead of searching services at design time, the template that would be used for matching the service can itself be integrated into the current service, deferring the search and matching process to runtime.

Of course, there is also a fourth case: That no service or service composition can be found that fulfils the template. In this case, a new service has to be created, thus starting the service development process again.

The service logic can be created in two ways: Either in the form of a Java method, or, using the VSDT, as a BPMN process, which is later either mapped to Java (JIAC agent beans) or interpreted directly. Which one to choose mainly depends on the ratio of service reuse to "original" service logic: In case the new service is mainly a composition of existing basic services, they can very well be modelled visually as business processes, but if they contain complex calculations or make extensive use of third-party libraries (that are not available as services), then implementing the services in plain Java is the better choice.

D. Testing the Implementation against the Specification

The last step before deployment is testing, to ensure that the services' implementations comply with their semantic descriptions. Of course, testing plays a well-established role in software engineering and is not particular to semantic service development. However, the presence of formal semantic descriptions impose both an obligation and an opportunity for (automated) unit testing.

On the one hand, while even a regular function or service that does not comply with its documentation is always a nuisance, a semantic service that violates its stated effect could threaten the functionality of the entire system it is embedded in, as automated planners will rely on that information. On the other hand, since the intended behaviour of the service has already been specified in its precondition and effect, writing the actual tests becomes very straightforward.

While this is currently not implemented in our approach, it would also be possible to automatically generate unit tests from the semantic service description, particularly the service's preconditions and according effects. For this, the input parameters can be generated, setting all attributes that are not specified in the precondition randomly; then, the expected output can be inferred from the service's effect, thus testing the actual result of the service invocation against the expected value.

In case the service does not comply with the tests (i.e., with its stated preconditions and effects), the usual course of action is, of course, to fix the service. However, in some cases this may also expose flaws in the service's input, output, precondition and effect (IOPE) descriptions. In this case, the process has to backtrack and update the semantic service description and adapt or extend the service's implementation accordingly.

E. Deployment and Runtime Monitoring

The final step is to deploy the new service to the runtime environment. Depending on whether the service has been implemented directly as a Java class (e.g., a JIAC agent bean exposing an accordant action), or in the form of a BPMN process diagram orchestrating different existing services, the deployment process is slightly different.

- In case the service has been implemented directly in Java and is meant to be a basic service to be used as a building block for other services, it is best to create a new agent exclusively for that service and to deploy it to the runtime server.
- In case of a service composition created as a BPMN process, the process diagram can be deployed to an already running process interpreter agent. This way, deployment and undeployment is very dynamic, and the interpreter also provides basic capabilities for runtime monitoring and user interaction. Alternatively, the process can also be automatically translated to Java code and deployed as in the above mentioned case.

In both cases, the services are deployed to the JIAC runtime environment and can be invoked as actions, and searched for using the semantic service matcher. Using the WSDL and REST integration beans, the services will also be exposed as WSDL or REST services, respectively, and can transparently use other services available in those formats.

IV. THE EMD USE CASE

In the project EMD (Extendable and adaptive E-Mobility Services), a use case within the transportation domain was constructed to demonstrate the use of the developed tools, the methodology, and the basic services, as depicted in Figure 5. Starting from the fundamental services, like reading the scheduled meetings from a calendar, getting the state of charge of a vehicle, scheduling the charging, or searching charging stations, this example constructs an adaptive extended service with the goal of supporting home visiting nurses during their daily rounds. Here, the idea is that if the state of charge of an electric car does not suffice for the whole schedule of visits for the day, the application will provide an alternative means of transportation for just enough time to charge the vehicle. This will lead the nurse to a few appointments via an intermodal route (including public transport, car or bike sharing vehicles, walking, taxis or any mobility service available). Finally, she returns to her vehicle when the vehicle's charging process has finished.

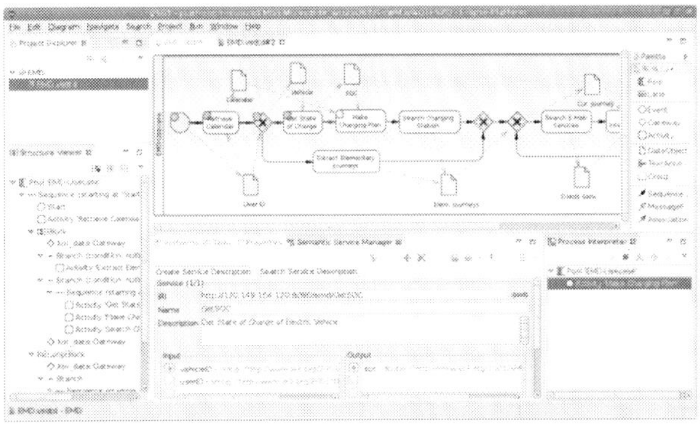

Figure 5. Example usecase for an extendible, adaptive mobility service. Top: VSDT editor showing process diagram; bottom: SSM view.

The search of the mobility providing services is the adaptive part of the service: Depending on the available services and the context of the user (e.g., carrying heavy equipment) the appropriate services are given to an intermodal routing service. Integrating the $SeMa^2$ service matcher into the service (shown as the "Search E-Mob Service") component, allows us to dynamically change the services which are used for the intermodal routing.

Describing all services semantically using the SSM allows the $SeMa^2$ to find fitting services at runtime. The semantic description of the services is done with the entities of the domain ontology created during the project. Since the whole process should not be composed automatically but using the VSDT editor to describe the interconnection of the service, the $SeMa^2$ is also part of the design process, finding existing service to be integrated into the developed process.

The service planner can then be used to create a first service composition which can be adapted using the VSDT. During the development the process can be debugged during its execution via the built-in BPMN process interpreter of the VSDT. This allows the inspection of the exchanged messages and the developer has the ability to add or remove specific services or to integrate transformation of the exchanged data formats.

V. Related Work

The foundation for an effective management of semantic services lies in a well-elaborated formalism for the semantic description of services. In this respect, a lot of research has been done and has led to a variety of approaches, some of them being lightweight, others coming up with a complete framework solution. The authors in [23] give a detailed overview about existing solutions, such as OWL-S, Semantic Annotations for WSDL and XML Schema (SAWSDL) or the Web Service Modeling Ontology (WSMO). Since the composition of services, which is an essential part of our framework, highly relies on formal expressions for preconditions and effects, we analysed OWL-S as the most suitable one embedding the rule language SWRL.

A comprehensive overview about approaches building upon these formalisms, such as development tools, matching and planning algorithms and the execution environment, is not feasible for this publication, therefore we refer to our related publications for this. Within the remaining section we shortly focus on other projects that present concepts for semantic service management.

The project Mercury [24] focused on automatic service discovery based on the user context. For the semantic description of the services different standards such as OWL-S and SAWSDL are supported. The project provides tool support for the user requests and enables the developer to insert the found services into a process chain. In contrast to our approach, Mercury can consider different semantic service formats, however, the user request does not allow to describe formal preconditions or effects, but is solely focusing on key words. Klan et al. [25] propose relevant requirements to an efficient semantic service management with respect to service matching. Furthermore, they define an evaluation methodology rating the results provided by semantic matchers according to user requirements. Within the project DIANE [26] a new service description model has been proposed that especially focuses on the expression of state transitions after service invocations. Furthermore, it provides the instance-based description of service requests, which makes the reasoning process more realistic. In contrast to that, Karastoyanova et al. [27] focus on the problem of semantic service management from a BPMN process perspective, providing an architecture for Semantic Business Process Management. They cover the whole lifecycle using the WSMO technology for the semantic part. However, what is missing in this work is an approach for automated service composition at runtime. The Framework PORSCE II [28] uses AI planning techniques like LPG-td [29] which implements a graph plan algorithm, to automatically create service composition, with the drawback of transforming the composition problem to a standard PDDL planning problem and thus losing the expressiveness of OWL and SWRL.

VI. Conclusion

In this paper, we presented a semantic service management methodology that covers the phases of service description modelling and deployment as well as service discovery and composition, both at design-time and at runtime, in order to generate adaptive and flexible systems in service-oriented environments. Most of the phases are supported by tools reducing the development effort. Furthermore, we presented an inclusion mechanism into a BPMN process environment called VSDT, where service templates can be specified within the process structure and dynamically matched to concrete services at runtime. Our whole approach has been included into a real environment, where services from the electric mobility domain have been linked to complex processes.

In the future, we will address the challenges for service composition that were formulated in Section II-A4. Among others, we intend to complete the integration of the specification for the description language SWRL and to facilitate the semantic annotation of services by further elaborating our tools. In doing so, we see a good opportunity to foster the usage of service planning approaches in real world applications.

Acknowledgements

This work is funded by the German Federal Ministry of Economic Affairs and Energy under the funding reference number 16SBB007A.

References

[1] M. Klusch, U. Küster, A. Leger, D. Martin, and M. Paolucci, "5th International Semantic Service Selection Contest - Performance Evaluation of Semantic Service Matchmakers," Nov. 2012, last access: 2016/03/07. [Online]. Available: http://www-ags.dfki.uni-sb.de/~klusch/s3/s3c-2012-summary-report.pdf

[2] J. Fähndrich, N. Masuch, H. Yildirim, and S. Albayrak, "Towards Automated Service Matchmaking and Planning for Multi-Agent Systems with OWL-S – Approach and Challenges," in Service-Oriented Computing – ICSOC 2013 Workshops. Cham: Springer International Publishing, 2014, pp. 240–247.

[3] P. A. Morris, "Combining expert judgments: A Bayesian approach," Management Science, vol. 23, no. 7, 1977, pp. 679–693.

[4] M. Stone, "The opinion pool," The Annals of Mathematical Statistics, vol. 32, no. 4, 1961, pp. 1339–1342.

[5] C. Genest, "Pooling operators with the marginalization property," The Canadian Journal of Statistics/La Revue Canadienne de Statistique, vol. 12, no. 2, 1984, pp. 153–163.

[6] D. Dyer. Watchmaker Framework. Last access: 2016/05/11. [Online]. Available: http://watchmaker.uncommons.org/ (2006)

[7] W. L. Goffe, G. D. Ferrier, and J. Rogers, "Global optimization of statistical functions with simulated annealing," Journal of Econometrics, vol. 60, no. 1-2, Jan. 1994, pp. 65–99.

[8] M. Klusch and P. Kapahnke. The Semantic Web Service Matchmaker Evaluation Environment (SME2). Last access: 2016/05/11. [Online]. Available: http://projects.semwebcentral.org/projects/sme2/ (2008)

[9] M. Ghallab, D. S. Nau, and P. Traverso, Automated Planning: Theory & Practice, D. E. M. Penrose, Ed. Morgan Kaufmann, 2008.

[10] H. Saboohi and S. A. Kareem, "A resemblance study of test collections for world-altering semantic web services," in Int. MultiConf. of Engineers and Computer Scientists (IMECS), vol. I, 2011, pp. 716–720.

[11] P. Doherty, W. Lukaszewicz, and A. Szalas, "Efficient Reasoning Using the Local Closed-World Assumption," in Agents and Computational Autonomy. Springer Berlin Heidelberg, Jan. 2003, pp. 49–58.

[12] E. Sirin, B. Parsia, B. C. Grau, A. Kalyanpur, and Y. Katz, "Pellet: A practical owl-dl reasoner," Web Semant., vol. 5, no. 2, Jun. 2007, pp. 51–53. [Online]. Available: http://dx.doi.org/10.1016/j.websem.2007.03.004

[13] E. Foundation. Eclipse. Last access: 2016/05/11. [Online]. Available: http://www.eclipse.org/ (2016)

[14] D. Martin et al., "OWL-S: Semantic Markup for Web Services," Website, Tech. Rep., Nov. 2004. [Online]. Available: http://www.w3.org/Submission/2004/SUBM-OWL-S-20041122/

[15] N. Masuch, C. Kuster, and S. Albayrak, "Semantic service manager–enabling semantic web technologies in multi-agent systems," in Proceedings of the Joint Workshops on Semantic Web and Big Data Technologies, INFORMATIK 2014, Stuttgart, Germany, 2014, 2014, pp. 499–510.

[16] M. Lützenberger, T. Konnerth, and T. Küster, "Programming of multiagent applications with JIAC," in Industrial Agents – Emerging Applications of Software Agents in Industry, P. Leitão and S. Karnouskos, Eds. Elsevier, 2015, pp. 381–400.

[17] T. Küster and A. Heßler, "Towards transformations from BPMN to heterogeneous systems," in Business Process Management Workshops, ser. LNBIP, D. Ardagna, M. Mecella, and J. Yang, Eds. Springer Berlin Heidelberg, 2009, vol. 17, pp. 200–211.

[18] OMG, "Business process model and notation (BPMN) version 2.0," Object Management Group, Specification formal/2011-01-03, 2011.

[19] T. Küster, M. Lützenberger, and S. Albayrak, "A formal description of a mapping from business processes to agents," in Engineering Multi-Agent Systems, ser. LNAI, M. Baldoni, L. Baresi, and M. Dastani, Eds. Springer International Publishing, 2015, vol. 9318, pp. 153–170.

[20] T. Küster, A. Heßler, and S. Albayrak, "Towards process-oriented modelling and creation of multi-agent systems," in Engineering Multi-Agent Systems, ser. LNAI, F. Dalpiaz, J. Dix, and M. B. van Riemsdijk, Eds. Springer International Publishing, 2014, vol. 8758, pp. 163–180.

[21] Stanford. Protégé. Last access: 2016/05/11. [Online]. Available: http://protege.stanford.edu/ (2016)

[22] E. Foundation. Eclipse Modeling Framework (EMF). Last access: 2016/05/11. [Online]. Available: https://eclipse.org/modeling/emf/ (2016)

[23] A. Barros and D. Oberle, Handbook of Service Description: USDL and Its Methods. Springer Publishing Company, Incorporated, 2012.

[24] K. Opasjumruskit, J. Expósito, B. König-Ries, A. Nauerz, and M. Welsch, "Service discovery with personal awareness in smart environments," Creating Personal, Social, and Urban Awareness through Pervasive Computing, 2013, pp. 86–107.

[25] F. Klan and B. König-Ries, "A user-centered methodology for the evaluation of (semantic) web service discovery and selection," in Proceedings of the 4th International Conference on Web Intelligence, Mining and Semantics (WIMS14). ACM, 2014, p. 18.

[26] U. Küster, B. König-Ries, M. Klein, and M. Stern, "Diane: A matchmaking-centered framework for automated service discovery, composition, binding, and invocation on the web," International Journal of Electronic Commerce, vol. 12, no. 2, 2007, pp. 41–68.

[27] D. Karastoyanova et al., "A reference architecture for semantic business process management systems," in Multikonferenz Wirtschaftsinformatik, 2008, pp. 1727–1738.

[28] O. Hatzi, D. Vrakas, and N. Bassiliades, "The PORSCE II framework: Using AI planning for automated semantic web service composition," Knowledge Engineering Review, vol. 28, no. 02, 2013, pp. 137–156.

[29] A. Gerevini, A. Saetti, I. Serina, and P. Toninelli, "LPG-TD: a fully automated planner for PDDL2.2 domains," in Proc. of 14th Int. Conf. on Automated Planning and Scheduling (ICAPS-04) International Planning Competition abstracts, 2004.

Cloud Computing in SMEs

Ileana Hamburg
Institut Arbeit und Technik, WH Gelsenkirchen
Gelsenkirchen, Germany
e-mail: hamburg@iat.eu

Sascha Bucksch
Institut Arbeit und Technik, WH Gelsenkirchen
Gelsenkirchen, Germany
e-mail: bucksch@iat.eu

Abstract – **Small and medium sized enterprises (SMEs) assure economic growth in Europe. Generally, many SMEs are struggling to survive in an ongoing global recession and are often reluctant to use research results and new technologies for business and learning. Cloud Computing offers many opportunities and could help companies to improve their business and use technology more efficiently. In this paper a short presentation of Cloud Computing and advantages for SMEs are given. The work in progress within the European project IN-CLOUD is presented in the paper. The results show that 70% of SMEs which answered to our research used Cloud services but they need more qualified staff in this field.**

Keywords-SME; Cloud Computing; European Cloud Computing Strategy; E-Learning; Erasmus +

I. INTRODUCTION

Small and medium sized enterprises (SMEs) assure economic growth in Europe, but the last financial crisis and the economic recession have hit SMEs hard in the EU28 and some of them have difficulties to survive and less resource to invest in new technologies [1].

Cloud Computing [2] offers many opportunities and can help companies to improve their business and use technology more efficiently. Some features i.e. on-demand services, broad network access, resource pooling, rapid elasticity and measured service distinguish Cloud from other computer networking models [3].

Cloud Computing could support SMEs' growth encouraging entrepreneurial practices at all levels [4]. But European SMEs are not making the best of the cost-effective solutions Cloud Computing has to offer i.e. avoiding large investments into hardware and software, entering the market more easily due to the cost-efficiency, attracting new customers by using new integrated Cloud Computing services. Universities/research can also benefit from cloud computing, as its storage capacity and economic viability ensure more efficient research management techniques in all fields. Cloud computing is thus an optimal solution for the innovation-driven alliance between universities and companies.

Cloud Computing reach interest in the corporate sector but some evidence a lack of professionals able to work in this field. According to the analyst firm IDC [5], in 2012 more than 1.7 million cloud computing jobs have remained unoccupied and the trend should lead to more than seven million cloud-related vacancies worldwide The European Commission has started several initiatives supporting the investment in entrepreneurship-boosting ICT and, in September 2012 has adopted a strategy for "Unleashing the Potential of Cloud Computing in Europe". The European Cloud Computing Strategy [6] includes three key actions; the most relevant is the creation of a "European Cloud Partnership" providing strategic options to turn Cloud Computing into an engine for sustainable economic growth, innovation and cost-efficient public and private services.

In this paper, after a short presentation of Cloud Computing and advantages for SMEs, the objectives of the European project IN-CLOUD and the progress work within this project are described.

The general objective of the project IN-CLOUD is to foster a partnership between research, higher education institutions and the corporate sector, in order to help SMEs to use Cloud Computing and to qualify new professionals able to support competitiveness and growth of European Companies and Universities, thanks to the advantages offered by the Cloud Computing technology. The eight partners of the project are education and research institutions, SMEs organisations, public administrations coming from Germany, Greece, Italy, Portugal, Spain and UK. IN-CLOUD uses the results of the project Smart PA () oriented to the use of Cloud Computing in public administration and coordinated by one of the authors.

In this paper, after a presentation of cloud computing in SMEs, the research methods used and some conclusions of the work done so far within the project IN-CLOUD are given.

II. CLOUD COMPUTING IN SMEs

By using Cloud services SMEs can avail of opportunities that allow them to compete in an innovative ICT environment, and give a level playing field required to succeed in business [8][9]. In the discussion with experts and SMEs, the following advantages of Cloud Computing emerged [10] – Figure 1:

- Up-to-date low-cost software solutions
- Unlimited data storage
- Access to data from anywhere and anytime
- High levels of security protocol that ensures business and data protection
- Improved business performance
- Simplified data management

Examples of services SMEs could offer to their clients could be a combination of Business Services, Application Software Services, Infrastructure Services, Integration and Development Services – Figure 1.

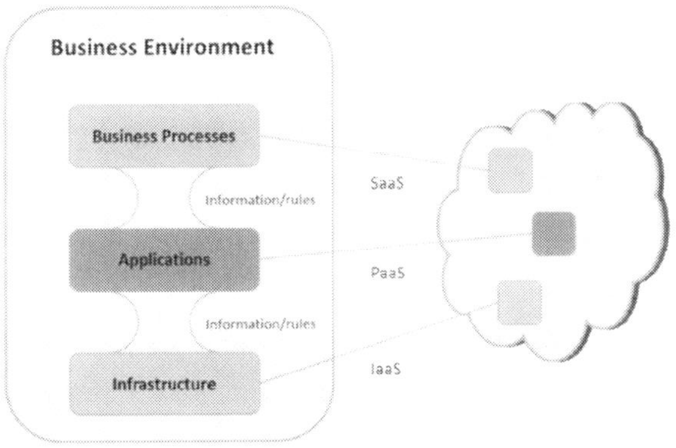

Figure 1. Advantages of Cloud Computing

There are also a number of limitations or issues with Cloud Computing. One of the main issues is the reliability, security, private and ownership of data [11][12] as well as the accessibility of this on a 24/7 basis, particularly when the Cloud service Provider (CSP) has an outage. Many companies will have problems about the lack of control over their ICT systems and the impact of a CSP on these [13][14].

These issues may inhibit an SME's decision to migrate to a Cloud Computing environment. In addition, there are other factors which may influence the decision which the authors discuss with companies like the followings:

- The lack of understanding of the infrastructure, cost, and appropriateness to the needs and scenarios of several companies from different business environments.
- Inadequate skill levels of users, managers, and entrepreneurs to use Cloud.
- The readiness of SMEs to adopt Cloud Computing from a business perspective.
- Less time to test Cloud services.

Cloud computing requires also new skills which are the bases for the development of didactic units within our project IN-CLOUD i.e.,:

- Business and financial skills
- Technical skills: depending on how much of the cloud will be built and managed in-house
- Enterprise architecture and business needs analysis
- Skills to work with the business, speak the language of business, as well as work with IT professionals
- Project management skills
- Contract and vendor negotiation working with CSP
- Security and compliance
- Data integration and analysis skills
- Mobile app development and management, being driven by the need to provide services that can be accessed by any and all devices, be they laptops or smartphones.

Besides advantages within business, Cloud Computing can be used for improving learning both in SMEs as well in Education. In the following we present E-Learning. E-Learning could address issues of time and cost in SMEs, by allowing employees to access learning resources remotely. The learning material is easy to keep updated; the trainers can integrate multimedia content which facilitates understanding and motivate the participants, but this form of learning is not used efficiently in SMEs.

Masud and Huang presented in [15], besides the general characteristics of an E-Learning system, a system architecture that combines the capabilities of learning with advantages of Cloud Computing services. Some aspects which could be improved by using Cloud Computing to implement E-Learning are scalability of E-Learning systems at the infrastructure level, development and assigning of resources only for determined tasks, need to configure and add new resources making the costs and resource management less expensive [15].

Pocailu and Vetrici described in [16] a plan for implementing an E-Learning system based on Cloud Computer architecture and the positive effects of using Cloud Computer technology are discussed.

Two main characteristics of Cloud Computing which could be an alternative to traditional ICT centres and could improve the E-Learning approaches in SMEs are the use of resources "on demand" and the transparent scalability so that the computational resources are assigned when they are necessary without the necessity of infrastructure understanding by the users. Costs related to computer infrastructure maintenance disappear [17]. The authors of the paper coordinated national and international projects about E-Learning methods and platforms. The experience of these projects will be used in the following projects.

Figure 2 shows the architecture of a platform for E-Learning with integrated Cloud services [18].

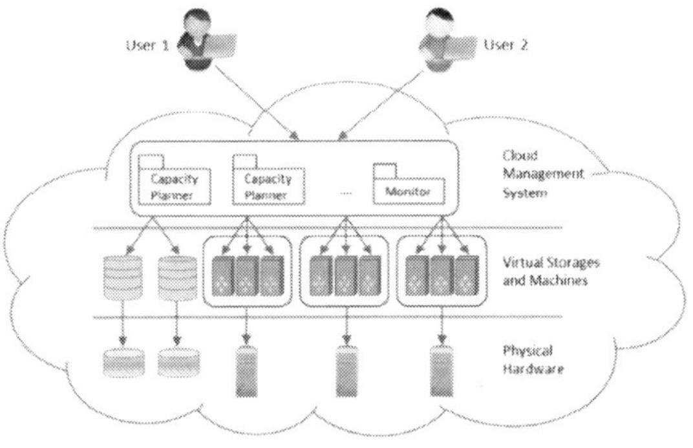

Figure 2. The architecture of a cloud computing platform for E-Learning [16]

III. RESEARCH METHODS

The IN-CLOUD project intends to operate pursuing the objectives of the European Cloud Computing Strategy [4] with the general objective of – fostering a partnership between 2 research institutions, 4 Universities, and 3 SMEs associations from 5 European countries, in order to qualify new professionals able to boost the competitiveness and growth of European Companies and Universities, thanks to the advantages offered by the cloud computing technology.

The advantages of working in cooperation with companies are:

- The needs of the companies and the requirements for qualifications could be taken into consideration at the beginning of the developments
- Testing of the didactic units and platform developed in the project could be conducted during the project period
- Exploitation of the results is ensured.

The used methods in the project IN-CLOUD to reach the objectives are the following:

- Analysis of the situation of the use and desire of ICT and Cloud Computing methods in SMEs of partner countries
- Analysis of the labour market requirements and of the necessary skills for SME staff in order to use Cloud Computing
- Development of qualification profiles for SME staff and Cloud Professionals
- Pilot actions to train SME staff based on the qualification profiles.

The first output of the IN-CLOUD, which started at the end of 2015, consists of a report that is the basis for the development of the other project activities. It includes a description of the Cloud Computing, an analysis of the awareness of the existing cloud computing technologies and services in the private and public sectors, a needs' analysis of technologies and services connected to Cloud Computing in the public and private sectors, an analysis of the professional skills required in the area of Cloud Computing and an analysis of the labour market actual situation and prospective of employability. The first design of didactic units that can satisfy the identified didactic needs will be also proposed as a result of this output.

The sent questionnaire contains questions about general company information, software usage and cloud computing. It was created with the help of Survey Monkey, an online survey development cloud-based company. It provides free, customizable surveys, as well as a suite of paid back-end programs that include data analysis, sample selection, bias elimination and data representation tools. Each partner searched for studies, publications, reports and projects about cloud computing.

We will present some results of the questionnaire including answers of all partner countries. 70% of 260 SMEs which answered use private or hybrid Cloud services. The following diagrams show some answers.

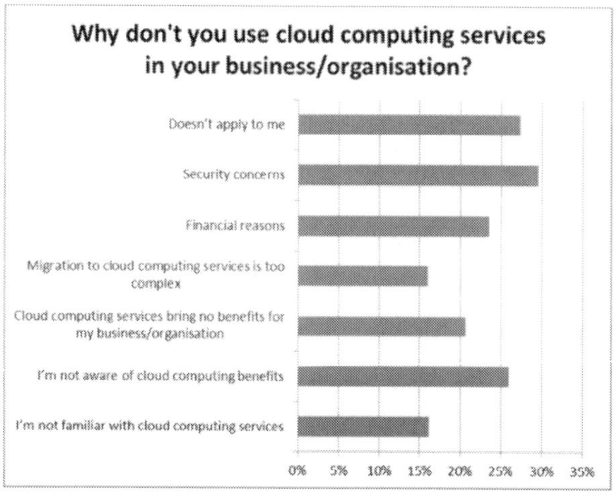

Figure 3. Results from the questionnaire on cloud computing made in all partner countries

Security stands as the top barrier for Cloud adoption which reflects that business are reluctant to trust in Cloud security capabilities.

Another problem is that also due to lack of information SMEs are not familiar with benefits of Cloud.

Figure 4. Results from the questionnaire on cloud computing made in all partner countries

Scalability, flexibility and Cost efficiency seem to be the top motivators for companies to use the Cloud.

The project IN-CLOUD also researches the economic impacts of cloud computing on different types of SMEs. The first conclusion is that it depends on region and sector; the IT sector mainly will have the most advantages. This impact in Europe will depend on how service providers, governments and managers understand it. European cloud services providers need to offer competitive prices.

A set of didactic units and a set of VET Qualifications with instruments to validate them are in the development as well as an E-Learning platform with Cloud Computing Services and training material including practical applications for companies.

The qualifications are:

- Certified Cloud Professional for Business

- Certified Cloud Professional for Public Administrations
- Certified Cloud Professional for Education
- Certified Cloud Technology Professional

The profiles include core units of learning outcomes, ECVET points acquired, the related performance description/ occupational standard, key activities, knowledge and skills, competences to be achieved during the qualification process.

For the qualification process different methods will be used based on the experience of the project partners:

- E-Learning platform with online modules, forum, exercises
- Videos with staff from companies
- Showcases with successful cloud implementations in SMEs

The IN-CLOUD project partners would like to cooperate with national governments in order to ensure an appropriate legal environment, procurement practices and energy prices. It will also depend on the willingness of managers to adopt the new practices necessary to exploit the technical and economic advantages of cloud computing.

IV. CONCLUSIONS

Small and medium sized companies remain vital for grow and innovation in the European economy but need support i.e. cooperation with research and education institutions in this context. Such cooperation is important to ensure the survival of these companies and encourage them to grow. In today's business world, SMEs are competing with a larger number of companies, many of these are multinationals; they have a greater number of staff and a wider pool of skills. SMEs should be helped to acquire the relevant strategic skills as quickly as possible to remain ahead of the competition by using latest technologies such as Cloud Computing for business and learning because most of them would like to use Cloud services.

In this context the steps within this project will cover the testing of the qualification units and the development of the E-Learning platform. The E-Learning platforms developed by the authors within other projects aimed at SMEs like ReadiSME and Archimedes will be the basis for it.

We are convinced that the project developments will help SMEs to increase innovation. The companies proved high motivation to qualify in the use of new technologies like Cloud Computing and E-Learning methods.

ACKNOWLEDGMENTS

This paper describes work within the on-going European project IN-CLOUD.

REFERENCES

[1] European Commission, "Annual Report on European SMEs 2013/2014: A Partial and Fragile Recovery", p. 10. http://ec.europa.eu/growth/smes/business-friendly-environment/performance-review/files/supporting-documents/2014/annual-report-smes-2014_en.pdf, 2014. Accessed on December, 28, 2015

[2] National Institute of Standards and Technology, NIST, "The NIST Definition of Cloud Computing," http://csrc.nist.gov/publications/nistpubs/800-145/SP800-145.pdf, 2011. Accessed on December, 28, 2015

[3] Lucchetti, R. and Sterlacchini, A. "The adoption of ICT among SMEs: Evidence from an Italian Survey", In: Small Business Economics 23, pp. 151-168, 2004

[4] https://ec.europa.eu/digital-agenda/en/european-cloud-initiative. Accessed April 2016

[5] IDC Report, "1.7 Million Cloud Computing Jobs Remain Unfilled, Gap Widening". http://cloudtimes.org/2013/01/09/idc-report-1-7-million-cloud-computing-jobs-remain-unfilled-gap-widening/. 2012. Accessed on December, 28, 2015

[6] European Commission, "European Cloud Computing Strategy," https://ec.europa.eu/digital-agenda/en/european-cloud-initiative/. 2012. Accessed on December, 28, 2015

[7] www.smartpuba.eu

[8] Layo, I. "Cloud computing advantages for SMEs," http://cloudtimes.org/2013/09/18/cloud-computing-advantages-for-smes/. 2013. Accessed on December, 28, 2015

[9] Ouf, S. and Nasr, M. "Business intelligence in the cloud," in IEEE Third International Conference on Communication Software and Networks (ICCSN2011), pp. 650-655, 2011.

[10] Hamburg, I. "Improving e-Learning in SMEs through cloud computing and scenarios". In: Gradinarova, B. (ed.): E-learning – instructional design, organizational strategy and management. Rijeka: InTech: pp. 481-498, 2015

[11] Cavalcanti, G. "Barriers to implementation of information and communication technologies among small- and medium-sized enterprises," The digital divide through the business lens, MBA., California State University, Fresno, pp. 57, AAT 1444963, 2006

[12] Shiels, H., McIvor, R. and O'Reilly, D. "Understanding the implications of ICT adoption: Insights from SMEs, Logistics Information Management," 16 (5), pp. 312-326, 2003

[13] Hamburg, I. and Marian, M. "Supporting knowledge transfer and mentoring in companies by e-learning and cloud computing," ICWL 2012 International Workshops, KMEL, SciLearn, and CCSTED, Sinaia, Romania, September 2-4, 2012; revised selected papers. Heidelberg: Springer: pp. 231-240, 2012

[14] Fernández, A., Peralta, D., Benítez, J.M. and Herrera, F. "E-learning and educational data mining in cloud computing: an overview," Int J Learning Technol, 9(1), pp. 25-52. 2014.

[15] Masud, A.H. and Huang, X. "Esaas a new education software model in e-learning systems." in M. Zhu (ed.), ICCIC 2011, Vol. 235 of CCIS, pp. 468-475, 2011

[16] Pocatilu, P. and Vetrici, M. "Using Cloud computing for E-Learning Systems," Proceedings of the 8th WSEAS International conference on data Networks, Communications, computers, Italy, 2009

[17] Hamburg, I. "Learning as a service – a cloud-based approach for SMEs." Service computation 2012: The Fourth International Conference on Advanced Service Computing, pp. 53-57, 2012

[18] Sulistio, A., Reich, C. and Doelitzscher, F. "Cloud infra-structure and applications – cloudia". In: Jaatun, M.G. , Zhao, G. and Rong, C. (Eds.): CloudCom, Vol. 5931 of Lecture Notes in Computer Science, Springer, pp. 583-588, 2009

Implementing a USB File System for Bare PC Applications

William Thompson, Ramesh K. Karne, Sonjie Liang, Alexander L. Wijesinha, Hamdan Alabsi, and Hojin Chang
Department of Computer and Information Sciences
Towson University
Towson, MD 21252, U.S.
e-mail: {wvthompson, rkarne, sliang, awijesinha, halabs1, hchang}@towson.edu

Abstract—**Bare machine computing applications including Web servers, Webmail servers, SIP servers and SQLite require a file system that can also be used with an OS such as Windows or Linux. However, conventional file systems are OS-dependent and cannot be used with bare PC applications, which run without any OS or kernel support. This paper describes the implementation of a novel FAT-32 based USB file system for a bare PC, and provides details of its internal structures and the file API. Implementing a bare machine file system is challenging because it does not use any standard system libraries and requires integrating the USB driver and FAT32 file system with the bare PC application. The file system can be used with any existing or future bare PC application.**

Keywords- bare machine computing; bare PC applications; FAT32; file system; USB.

I. INTRODUCTION

File systems provide a means for organizing and retrieving the data needed by many computer applications. Typically, they are closely tied to the underlying operating system (OS) and mass storage technology. Bare machine file systems are, in contrast, independent of any OS or platform. Such a file system can be used with computer applications that run on a bare machine with no OS, and also in a conventional OS environment. The file system can serve as a basis to support future bare machine database management systems, big data systems, and Web and mobile applications that eliminate OS overhead and cost. Furthermore, it can be used in bare machine security applications that provide protection from attacks targeting OS vulnerabilities. In earlier work [14], a lean USB file system for a bare PC was described and relevant design issues were discussed. This paper focuses on the implementation and internals of a bare machine USB file system. It also defines a file API for bare PC applications.

The file system depends on the USB architecture [17], USB Mass Storage Specification [21], USB Enhanced Host Controller Interface Specification [6], FAT32 standard [15],

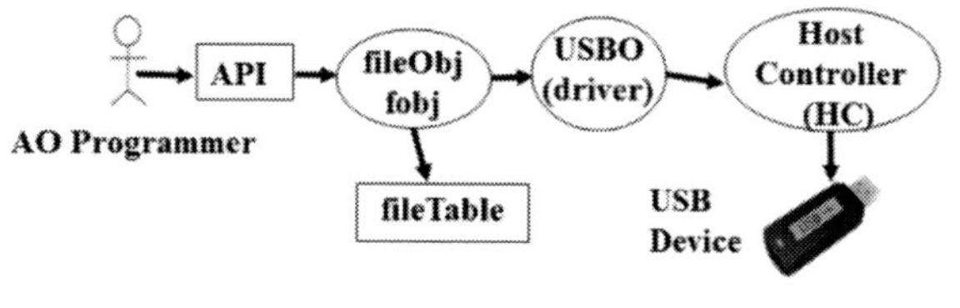

Figure 1. Bare machine USB file system.

and the bare machine computing paradigm. The file system is stored on a USB along with its application. The USB layout is similar to a memory layout providing a linear block addressing (LBA) scheme. That is, a USB address map is similar to a memory map. However, a USB is accessed with sector numbers that are directly mapped to memory addresses. It uses small computer system interface (SCSI) commands that are encapsulated in USB commands. Thus, a bare PC USB driver that works with this file system is needed [12]. The FAT32 standard is complex and has a variety of options that are needed for an OS based system as it is required to work with many application environments. The FAT32 options implemented in this system and the file API are designed for bare PC applications.

Bare PC applications are based on the Bare Machine Computing (BMC) or dispersed OS computing paradigm [10]. This paradigm differs from a conventional approach as there is no underlying OS to manage resources. This means that the application programmer also has to deal with system programming aspects. Resident mass storage is not used in a bare PC, so applications are stored in a portable device such as a USB drive or in the cloud. The application is written primarily in C/C++ (with some assembly code) and runs as an application object (AO). An AO includes its own interfaces to the hardware [11] and the necessary OS-independent device drivers. Bare PC applications include Web servers [9], split servers [18], server clusters [19], email servers [5], SIP servers and user agents [1], and peer-to-peer VoIP systems [8].

The rest of the paper is organized as follows. Section 2 discusses related work. Section 3 describes the file API for bare PC applications. Section 4 gives details of file system internals. Section 5 presents functional operation. Section 6 contains the conclusion..

II. RELATED WORK

There are many approaches to reduce OS overhead, use lean kernels, or build a high-performance OS such as Exokernel [4], IO-Lite [16], and Palacios and Kitten [13]. While the BMC paradigm somewhat resembles these approaches, there is a significant difference in that bare machine applications run without any centralized code in the form of an OS or kernel. Flash memory has been used for mass storage devices as in the Umbrella file system [7], which also integrates two different types of storage devices. In [2], it is shown how to improve performance by adding cache systems at a driver level. In [3], a FAT32 file system for high performance clusters is implemented.

```
h= createFile(fn, saddr, size, attr)
deletFile (h)
resizeFile (h, size)
flushFile (h)
flushAll ()
```

Figure 2. File API functions.

In [14], the design of a lean USB file system for bare PC applications was discussed and an initial version of the file system was built and tested. That work showed the feasibility of developing a file system without any OS support. However, the file system was not easy to modify or use with existing bare PC applications. This paper describes the implementation of an enhanced USB file system with a simple file API for bare PC applications.

III. FILE API

In a bare PC application, code for data and file systems reside on the same USB. In addition to the application, the USB has the boot code and loader in a separate executable, which enables the bare PC to be booted from the USB. The application suite (consisting of one or more end-user applications) is a self-contained application object (AO) [11] that encapsulates all the needed code for execution as a single entity. For example, a Webmail server, SQLite database and the file system can all be part of one AO. Since no centralized kernel or OS runs in the machine, the AO programmer controls the execution of the application on the machine. When an AO runs, no other applications are running in the machine. After the AO runs, no trace of its execution remains.

An overview of the USB file system for bare PC applications is shown in Figure 1. The simple API for the file system consists of five functions to support bare PC applications. These are (1) createFile(), (2) deleteFile(), (3) resizeFile(), (4) flushFile() and (5) flushAll(). These functions provide all the necessary interfaces to create and use files in bare PC applications. The fileObj (class) uses a fileTable data structure to manage and control the file system. A given API call in turn interfaces with the USBO object, which is the bare PC device driver for the USB [12]. This device driver has many interfaces to communicate directly with the host controller (HC). The HC interfaces with USB device using low-level USB commands.

Figure 2 lists the file API functions, and Figure 3 shows an example of their usage. The parameters for the createFile() function are file name (fn), memory address pointer (saddr), file size (size) and file attributes (attr); it

```
char *ptr;
char *readArray;
FileObj fobj;
h = fobj.createFile(fileName,
   &startAddress, &fileSize, attr);
ptr = (char *)startAddress;
for(i = 0; i < fileSize; i++)
    ptr[i] = 0; //write to file
for(i = 0; i < fileSize; i++)
    readArray[i] = ptr[i]; //read from
file
fobj.flushFile(h);
```

Figure 3. File API Usage.

```
GetReservedSectors() 0xe - 0xf (0x0236)
GetNumOfFats() 0x10 (02)
GetNumOfSectorsPerFat() 0x24 - 0x27 (0x0ee5)
GetSectorsPerCluster() 0x0d (08)
GetNumOfSectorsInPart() 0x20 -0x23 (0x003bafff)
GetClusterOfStartRootDir() 0x2c - 0x2f (02)
GetNumOfClustersInRootDir() (third entry in FAT, 04)
GetFATEntryPoint()
GetDirectoryEntryPoint()
```

Figure 4. USB parameters

returns a file handle (h). The file handle is the index value of the file in the fileTable structure, which has all the control information of a file. This approach considerably simplifies file system design as it can be used as a direct index into the fileTable without the need for searching. The deleteFile(h) function uses the file handle to delete a file. When a file is deleted, it simply makes a mark in the fileTable structure and its related structures such as the root directory and FAT table. The resizeFile() function is used to increase or decrease a previously allocated file size. Thus, an AO programmer needs to keep track of the growth of a file from within the application. The flushFile() function will update the USB mass storage device from its related data structures and memory data. An AO programmer has to call this function periodically or at the end of the program to write files to persistent storage. The flushAll() interface is used to flush all files and related structures onto the USB drive. Note that the programmer gets a file address, uses it as standard memory (similar to memory mapped files), and manages the memory to read and write to a file. There is no need for a read and write API in this file system. All standard file IO operations are reduced to the list shown in Figure 2.

A significant difference between the bare PC file system and a conventional OS-based file system is that an AO programmer directly controls the USB device through the API. That is, a user program directly communicates with the hardware without using an OS, kernel or intermediary software. For instance, the createFile() function invokes the

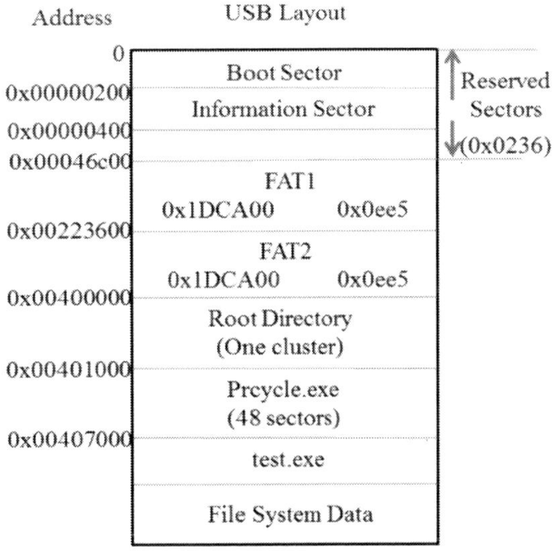

Figure 5. USB layout.

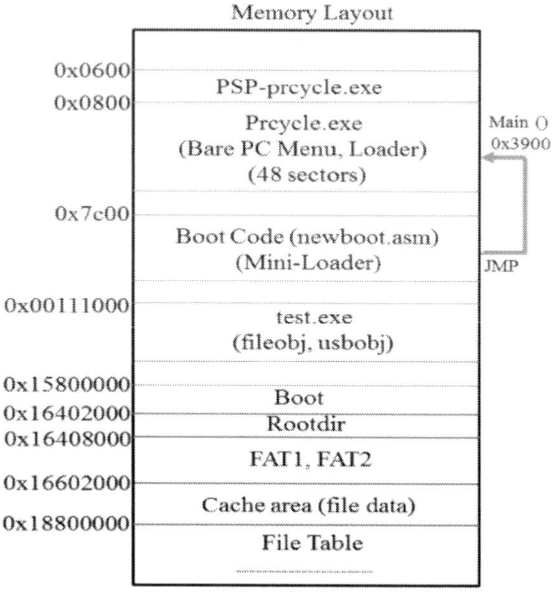

Figure 6. Memory map

ileObj function, which in turn invokes the USBO function. The latter then calls the HC low-level functions. In this approach, an API call runs as a single thread of execution without the intervention of any other tasks. Thus, writing a bare PC application is different from writing conventional programs as there is no kernel or centralized program running in the hardware to control the application. These applications are designed to run as self-controlled, self-managed and self-executable entities. In addition, the application code does not depend on any external software or modules since it is created as a single monolithic executable.

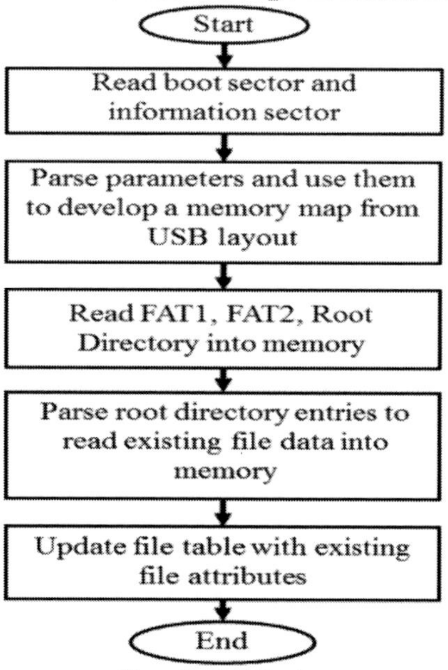

Figure 7. Initialization.

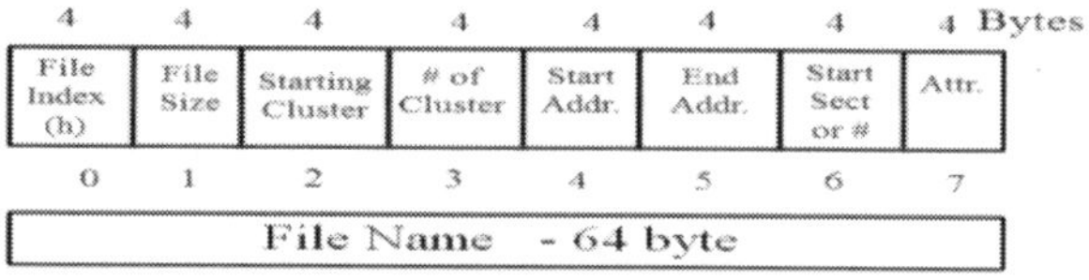

Figure 8. File Table Entry (FTE)

IV. FILE SYSTEM INTERNALS

Building a USB file system for bare PC applications is challenging. The system involves several components and interfaces, and it is necessary to map the USB specifications to work with the memory layout in a bare PC application and the bare machine programming paradigm. Details of file system internals are provided in this section to illustrate the approach.

A. *USB Parameters*

Each USB has its own parameters depending on the vendor, size and other attributes. Some parameters shown in Figure 4 are used for identification and laying out the USB memory map. These parameters are analogous to a schema in a database system and are located in the 0th sector.

B. *USB and Memory Layout*

Figure 5 displays the USB layout for a typical file system with 2GB mass storage. The boot sector contains many parameters as shown in Figure 4. The reserved sectors parameter is used to calculate the start address of FAT1 table. The number of sectors per FAT defines the size of FAT1 and FAT2 tables, which are contiguous. The root directory entry follows the FAT2 table as shown in Figure 5.

The number of clusters in the root directory and number of sectors per cluster defines the starting point for the files stored in the USB. The root directory has 32 byte structures for each file on the USB. These 32 byte structures describe the characteristics of a FAT32 file system. The layout in Figure 5 shows two files prcycle.exe and test.exe. The first file is the entry point of a program after boot and the second one is the application. Other mass storage files created by the application are located after test.exe. The bare PC file system has to manage the FAT tables, root directory and file system data.

The USB layout and its entry points are used to map these sectors to physical memory. A memory map is then drawn as shown in Figure 6. During the boot process, the BIOS will load the boot sector at 0x7c00 and boot up the machine. This code will run and load prcycle.exe using a mini-loader. When prcycle.exe runs, it provides a menu to load and run the application (test.exe). The original boot, root directory and FATs as well as other existing files and

```
usbo.ResetUSBPluggedIn()
usbo.ReadUSBDesc()
usbo.SetupUSB()
usbo.ClearFeature()
usbo.WriteOp()
usbo.ReadOp()
```

Figure 9. USB operations.

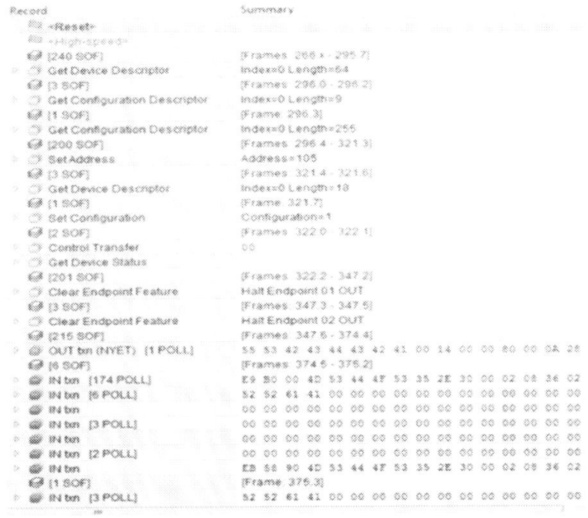

Figure 10. Analyzer trace.

data in the USB are also stored in memory to manage them as memory mapped files. The cache area stores all the user file data and provides direct access to the application program. In this system, the USB and memory maps are controlled by the application and not by middleware.

C. *Initialization*

The Figure 7 illustrates the initialization process after the bare PC starts. During initialization, existing files from the USB are read into memory and file table attributes are populated. In addition, FAT tables and other relevant parameters are read and stored in the system. If the file data size is larger than the available memory, then partial data is read as needed and the file tables are updated appropriately. A contiguous memory allocation strategy is used to manage real memory. Because the file handle serves as a direct index to the file table, the file management system is simplified.

D. *File Table Entry (FTE)*

The FTE is a 96-byte structure as shown in Figure 8. The file name is limited to 64 bytes including name and type. 32-byte control fields are used to store the file control information needed to manage files. These attributes are derived from the root directory, FAT tables and memory map. The file index is the first entry in the FTE and it indicates the index of the file table. The index is also used as a file handle to be returned to the user for file control.

E. *File Operations*

The five file operations in the bare PC system use the data structures file table and device driver interfaces.

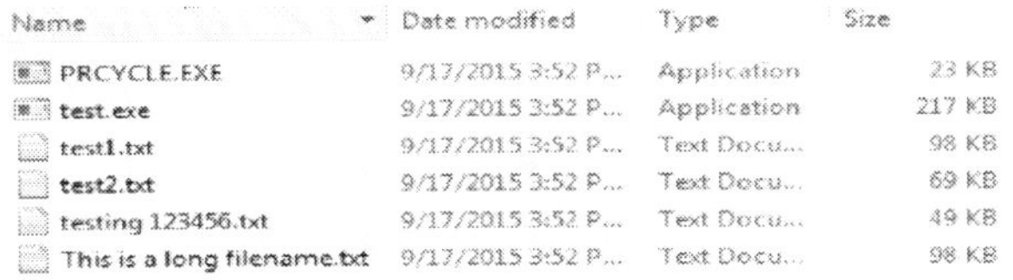

Figure 11. Windows trace.

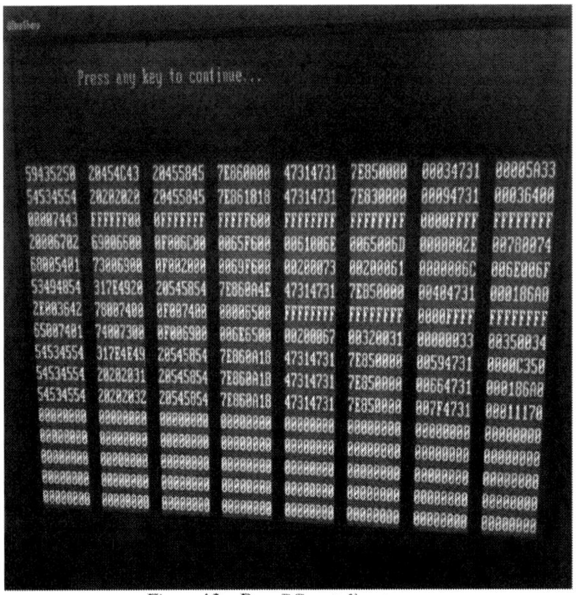

Figure 12. Bare PC root directory.

The file system only covers a single directory structure. When createFile() is called, it first checks the file table for any existing file using the file name. If this file does not exist, a new file is created with the given file name and requested file size. Then an entry is made in the file table, memory is assigned, and the root directory and FAT entries are created for the file. When flushFile() is called, it updates the USB and the call returns the file handle, which is an index into the file table. Similarly, deleteFile() will delete the file from the file table and flushAll() will update the USB with all the USB data fields. The resizeFile() interface simply uses the same entry with a different memory pointer and keeps the data "as is" unless the size is reduced. When the size is reduced, the extra memory is reset. All API calls and their internals are visible to the programmer.

F. *File Name*

The file system supports both short and long file names. At present, long file names are limited to 64 characters by design since they introduce difficulties when creating the root directory and file table entries. The FAT32 root directory structure also results in complexity that affects file system implementation.

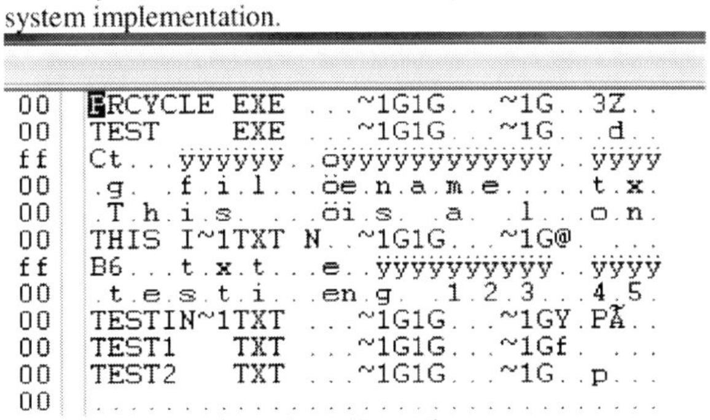

Figure 13. USB root directory.

G. *System Interfaces*

The The USB file system runs as a separate task in the bare PC AO. The AO has one main task, one receive task and many application tasks such as server threads. The main task enables plug-and-play when the USB drive is plugged into the system. Each USB slot in the PC is managed as a separate task. Tasks and threads are synonymous in bare PC applications as threads are implemented as tasks in the system. Each event in the system is treated as a single thread of execution without interruption. Thus, each file operation runs as one thread of execution. There is no need for concurrency control and related mechanisms in a bare PC application. The files generated in the bare PC system can be read on any OS that supports FAT32 such as Windows, Linux or Mac.

V. OPERATION

The file system is written in C/C++, while the device driver code is written in C and MASM. The MASM code is 27 lines and provides two functions that read and write to control registers in the host controller. The fileObj code is 4262 lines including comments (30% of the code), and one class definition. State transition diagrams are used to implement USB operations and their sequencing. For example, some of the state transitions occurring during the initialization process are shown in Figure 7. The fileObj in turn invokes the USB device driver calls shown in Figure 9.

File operations can be done anywhere in the bare PC application. The task structure that runs in the bare PC file system is similar to that used for bare Web servers [9], and runs on any Intel-based CPU that is IA32 compatible. Bare PC applications do not use a hard disk; instead, the BIOS is used to boot the system. The file system, boot code and application are stored on the same USB. A bootable USB along with its application is generated by a special tool designed for bare PC applications. The USB file system was integrated with the bare PC Web server for functional testing.

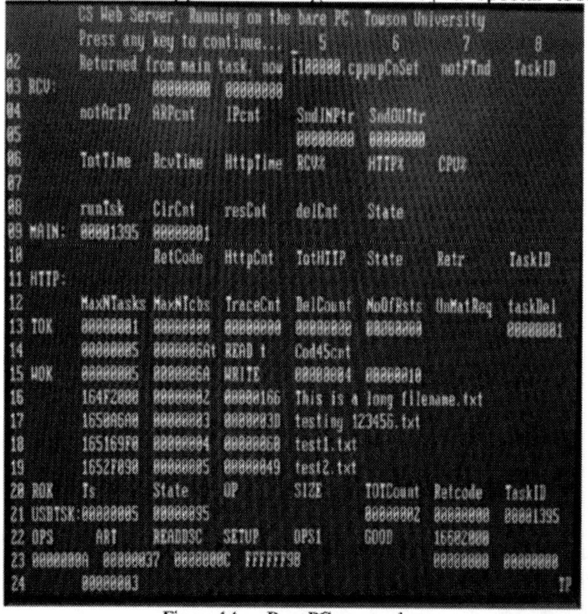

Figure 14. Bare PC screen shot.

The operation of the bare PC file system is demonstrated by having two existing files (prcycle.exe and test.exe) on the USB along with the boot code. Small and large files are created by the application with file sizes varying up to 100K. To demonstrate file operations, four files were created and tested as described here in addition to the two files prcycle.exe and test.exe on the USB (after the program runs, there a total of six files on the USB). The data were read from the files and also written to them using the file API. A USB analyzer [20] was used to test and validate the file system and the driver. Figure 10 shows a sample trace from the analyzer that illustrates reset, read descriptors, set configuration and clear. These low level USB commands are directly controlled by the programmer (they are a part of the bare PC application).

Figure 11 shows the six files that exist on the USB displayed on the screen of a Windows PC. The four created files can be read from the Windows PC. Figure 12 shows the file system in the bare PC root directory in memory. This directory is used to update the files until they are flushed. Figure 13 shows the root directory entries on the USB after the program is complete. Figure 14 is a screen shot on the bare PC showing the four files (short and long) created successfully by the system. The bare PC screen is divided into 25 rows and 8 columns to display text using video memory. This display is used by the programmer to print functional data, and for debugging. The programmer controls writing to the display directly from the bare PC application, with no interrupts used for display operations.

VI. CONCLUSION

We described the implementation of a novel bare machine USB file system designed for applications that run without the support of any OS environment/platform, lean kernel or embedded software. We also presented a file API for bare PC applications. The file system enables a programmer to build and control an entire application from the top down to its USB data storage level without the need for an OS or intermediary system. This implementation can be used as a basis for extending bare PC file system capabilities in the future. The file system can be integrated with bare PC applications such as Web servers, Webmail/email servers, SIP servers and VoIP clients.

REFERENCES

[1] A. Alexander, A. L.Wijesinha, and R. Karne, "Implementing a VoIP SIP server and a user agent on a bare PC", 2nd International Conference on Future Computational Technologies and Applications (Future Computing), 2010, pp. 8-13.

[2] Y. H. Chang, P. Y. Hsu, Y. F. Lu, and T. W. Kuo "A driver-layer caching policy for removable storage devices", ACM Transactions on Storage, Vol. 7, No. 1, Article 1, June 2011, p1:1-1:23.

[3] M. Choi, H. Park, and J. Jeon, "Design and implementation of a FAT file system for reduced cluster switching overhead",

International Conference on Multimedia and Ubiquitous Engineering, 2008, pp. 355-360.

[4] D. R. Engler and M.F. Kaashoek, "Exterminate all operating system abstractions", Fifth Workshop on Hot Topics in Operating Systems, USENIX, 1995, p. 78.

[5] G. H. Ford, R. K. Karne, A. L. Wijesinha, and P. Appiah-Kubi, "The design and implementation of a bare PC email server", 33rd IEEE Computer Software and Applications Conference (COMPSAC), 2009, pp. 480-485.

[6] Intel Corporation, Enhanced host controller interface specification for universal serial bus, March 2002, Rev 1, http://www.intel.com/technology/usb/download/ehci-r10.pdf [retrieved: April 8, 2016]

[7] J. A. Garrison and A. L. N. Reddy, "Umbrella file system: Storage management across heterogeneous devices", ACM Transactions on Storage (TOS), Vol. 5, No. 1, Article 3, March 2009.

[8] G. Khaksari, A. Wijesinha, R. Karne, L. He, and S. Girumala., "A peer-to-peer bare PC VoIP application", IEEE Consumer Communications and Networking Conference (CCNC) 2007, pp. 803-807.

[9] L. He, R. K. Karne, and A. L. Wijesinha, "The design and performance of a bare PC Web server", International Journal of Computers and Their Applications, IJCA, Vol. 15, No. 2, June 2008, pp. 100-112.

[10] R. K. Karne, K. V. Jaganathan, N. Rosa, and T. Ahmed, "DOSC: dispersed operating system computing", 20th Annual ACM Conference on Object Oriented Programming, Systems, Languages, and Applications (OOPSLA), 2005, pp. 55-61.

[11] R. K. Karne, K. V. Jaganathan, and T. Ahmed, "How to run C++ applications on a bare PC", 6th ACIS Conference on Software Engineering, Artificial Intelligence, Networking and Parallel/Distributed Computing (SNPD) 2005.

[12] R. K. Karne, S. Liang, A. L. Wijesinha, and P. Appiah-Kubi, "A bare PC mass storage USB device driver", International Journal of Computers and Their Applications, Vol 20, No. 1, March 2013, pp. 32-45.

[13] J. Lange et al., "Palacios and Kitten: New high performance operating systems for scalable virtualized and native supercomputing", 24th IEEE International Parallel and Distributed Processing Symposium (IPDPS), 2010, pp. 1-12.

[14] S. Liang, R. Karne, and A. L. Wijesinha, "A lean USB file system for bare machine applications", 21st Conference on Software Engineering and Data Engineering (SEDE), 2012, pp. 191-196.

[15] Microsoft Corp, "FAT32 file system specification", http://microsoft.com/whdc/system/platform/firmware/fatgn.rn spx, 2000. [retrieved: April 8, 2016]

[16] V. S. Pai, P. Druschel, and W. Zwaenepoel. "IO-Lite: A unified i/o buffering and caching system", ACM Transactions on Computer Systems, Vol.18 (1), Feb. 2000, pp. 37-66.

[17] Perisoft Corp, Universal serial bus specification 2.0, http://www.perisoft.net/engineer/usb_20.pdf. [retrieved: April 8, 2016]

[18] B. Rawal, R. Karne, and A. L. Wijesinha, "Splitting HTTP requests on two servers", 3rd Conference on Communication Systems and Networks (COMSNETS), 2011, pp. 1-8.

[19] B. Rawal, R. K. Karne, and A. L. Wijesinha. "Mini Web server clusters for HTTP request splitting", IEEE Conference on High Performance, Computing and Communications (HPCC), 2011, pp. 94-100.

[20] Total Phase Inc., USB analyzers, Beagle, http://www.totalphase.com. [retrieved: April 8, 2016]

[21] Universal serial bus mass storage class, bulk only transport, revision 1.0, 1999, http://www.usb.org [retrieved: April 8, 2016]

A XBRL Financial Virtual Assistant

Adalberto Alves Abraão
Programa de Pós-Graduação em Sistemas e Computação
Universidade Salvador - Unifacs
Salvador, Brazil
e-mail: adalbertoabraao@gmail.com,

Paulo Caetano da Silva
Programa de Pós-Graduação em Sistemas e Computação
Universidade Salvador - Unifacs
Salvador, Brazil
paulo.caetano@pro.unifacs.br

***Abstract*— Nowadays, by means of stock exchanges, it is possible to invest in globally located enterprises. It is a market in which it is possible to obtain great profits, but it also conveys great risks of loss. In order to decrease risks, it is important to know the financial strength of the enterprises, through specific indicators, to ask what their values are, for example, "What is the leverage ratio of the company X currently?". Financial consultancy emerges for that need, but it is very expensive. An alternative is to search for the answers by themselves on enterprises websites or from the regulatory agencies. Such tasks require time, calculations and analyses. With the aim at facilitating the obtaining of financial information about the enterprises for any investors, a virtual financial assistant is presented in this paper which answers to the questions of financial type made by the user, interacting by means of a natural language. The assistant utilizes financial information from analytic Online Analytical Processing (OLAP) queries at eXtensible Business Reporting Language (XBRL) database. The architecture of the virtual assistant is presented as well as details a prototype's implementation. As a result, we expect that the assistant correctly answers the user's questions, asked in a natural language and related to financial indexes of given enterprises.**

Keywords- Virtual Assistant; XBRL Financial Virtual Assistant; Financial Virtual Assistant; LDQM application; NLP application; Virtual Financial Assistant Architecture.

I. INTRODUCTION

In a globalized world, electronic interconnections, by means of telecommunication nets and information systems are crucial for the global financial transactions. Stock market is one of the sectors in which the investors act almost entirely online. An environment where, nowadays, it is possible to operate in almost all stock exchanges throughout the world from a computational system with internet access. It is a high-risk market that can provide a high rate of profit over investments but also a great loss. In order to increase success rate, it is vital that the analyses for the decision making are correct and based on authentic and as much as possible updated information. Part of that analysis consists of the identification of the enterprises financial strength, while suggesting typical questionings such as: "What is the leverage ratio of the company X currently?"; "What is the net profit of the company Z in the second quarter of the year Y?" and so on.

Many investors search for the most diverse financial information enterprises by means of reports published online in electronic format Portable Document Format (PDF), HyperText Markup Language (HTML) or text. Many regulatory agencies are currently demanding that those reports be published in XBRL [15], a technology that have features that enable to identifies the fraudulent manipulations more quickly, among other functionalities.

Normally, the investors pay for expensive services of financial assistance in order to obtain information and complete consultancy. However, for retail investors, which mostly do not have assistants, collecting and analyzing information present far greater risks. The available virtual assistants on the web or on smartphones could be alternatives to financial consultancy. However, in general, these software are proprietary and they do not give satisfactory answers to the financial queries.

The non-existence of a virtual financial assistant, capable of being an alternative to a financial consultancy to a retail investor, motivated the creating a virtual financial assistant. A computational system capable of answering questions in a natural language utilizing the financial jargon based on data from reliable financial reports and of high availability.

So, the aim of this paper is to present the architecture and a prototype of a virtual financial assistant which answers to the user's financial questions with XBRL database, interacting by a natural language.

The rest of the article is organized as follows: Section II describes papers and implementations related to virtual assistants. Section III presents the architecture of the proposed virtual financial assistant. Section IV presents the prototype implementation details and its evaluation. Section V shows the conclusion.

II. VIRTUAL ASSISTANTS

The term Virtual Assistant can have many nomenclatures and denominations. For Paraiso et al. [2], Personal Assistants are agents who help people to perform their daily chores. In another work, Zambiasi et al. [9], the authors denominate as

Personal Assistant Software (PAS), software that help people with their daily activities. They affirm that this kind of software has several denominations and characteristics identified by various authors and one can hardly reach a final definition.

The term Embodied Conversational Agent (ECA) is defined by Eisman et al. [3] as an intelligent system represented by a character capable of getting involved in a conversation with a human being. Helping the user to accomplish a given set of tasks is its main function.

The various denominations are directly linked to the actions performed by the assistants. In this regard, Medina et al. [6] affirms that these denominations distinguish the existent assistants as of general purpose and of specific domain. The first ones are useful for providing information about climate, about how to get to a given location or even for performing some actions such as making an appointment, elaborating and sending a message. The second ones serve to answer the questions about a specific domain. Next, works related to this article are cited and analyzed.

The project of a personal assistant with interaction via voice through dialogs in natural language which helps the user in a governmental system was described by Paraiso et al. [2]. They have created a personal assistant that is used as an interface among users and a multi-agent system. Its architecture was divided in three main parts: interaction with the user, performed through Graphic Speech User Interface modules (GSUI); the processing of expressions, performed by the Linguistic Modules (LU) that, supported by ontologies, interprets user interactions by means of syntactic analysis and conversions; dialog management, performed by Agency Modules (AM) which activates the external events execution by means of the agents and controls the dialog and the assistance.

There is a voice conversation interface which allows the user to interact with the software using their own terms in addition to a taxonomy to deal with the users expressions, allowing to analyze if the sentence is well formed and in accordance with the grammatical structure. A personal assistant that can activate service agents locally is dedicated to each user. Those agents, in turn, can delegate sub-tasks to other service agents in order to complete a complex task. The agents are independent and exchange information with each other and with the personal assistant.

The user interface architecture and similar requirements of the proposed personal assistant, like the limited and well-known domain, presented by Paraiso et al. [2] have been contributions to this work.

A framework for projecting virtual assistants of multilingual closed domain that can be integrated to websites was presented by Eisman et al. [3]. The knowledge, i.e., domain, is stored in regular expressions and in an ontology. The regular expressions have the function of construct a syntax to facilitating the acknowledgement of the user queries. Ontology, in turn, supports the choice process of the next action to be performed and the adequate answer creation. That system was designed by using a client-server architecture and it was implemented in three modules The Natural Language Understander (NLU) which recognizes the questions elaborated by the user; The Dialog Manager (DM), which determines what, when and how the assistant is supposed to do; And the Communication Generator (CG), responsible for generating a specific answer that encompasses an action.

The authors presented a virtual assistant implementation based on the framework that supplies information about courses and services offered by a university. Although the framework has been designed to support assistants which help with the navigation in private websites, it has served as an inspiration for the proposed Financial Virtual Assistant.

Zambiasi et al. [9] presented a conceptual model and reference architecture for personal assistance software, which according to them, are inter-agent software and also integrated to corporative business environments, adaptive and inter-operatives with various sub-systems and sources of information and activities. The model and the architecture presented are based on Service Oriented Architecture (SOA).

PAS behaviors are a composite of services available on the web and they are chosen by the user to define the activities which the assistant may execute. The architecture proposed by Zambiasi et al. [9] facilitates the addition of new behaviors to PAS in a dynamic manner. All in all, the assistance that will be performed by PAS it will depend on the behaviors it possesses, and those, in turn, are included through the orchestration or configuration of the available selected services. Although the assistant, focus of this study, does not presume to be a PAS, the study greatly contributes for this work mainly in defining general architectural requirements for the assistant implementation and also with the identification of its main elements. A disadvantage is related to PAS do not process user queries made in natural language.

Within the study field of virtual assistance software there are important academic advances, the same way there are advances on the software development market. Currently, it is possible to perceive the utilization of virtual assistants in various situations, , on social nets, car selling websites, also bookstores and integrated in the smartphones operational systems.

Sys Virtual Assistant [14] by Synthetic Intelligence Network is a virtual assistant software of general purpose, whose main objective is helping users with the interaction man-machine, human-computer interaction (HCI). It works completely in the local machine, without sending data for any server. That feature is relevant in favor of data privacy and the security of the users. Its architecture is based on an Natural Language Processor (NLP) interacting with a collection of modules, or plugins, responsible for the functionalities. It is possible to modify, include or exclude modules, which allows a developer to configure the behavior of the assistant and thus define a new purpose. The utilization of the NLP facilitates the task of mapping the user phrases to perform the assistant software functions.

Although the type of sys virtual assistant is general purpose, one of its great advantages is the possibility of increase its knowledge through the addition of new plugins, which allows the creation and addition of a financial knowledge module. That resource is supported by the platform also developed by SYN network called The Syn Engine [14] that does not require a great computational power to work. It is available through user licenses among which there is a free version. However, there are some disadvantages of the Sys Virtual Assistant such as not being multilingual, and there are only two compatible software environments currently.

The Assistant.ai [13] by Speaktoit Inc is also an assistant of general purpose. It answers not only to questions made by the user but it also suggests assistance based on information from the schedule and its present location. It is multilingual and multiplatform and it can be used in several operational systems or in a given web browser. One of the disadvantages of this assistant is the most advanced features are only available on the charged version. Furthermore, some private user information, such as localization and names on its contacts list are sent to the enterprise servers in order to create the context environments, what may infringe issues related to the user information privacy.

One of the most interesting assistant features is supported by the Application Programming Interface (API) in which it was developed. It is called Api.ai [12] and it is composed by three modularized components: speech recognition, natural language understanding (NLU) and Conversation Management (CM), and user-fulfillment. The NLU and the CM are part of the platform's main component, responsible for knowledge manipulation and part of dialog management. The NLU allows the insertion of queries user patterns in order to generate the domain grammar, as well as a dictionary of terms and their synonyms. A relevant contribution of that platform for this work is the capacity of creating new domains, defining behaviors and thus, generating assistants of specific purpose.

There are several other available assistants on the web or integrated in the main operational mobile systems, but none of them corresponds to the financial scope proposed in this work.

III. VIRTUAL FINANCIAL ASSISTANT ARCHITECTURE

The architecture of the virtual financial assistant was designed for a distributed environment. It is composed by four layers: Presentation; Orchestration; Understanding / Knowledge; and Data.

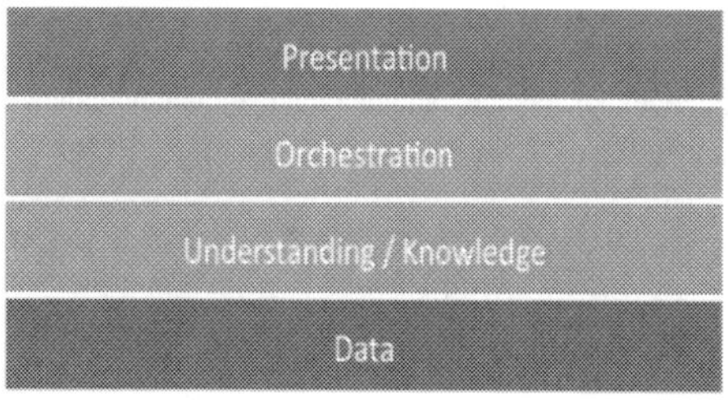

Figure 1. Architecture of the Virtual Financial Assistant in layers.

Figure 1 illustrates the assistant architecture, whose layers are discussed as follows.

Presentation: user layer interface. Responsible for dealing with the users events and for directing them to the Orchestration layer. It also has the responsibility of receiving the information returned from the Orchestration layer and presenting them to the user in an adequate format: text, image, animation, speech.

Orchestration: it is the layer that coordinates the assistant. It accesses the services of the Understanding / Knowledge in order to fulfill the requirements of the Presentation layer.

Understanding / Knowledge: that layer represents the knowledge domain. It is responsible for dealing with the understanding of the questions elaborated by the users and for the knowledge manipulation. It accesses the data layer in order to respond to the requirements of the Orchestration layer.

Data: Layer that represents the data repositories that can be a database or a set of documents, i.e., eXtensible Markup Language (XML), JavaScript Object Notation (JSON). It makes available data for the layer Understanding / Knowledge.

The components of each layer will be described below, according to what has been shown in the Figure 2.

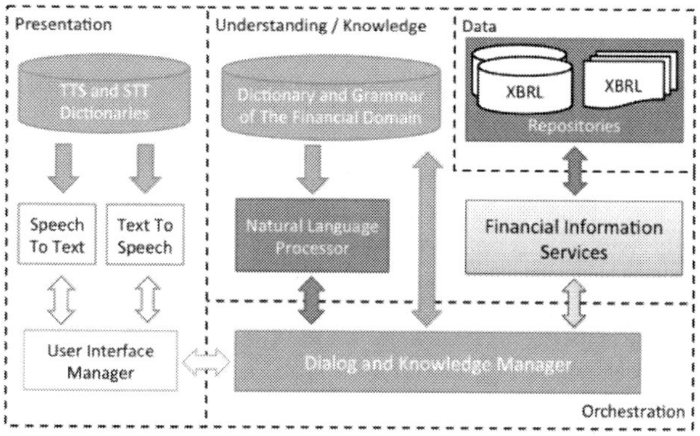

Figure 2. Virtual Financial Assistant Architecture.

A. *Presentation Layer*

It is the layer responsible for the interaction of the assistant with the user. It is formed by the following components: Speech To Text (STT); Text To Speech (TTS), TTS and STT Dictionaries and The User Interface Manager;

1) The Speech To Text: It is the responsible for the user speech recognition (encapsuled in audio streaming) and for text conversion. Normally, it is multilingual, funcionality suportted by dictionaries of specific word/voice for each language. It communicates with The User Interface Manager (UIM). Some of the factors that determine its quality are the precision and the velocity of voice recognition. If it is not obligatory that the assistant has support for speech recognition, the STT is optional.

2) The Text To Speech: it is responsible for converting a text into speech. Similar to STT, it accesses dictionaries of specific word/voice for each language to make multilingual conversions available. It serves the UIM. The TTS is obligatory only when it is pre-established that the assistant interacts with the user by means of voice. Some factors determine its quality, such as pronunciation and intonation in speech performance.

3) The TTS and STT Dictionaries: They make available data in order to facilitate the correct identification of the words embedded in the voice streaming or to facilitate the correct creation of the voice streaming. They are elaborated specifically for each language. The bigger the quantity of available dictionaries, the bigger the multilingual capacity of dealing with the speech of the assistant.

4) The User Interface Manager: It is responsible for collecting the information inserted by the user and directs them to The Dialog and Knowledge Manager; in addition, it is responsible for obtaining its answer and returning it to the user in an adequate format, such as: text, image, animation and speech.

B. Understanding / Knowledge Layer

It is the layer responsible for understanding the questions elaborated by the user, resolving them and directing the answers to the layer Orchestration. The Natural Language Processor, which deals with the sentences in natural language made by the user; Dictionary and Grammar of the financial domain, which define the syntax rules for the sentences of the user and the dictionary of financial terms domain; Financial Information Services, which provide specialized financial information are constituent parts of it.

1) The Natural Language Processor: Its main responsibility is to understand the user sentence, made in a natural language and to extract information from it, which allows a computational system to execute proceedings in response to it. In order to manipulate knowledge, NLP depends on the dictionary and the domain grammar, that is, whenever receiving one expression to be processed, it consults them in order to understand what the user had sentenced.

In case NLP does not find a pattern coherent with the question made, it warns The Dialog and Knowledge Manager (DKM) that it could not recognize the user expression. If it could understand the expression, the process result of conversion is returned to the DKM, by means of pre-established and known parameters.

2) Dictionary of The Financial Domain: It defines which words of the financial domain vocabulary are expected. In addition, it allows the definition of synonyms for the terms, in order to facilitate the process of understanding. Words, names of artifacts, documents, indexes, words related to financial domain must be represented in the dictionary.

3) Grammar of The Financial Domain: it defines the syntax of the sentences, that is which patterns of queries that can be elaborated by the user and which parameters will be extracted from them. The more representative and integrated the dictionary and the grammar are, the more precise it will be the assistant towards understanding what the user is asking in relation to the domain.

4) The Financial Information Services (FIS): They are responsible for dealing with the data and for making available information from the financial domain required by DKM. One example of dealing with data can be accessing data, calculating indicators and analyzing the financial risks.

The quantity, the versatility and the complexity of the information made available by this consulting service are the main responsible features for the level of sophistication of the answers given by the assistant. They can be made available by internet service providers of financial information widespread at any place by means of web service. One of the premises is that they have to be fast, once the consultations need answers within seconds.

C. The XBRL Repositories Layer

The XBRL Repositories is the layer responsible for supplying the financial data. It can be formed by XBRL instances or by XBRL relational database.

These repositories must be made available and administered periodically by reliable institutions, fact that will guarantee that the answers are based in current and authentic data.

D. The Orchestration Layer

It is the layer that coordinates the whole system and it is composed by the Dialog Knowledge Manager, component responsible for keeping a dialog with the user and for managing knowledge. This layer is the behavior manager of the assistant.

1) The Dialog and Knowledge Manager

The Dialog and Knowledge Manager (DKM) is the coordinator of the whole system. It is responsible for keeping a dialog with the user similarly to a conversation between people. A typical transaction of the DKM starts right after receiving a sentence of the user sent by the UIM. It sends the message to the NLP and waits for the parameters of the answer. In accordance with those parameters, it will select and request the available FIS services. After receiving the messages from the selected services, it builds up the answer and forwards it to the UIM, closing the transaction and waiting for the next solicitation.

When the NLP gives a signal that the user sentence was not recognized, the DKM does not activate any services. Only it informs the user about what has occurred via UIM.

DKM allows the assistant to incorporate new pieces of knowledge, as in the case of learning a new term of domain. The addition of new patterns or behaviors can be dynamically done. The questioning patterns for the services that will be activated in order to respond to them are mapped inside the DKM. In short, it defines the assistant behaviors through the management of the grammar, of the domain dictionary and of the services selection which will supply the adequate information. It is the master of knowledge manipulation.

IV. VIRTUAL FINANCIAL ASSISTANT IMPLEMENTATION

Many software companies provides STT and TTS components in various forms, either by services or by browser plugins, and the most of them are free. Two clients were implemented: a mobile application and a web page application. The android mobile operational system was chosen because it provides the STT and TTS components for free. The software development environment for it is free and is installed at the majority of mobile devices. The web page application was developed in Javascript language making the assistant available for any Operational System.

There are some NLPs currently available, many of them proprietary ones. The selection criteria utilized for chose the NLP, as shown in Table I, were:

1. Available functions /API to create new domains;
2. Provides questions grouping and customized parameters as a service;
3. Multilingual;
4. Availability for several platforms;
5. Proprietary solution;
6. Free license charge for evaluation and study;
7. Maintenance of the Grammar and the dictionary without code updates.

For the presented proposition in this job, the API.AI NLP [12] was utilized.

The more typical expressions and terms of financial jargon are entered in grammar and vocabulary, respectively, the greater the NLP ability to understand the financial user queries. Some financial queries patterns were used in the prototype grammar to increase the financial knowledge, for example, "What is the leverage ratio of the company X in 2013", or "What is the net income of Z company". These patterns, depending on the NLP, can be configured in various manners, for instance, utilizing regular expressions, specific languages or rules defined by NLP itself for build the syntax.

Some patterns that use the English language structure were registered on the grammar of American version and several patterns that use Portuguese language structure were registered on the grammar of Brazilian version. The construction of the Portuguese syntax patterns requires more effort than the English patterns because of the greater amount of syntax rules of the Portuguese language in relation to the English language.

TABLE I. SELECTION CRITERIAS OF NLP

NLP platform name	Provider	Criterias						
		1	*2*	*3*	*4*	*5*	*6*	*7*
API.AI	Speaktoit	x	x	x	x	x	x	x
Cortana Plataform	Microsoft	x	o	o	x	x	o	-
Google Now Plataform	Google Inc	x	o	o	x	x	x	-
Syn Engine	Synthetic Intelligence Network	x	x	x	o	Only two	x	o
Siri Plataform	Apple	x	o	o	x	o	x	-

A. Dictionary of terms

Concepts and entities of the Financial Domain have to be in the dictionary of terms. We grouped these terms in a feature of the selected NLP named "Entity". Each entity has a list of terms and each terms has its synonymous. For the prototype, we created following four entities: BalanceSheetsFinancialConcept Company, YearPeriod, CommandExpressions. Objectives and descriptions of each one are described as follows.

1. BalanceSheetsFinancialConcept: Contains the main financial concepts of Company Balance Sheets. We created two dictionaries of financial terms, and the majority of registered terms there were derived from XBRL taxonomies. US-GAAP 2013 [16] for questions in English language and BR-GAAP for questions in Portuguese language. The fragment of the BalanceSheetsFinancialConcept entity is shown in Table II.
2. Company: Contains target company names. Table III shows a fragment of the Company entity.
3. YearPeriod: List of the financial quarter symbols. Example: The first quarter is Q1;
4. CommandExpressions: Entity created for grouping command expressions that can be said by the user, as "What is", "Show me", "Inform". The grammar rules becomes smaller, by the use of it. Table IV lists this command expressions.

When an NLP recognizes a given set of words, it substitutes them for the pattern word defined in the dictionary of terms. For example, in similar fashion, a supposed user expression "What is the debt-to-equity ratio of Petrobras in 2013" after going through the process of substitution, it will be transformed into: "Show me the leverageRatio of Petroleo Brasileiro in 2013".

TABLE II. BALANCESHEETSFINANCIALCONCEPT ENTITY

Financial Concept Name	Synonymous
Assets	*Assets,Total assets*
Cash and cash equivalents	*Cash,Cash and cash equivalents*
EBITDA	*EBITDA,ebitda,"Earning Before Interests, Taxes, Depreciation and Amortization"*
leverageRatio	*leverageRatio,leverage ratio,debt-to-equity, debt to equity, leverage*
Net Income	*netIncome,Net Income,NI*
Short-term investments	*Short-term investments*
Total liabilities	*Total liabilities,Current liabilities*
Total liabilities and stockholders' equity	*Total liabilities and stockholders' equity, liabilities and stockholders' equity*
Total current assets	*Total current assets,Current assets*

TABLE III. COMPANY ENTITY

Company name	Synonymous
Apple Inc	*Apple Inc,Apple*
IBM	*IBM*
Google Inc	*Google Inc,Google*
Microsoft Inc	*Microsoft Inc,Microsoft*
Petroleo Brasileiro	*Petroleo Brasileiro,Petrobras*

B. *The rules of grammar*

After the process of substitution, the NLP confronts the query with the configured patterns in grammar. For example, in order to make the NLP, used in this proposition, understand the questions cited previously, the following rules of syntax were established:

"@CommandExpressions @BalanceSheetsFinancialConcept:financialConcept of @Company:companyName in @sys.number:year"

or

" @BalanceSheetsFinancialConcept:financialConcept of @Company:companyName [at,in,of,on fiscal year, in fiscal year,of fiscal year,of year, year] @sys.number:year".

The positioning of words, entity names and parameter names defines a pattern of questions expected. The symbol at sign identifies the name of the entity and the name after the colon identifies the parameter expected at that position.. Words or Entity names between square bracket symbols are considered optional.

From that example, supposing the question "What is the leverage ratio of Petrobras in 2013", the result of the NLP, after dealing with the question, will be a set of parameters and values extracted from the sentence.

@action = CompanyRatioService
$financialConcept = leverageRatio
$companyName = Petroleo Brasileiro
$year=2013

The selected NLP offers a resource to organize groups of pattern questions that is called "Intent". In each Intent, the programmer defines the rules and specifies the parameters that must be filled by NLP. In Table V, "What is The Financial Concept of Balance Sheets at Period" intent is presented.

There are also some parameters for each intent that are only defined by the developer, one of them is @Action. In the prototype the parameter @Action was used to identify the name of the class that will handle the parameters sent by each intent. NLP encapsulates all the parameters in a response object in the data format JavaScript Object Notation (JSON).

TABLE IV. COMMAND EXPRESSION ENTITY

Command	Expression
Whatis	*What is,Give me,Give,Would you tell me,Show me,Show*

TABLE V. WHAT IS THE FINANCIAL CONCEPT OF BALANCE SHEETS AT PERIOD INTENT

Id	Rule
1	*@CommandExpressions @BalanceSheetsFinancialConcept:financialConcept of @Company:companyName [in,on] @YearPeriod:yearPeriod [at,in,on fiscal year, in fiscal year,of fiscal year,of year, year] @sys.number:year*
2	*@CommandExpressions @BalanceSheetsFinancialConcept:financialConcept of @Company:companyName [at,in,of,on fiscal year, in fiscal year,of fiscal year,of year, year] @sys.number:year*
3	*@CommandExpressions @Company:companyName @BalanceSheetsFinancialConcept:financialConcept [at,in,of,on fiscal year, in fiscal year,of fiscal year,of year, year] @sys.number:year*
4	*@CommandExpressions @Company:companyName @BalanceSheetsFinancialConcept:financialConcept [in,on] @YearPeriod:yearPeriod [at,in,of,on fiscal year, in fiscal year,of fiscal year,of year, year] @sys.number:year*
5	*[at,in,of,on fiscal year, in fiscal year,of fiscal year,of year, year] @sys.number:year @CommandExpressions @BalanceSheetsFinancialConcept:financialConcept of @Company:companyName*
6	*[in,on] @YearPeriod:yearPeriod [at,in,of,on fiscal year, in fiscal year,of fiscal year,of year, year] @sys.number:year @CommandExpressions @BalanceSheetsFinancialConcept:financialConcept of @Company:companyName*

We created the following four intents for help to keep the state of the dialog with user: "Change Company", "Change Financial Concept", "Change Period", "Change Financial Concept And Period". This feature avoids that users have to make a complete question for each interaction.

C. *The services mapping*

After the DKM receives the response object of NLP it extracts the @Action parameter and through its built-in mapping forwards to the corresponding class and waits for the response. This mapping is done by a factory pattern class type allowing addition of new classes to handle new services and parameters without quite code. The classes added to the inventory of this factory should extend the standard abstract class called FinancialService. In addition, the code required to access the financial services must include a method for treating the parameters encapsulated in objects of a class named FinancialParametersRequest and other method named getResponse that aim to return the result of the service.

In the cited example the @Action informs that the CompanyRatioService Class must be invoked to treat the rescued parameters.

If it does not find a coherent pattern with the asked question, the NLP will send the empty @action parameter to DKM. When this occurs, a created exception UnknownFinancialServiceException is launched and treated by the DKM which, in turn, sends to the user the following message:

"I'm Sorry! I didn't understand your question!"

For the prototype proposed, a web service of FIS was designed to analyze the financial situation of enterprises. This analysis involves the evaluation of several values and/or variations of the economic indexes of the enterprise within a time period. This web service of FIS is called by the CompanyRatioService Class.

The OLAP queries are the most adequate so that the most complex analyses of risks, performed under the perspective of many dimensions, or business views, typical of economic evaluations may be performed with acceptable flexibility and performance. However, it is complex to perform OLAP queries in XBRL artifacts or database or documents based in XML. In this case, Link Based Multidimensional Query Language (LMDQL) [8][7], can be use to decrease this complexity. It is a specified language for performance of OLAP queries in XBRL documents. Furthermore, there is the definition of specific operators in LMDQL for the financial analysis, considerably decreasing the complexity of the queries and of the orchestration work.

The assistant can answer to typical questions with these operators, such as those ones related to the level of the enterprise debt's using the operator *GrauAlavancagemFinanceira (Financial Leverage Degree)*[7], (available in LMDQL). There are also more complex operators such as those of enterprises evaluation statistical models, which allow the assistant the "capacity" of indicating enterprises with good economic strength, widening the sophistication of financial queries. There is an example of a LMDQL, query (1), to obtain the index of risk exposition.

```
SELECT {#GrauAlavancagemFinanceira#} ON COLUMNS,
{([Exposure Class])} ON ROWS from [Capital Requirements SA]
where [Time].[2013]                                        (1)
```

For this prototype, the *getMeasurementTime* was one of the implemented web services. It has as entry parameters: the enterprise name registered on SEC, the financial measurement name and the period desired. The financial measurement, "leverage ratio" was mapped in order to perform the OLAP query utilizing the operator *GrauAlavancagemFinanceira* in the XBRL repository.

Example (2) is part of the *getMeasurementTime* web service specification:

```
<message name="getMeasurementTimeRequest">
  <part name="measurement" type="xs:string"/>
  <part name="companyName" type="xs:string"/>
  <part name="time" type="xs:string"/>
</message>
<message name="getMeasurementTimeResponse">
  <part name="value" type="xs:integer"/>
</message>
<portType name="financialMeasurement">
  <operation name="getMeasurementTime">
    <input message="getMeasurementTimeRequest"/>
    <output message="getMeasurementTimeResponse"/>
  </operation>
</portType>                                              (2)
```

So, the versatility and simplicity provided by LMDQL queries, encapsulate in the services, allow a high level of sophistication to the financial answers supplied by the assistant.

The Securities and Exchange Commission, from the USA is an institution which makes available in one of its sites several XBRL database containing information from many enterprises registered in the agency. The quantity of available data of these repositories is a limitation of the range of the answers of the assistant. Furthermore, the correctness of the data implicates directly in the correction of the assistant answers.

For a low coupling configuration, the "DKM", that is part of Orchestration layer, must be implemented in a server environment and the Presentation layer in a Client environment. The possibility of modifying the assistant behavior in a single location for all clients is the main reason, i.e., it is easier to perform the maintenance of the mapping in a single code, with the advantages such as intervention speed, lower probability of code update failures, smaller tests quantity, lower alteration costs.

D. The Evaluation of the Prototype

In order to validate the prototype, some components of architecture were implemented as described as follows:

- A mobile Android application and a Javascript application to represent UIM.
- Two versions of dictionaries, the American version and the Brazilian version as part of UK.
- A Python Web Service as proxy of NLP.
- Several JAVA Classes as part of Orchestration
- A Java Webservice to access XBRL data.

We loaded 542 not duplicated terms extracted from US-GAAP taxonomy on the American financial dictionary. The mapping of two type of user questions to the corresponding services activation was done. Questions related to the available information about items in the financial statements, reports which display the situation of the organization in a given moment, were mapped to activate a web service called *getMeasurementTime*.

In our experiments we used the following eleven questions (3) for question answering over tree assistant: Our prototype, SIRI [11] and Google Now [4]. The last two are of the most used commercial assistants on the market. We did not compare with other financial virtual assistant because did not found anything similar.

1. *"What is the net income of Petrobras in 2013?"*
2. *"Give me the leverage of Microsoft of fiscal year 2014?"*
3. *"Show me the leverage of Microsoft in the fourth quarter of fiscal year 2014?"*
4. *"What is the leverage of Apple Q4 2014?"*
5. *"What is the Total assets of Petrobras in the second quarter of fiscal year 2014?"*
6. *"Give me the Total assets of Microsoft of fiscal year 2014?"*
7. *"What is the Petrobras Total assets of fiscal year 2014?"*

8. *"Show me the Microsoft' Total assets in the second quarter of fiscal year 2013?"*
9. *"In fiscal year 2013, what is the leverage of Petrobras?"*
10. *"In the second quarter of year 2013, what is the leverage of Apple?"* (3)

All questions were understood and correctly answered. by our prototype. For the first question, its response was presented as follow:

"The net income of Petroleo Brasileiro was U$10,832 million in 2013."

The responses of Google Now for all question were a list of web links about each query supported by Google Web Search engine [5]. The tree first presented summaries of these lists contained the solicited data in the first lines.

The SIRI answered the questions showing and speaking a following text before present a list of links about the question. e.g., :

"Here's what I found on the web for 'What is the net income of Petroleo Brasileiro in 2013'.

The SIRI uses Bing Web Search [1] to supports the answers. The SIRI answers about the 7th, 8th and 10th questions were different than others. In this case, SIRI identified every parameters and showed an answer expression on the screen, similar to our prototype. SIRI acted like an assistant at 30% of the experiment questions. However, the responses about these question were wrong.

Google Now only acted like a web search assistant for 100% of questions.

Also, we evaluated if these assistant keeps the history and the state of the user dialog. After a complete question, e.g., *"Give me the leverage of Microsoft of fiscal year 2014?"*, we used the short questions over the assistants as a sequence. e.g., On the first, "Now show me at 2014". On the second, "Give me the EBITDA". Then, the last short question of the sequence was "And about Apple". These queries have the objective to change the year, the financial concept and the company of the initial complete query, respectively. This feature allows the user ask short questions based on the first complete question. i.e., similar to human conversation, if the user wants to change some attributes of the original question, it is not necessary to ask a new complete question for each interaction.

In our experiment the prototype changed the corresponding parameter of the initial query and answered to the user for each interaction. All responses provided by our prototype were correct. However, Google Now and SIRI understood each interaction as a new query, so, all questions were submitted to their search engines, respectively. All answers, provided by them, had no relationship with the first complete question. Also, the first answers and the third answers had no relationship with the financial theme, respectively. As result of this experiment, we certified that the minimal tracking of state of the dialogue, between a user and an assistant, was only done by our prototype. In this case, it happened because only our prototype answers to the user after it analyzes both the new question and the previous question. This behavior is different from the SIRI and the Google Now, which always process each new question as if it was a new complete question, without any relation with previous question.

Our approach is a positive contribution in this area of research, because it presents an architecture for virtual closed domain assistants based on services, especially the NLP service.

We consider that the prototype of the financial virtual assistant produced based on the proposed architecture is a viable alternative and it proves the effectiveness of architecture. However, there are still some necessary evaluations to do like performance and accuracy test on manipulating a big list of services, datasources, items of dictionaries and items of grammar.

Although this work is a positive contribution, there are some limitations. Firstly, the quantity of utilized companies was little, about ten companies. Secondly, the prototype was not evaluated by investors about effectiveness. Thirdly, the comparison with others similar financial assistants was not done because they do not exist or are unknown for us.

V. CONCLUSION

When an investor gets the right information about the companies in a risky market, e.g., the stock market, quickly and easily, he has a great competitive advantage. For this context, this work presented the details of a virtual financial assistant prototype as an alternative solution to support the small investor.

This virtual financial assistant is a service-oriented computer system whose answers are based on the available financial information of companies in XBRL. The user can interact with it through natural language, supported by a service NLP and a dialog management unit. Its understanding degree of the financial questions and the sophistication level of its answers can be expanded, especially with the use of financial services that encapsulates OLAP analytic queries for XBRL database, as exemplified in this work.

An architecture for implementation of the closed domain virtual assistants, based on domain information services, in which the assistant was based, was also presented.

As evaluation of the prototype, financial questions in natural language were submitted to the prototype, which understood and answered all the questions correctly. The evaluation of the dialog manager feature of the prototype was also done and returned positive results.

We concluded that the architecture has been validated and we recognized enough potential of the prototype to be a viable alternative to traditional existing financial assistance.

In future work, the financial virtual assistant could compare the financial health of companies and, based on the share value of the selected companies, the assistant could notify the user when is a good moment to buy or to sell the shares in a company.

REFERENCES

[1] Bing, Microsoft Corporation. [Online]. Available from: http://www.bing.com. [retrieved: 05, 2016]

[2] E. C. Paraiso, and J-P A. Barthès, "A Voice-enabled Assistant in a Multi-agent System for e-Government Services," Conference: Advanced Distributed Systems: 5th International School and Symposium. Jan. 2005. pp. 495–503. ISSN: 0302-9743, ISBN: 978-3-540-31674-9.

[3] E. M. Eisman, and V. López, "A framework for designing closed domain virtual assistants," Expert Systems with Applications, vol. 39, Issue 3, pp. 3135–3144, Feb. 2012, doi:10.1016/j.eswa.2011.08.177.

[4] Google Now. Google Inc. [Online]. Available from: https://www.google.com/landing/now/. [retrieved: 04, 2016]

[5] Google Web Search. Google Inc. [Online]. Available from: https://www.google.com. [retrieved: 05, 2016]

[6] J. Medina, E. M. Eisman and J. L. Castro, "Virtual Assistants platforms 3.0," Transl. IE Comunicaciones: Revista Iberoamericana de Informática Educativa, n. 18, pp. 41–49, Dez. 2013, [Online] Available from: http://dialnet.unirioja.es/descarga/articulo/4468692.pdf. [retrieved: 04, 2016]

[7] M. A. P. da Silva, and P. C. da Silva, "Analytical Processing for Forensic Analysis," IEEE 18th International Enterprise Distributed Object Computing Conference Workshops and Demonstrations (EDOCW), 2014 pp. 364-371, http://dx.doi.org/10.1109/EDOCW.2014.60.

[8] P. C. da Silva, and V. C. Times, "Analytical Processing over XML and XLink. International," Journal of Data Warehousing and Mining, vol. 8, pp. 52, 2012. ISSN: 1548-3924, EISSN: 1548-3932, doi: 10.4018/IJDWM.

[9] S. P. Zambiasi, and R. J. Rabelo, "A Proposal for Reference Architecture for Personal Assistant Software Based on SOA," IEEE Latin America Transactions, vol. 10, pp. 1227–1234, Jan 2012. ISSN 1548-0992, doi: 10.1109/TLA.2012.6142466.

[10] Securities and Exchange Commission U.S. [Online] Available from: http://xbrl.sec.gov. [retrieved: 05, 2016]

[11] SIRI. Apple Inc. [Online]. Available from: http://www.apple.com/ios/siri/. [retrieved: 05, 2016]

[12] Speaktoit. API.AI. [Online]. Available from: https://api.ai. [retrieved: 04, 2016]

[13] Speaktoit. Assistant.ai. [Online]. Available from: https://assistant.ai. [retrieved: 05, 2016]

[14] Synthetic Intelligence Network, SYN: Syn Virtual Assistant, 2015. [Online]. Available from: http://syn.co.in/Syn-Virtual-Assistant.aspx. [retrieved: 05, 2016]

[15] XBRL Consortium. XBRL. [Online]. Available from: https://www.xbrl.org. [retrieved: 05, 2016]

[16] XBRL US. 2013 US-GAAP taxonomy. [Online]. Available from: https://xbrl.us/xbrl-taxonomy/2013-us-gaap/. [retrieved: 05, 2016]

OLAP-based Sustainability Report Auditing

Daniela C. Souza
Master in Systems and Computing
Universidade Salvador (UNIFACS)
Salvador, Brazil
dannyscosta@msn.com

Márcio Alexandre P. Silva
Master in Systems and Computing
Universidade Salvador (UNIFACS)
Salvador, Brazil
marcio.alexandre83@gmail.com

Paulo Caetano da Silva
Master in Systems and Computing
Universidade Salvador (UNIFACS)
Salvador, Brazil
paulo.caetano@pro.unifacs.br

Abstract — **In the last decades, companies have adopted environmental control and protection systems and have also been encouraged to demonstrate their results through the use of indicators in which the efforts made are presented. The adoption of XBRL by the Global Reporting Initiative (GRI) in the disclosure of sustainability reports contributes to the increase of their quality. However, the great heterogeneity of enterprise information systems is an obstacle to the use of the GRI guidelines in the corporate setting and for efficient auditing. In this paper, a service framework to audit sustainability reports based on the GRI rules is proposed. We also present operators that are called GRI operators and are implemented in an OLAP server, which aims to conduct analytical processing of sustainability reports to validate their compliance with the GRI guidelines.**

Keywords: Sustainability Report Auditing; OLAP; Global Report Initiative; SOA; XBRL.

I. INTRODUCTION

For decades, sustainable development has been an important topic in companies, mainly for those that are market leaders. Each company establishes its own sustainability approaches, seeking to develop better practices in order to create competitive advantages. Therefore, the disclosure of non-financial data has gained great importance for company success and sustainability reports have become a divulgation tool for acquiring competitive advantages and increasing the organizational image. Many companies use a specific model for building sustainability reports; however, the proposed standard by Global Reporting Initiative (GRI) has relevant and acceptable representation worldwide. According to GRI, the elaboration of Sustainability Reports is a measuring and divulgation practice, which is a responsibility of each company, whose results must be sent to stakeholders so they may analyze its performance in environmental, social and economic terms.

Although the adoption of GRI guidelines has contributed to the standardization of sustainability data, companies have been facing challenges, such as (a) diversity of computer systems and (b) the difficulty to perform an audit that is able to monitor data continuously, given it may not be trivial to capture large data in different systems and formats. In this context, the adoption of a Service Oriented Architecture (SOA) is a solution to mitigate flexibility and integration problems in software applications. SOA should be considered to improve (i) company productivity, (ii) alignment with business, (iii) agility for attending new demands, and (iv) service reuse [9].

Continuous Auditing is a technology innovation of the traditional audit, which is based on automation and, though its concepts have been established for almost two decades, in practice it is still something new [4]. Currently, technologies allow continuous auditing; however, some challenges must still be overcome, such as data acquisition in real time, as well as the scope and flexibility of audits. To solve this problem, a service-based framework is proposed in this work, in which analytical processing can be executed on eXtensible Business Reporting Language (XBRL) documents, allowing continuous auditing based on GRI sustainability guidelines.

After the introduction, this paper is structured as follows: Section II introduces a review of related literature; in Section III, the proposed model based on SOA is discussed; Section IV presents an analysis of the compliance of sustainability reports with GRI guidelines; Section V discusses Link Based Multidimensional Query Language (LMDQL) [19]-[23] operators (based on GRI rules), which can perform analytical processing on XBRL/GRI data; Section VI includes the conclusions and future work and, finally, the references are presented.

II. LITERATURE REVIEW

A model for continuous auditing is proposed to help stakeholders in decision-making processes in companies [25]. The integrity of data in financial reports is currently questionable; however, continuous auditing is an effective way to ensure safety and to facilitate early detection of fraud in financial reporting [14].

A study about integration on information systems and auditing which revealed several future challenges for audits due to business information systems is shown in Kanellou and Spathis [13]. These authors also state that continuous audit and monitoring can help stakeholders in the detection of errors and financial fraud.

A model is proposed for auditing through software systems called Continuous Auditing Web Service (CAWS), which is based on Web Service and XML technologies [16]. This model has been developed in order to reduce complexity in the transmission of data and to aggregate security to software systems, and for that the following technologies have been used: XML, WS-BPEL (for the composition of new services) and Web Service (for avoiding incompatibility in data access and exchange).

A collaborative model based on SOA for audit systems is proposed, which uses XML standards and data transformation applications (developed by companies and software vendors) [6].

The adoption of XBRL by GRI provides greater facility in the collection and analysis of sustainability data, besides significantly influencing the improvement of quality of data that composes the report is discussed in Leibs [24].

Recent advances in information technology have encouraged the search for means which are able to verify the integrity of transactional data, which brings many benefits to auditing particularly through continuous monitoring, in order to guarantee operations are made in an environment where information technology is intensively used [1].

Regarding the standardization of sustainability reporting, GRI has strong representation, to be considered an international standard widely accepted, which allows organizations to inform their sustainable practices in relation to environmental, social and economic dimensions. Many organizations use the GRI standard; however, studies show that although organizations declare themselves strategically sustainable, there are attempts to camouflage the indicators that are disclosed in sustainability reports, as well as the omission of relevant negative information, which puts at risk the interpretation of corporate performance and the impact of the company's programs. Therefore, this article seeks to fill a gap that previous studies have left, with regard to the lack of automated controls that allow the audit of reports issued by organizations. Then, it is also intended to verify if the reports are in compliance with the guidelines proposed by the GRI. To address this issue, a service framework is presented to audit sustainability reports with operators that evaluate the compliance of sustainability reports to the GRI guidelines, which can be seen in section V.

III. A SERVICE FRAMEWORK FOR SUSTAINABILITY REPORTS

The framework proposed in this paper is divided into two conceptual layers: (1) integration infrastructure, which is intended promote the access and retrieval of data within the informational structure of the company. In this layer we can find the corporative environment, extraction services and standardization services; and (2) Global Reporting Initiative, whose function is to integrate the architecture proposed by the GRI to the informational scenario of the organization. In this layer we can find persistence, auditing and distribution services. The services are materialized in the form of Web Services to meet the necessary integration in order to design the collection environment and the recovery of sustainability data. Thus, all adjacent layers of the model can consume this data. Figure 1 illustrates the framework proposed using SOA, XBRL, GRI and Continuous Auditing.

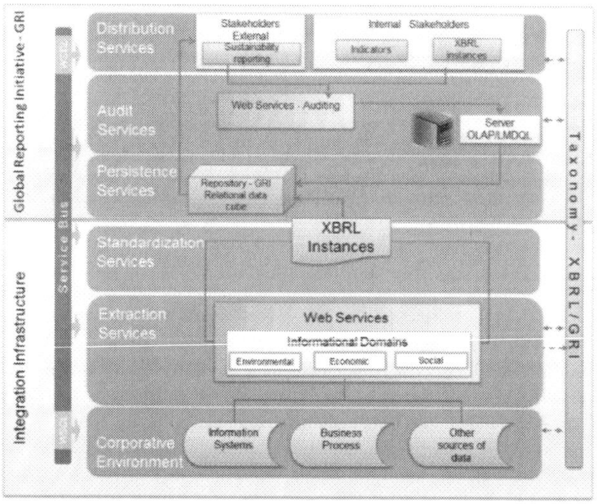

Figure 1. Service Framework for Sustainability Report. [5]

A physical and logical infrastructure is proposed to provide effective communication among the many layers of the model. The physical one is based on a service bus and the logical one is responsible for the representation of data using XBRL technology.

- *Service Bus XBRL:* Enterprise Service Bus (ESB) has the function of granting access to resources provided among the layers, which allows the exchange of messages. The implementation of service bus enables the connection of software systems developed on different platforms, integrating them as services. The communication interface of the services on the bus is made through their WSDL documents. In ESB, through the SOAP protocol, the consumption and provision of services of all layers of the framework are allowed.
- *XBRL-GRI Taxonomy*: The XBRL-GRI taxonomy standardizes the representation of data, as well as how to perform its exchange, which facilitates the connection of all layers in the proposed model. This allows all layers to have the necessary infrastructure to use the facts reported in XBRL instances [12].

From this physical and logical communication infrastructure, six layers are defined.

- *Corporate Environment*: The corporate environment layer is composed of information systems that store data related to the scope of sustainability. It is understood as the scope of sustainability the set of data required according to the GRI guidelines.
- *Extraction Services*: The extraction services layer gathers the necessary services for the integration of data. These services are responsible for collecting the data that is available in the corporate environment to be converted into XBRL format, according to the guidelines proposed by the GRI.
- *Standardization Services*: This layer is intended to standardize the form of the representation of data in the

Extraction Services and *Corporate Environment* layers through the XBRL-GRI taxonomy. This layer is connected to extraction services layer through Enterprise Service Bus (ESB), where data is retrieved and organized, creating the XBRL instance with the data related to sustainability performance.

- *Persistence Services*: The function of this layer is to store the sustainability reports of the organization through a data repository. This will allow retrieving and analyzing data of specific reports. From the several XBRL instances stored, queries can be executed, providing the use of analysis techniques and knowledge discovery (e.g., OLAP, data mining, trend analysis) to support decision-making related to sustainability.
- *Audit Services*: the Audit Services layer consists of two components: Web Services Auditing and OLAP/LMDQL Server. In the former, are the services that are designed to audit the sustainability reports based on the GRI guidelines. The latter is a tool that will allow stakeholders to generate queries for the analysis of sustainability data [20].
- *Distribution Services*: In this layer, the sustainability data of the organization is made available. It is conceptually subdivided into two categories: (1) internal stakeholders, whose function is to carry out a continuous monitoring of sustainability indicators and (2) external stakeholders, who1ª avaliação11se focus is on the use of reports in order to know the sustainable practices of the organization. Thus, the distribution layer is of fundamental importance in the process of engagement and performance maintenance of the organization sustainability, benefiting all stakeholders, since it is an important feature to track the organization's sustainability initiatives.

It is expected that through this architecture it will be possible to provide the necessary means to mitigate problems of access and standardization of data on the sustainable performance of organizations. In the next section the analysis of sustainability reporting compliance is presented.

IV. ANALYSIS OF SUSTAINABILITY REPORTS COMPLIANCE

This section presents three analytical levels of compliance of reports based on GRI guidelines, which are GAPIE (Degree of Full Compliance), GEE (Degree of Effective Disclosure) and GRIConformity (Degree of Compliance). Through these indices it is expected to evaluate the level of disclosure of sustainability data in organizational reports issued based on the GRI guidelines.

The GRI guidelines are developed through a process that involves a network of stakeholders, including company representatives, workers, financial markets, auditors and specialists in several areas. One of the main aspirations of GRI is that sustainability reporting reaches the same level of accuracy, comparability, credibility and verifiability expected of a financial report. To define the content of reports, GRI uses three main principles called Indicators, Aspects and Categories to describe two types of content: general and specific [2].

The "Core" option contains the essential elements of a sustainability report. It provides grants for the organization to report the impact of their economic, environmental, social and governance performance, requiring a report of at least one indicator related to each material aspect identified. The "comprehensive" option requires disclosure of additional information about the strategy, analysis, governance, ethics and integrity of the organization.

According to the GRI, indicators are qualitative or quantitative information associated with the organization. This provides information about the performance or economic, environmental and social impacts of the organization related to material aspects; Aspects relate to topics that each Category covers; and Categories represent each of the three macro-elements that comprise the GRI guidelines, which represent the dimensions of sustainability [12]. From these definitions, two are the types of GRI reports: General Standard Disclosure and Specific Standard Disclosure. Based on the GRI guidelines, the authors Dias [7] and Carvalho and Siqueira [3] propose two indices for the analysis of compliance of sustainability reports: the degree of effective disclosure (GEE) and the degree of full compliance (GAPIE). The degree of effective disclosure (GEE) is intended to measure the percentage of the amount of data reported by the organization in relation to all data according to the GRI guidelines [3]. The degree of full compliance allows establishing the percentage of compliance of each company in relation to what was required by GRI [3]. For the treatment of data, first the data that organizations report on sustainability reports are classified according to the information required by the essential indicators of GRI; then, the calculations of GAPIE and GEE are made. For this classification, the criteria defined by Dias [7] and Carvalho and Siqueira [3] are followed, as shown in Table I and II.

TABLE I. BASIS FOR INFORMATION CLASSIFICATION

CATEGORY: SHOWN		
CLASSIFICATION	***ABREVIATION***	***DEFINITION***
FULL COMPLIANCE	FC	When all the data required by the GRI-G4 guidelines is provided by the organization.
PARTIAL COMPLIANCE	PC	When only part of the data required by the GRI-G4 guidelines is provided by the organization.
DUBIOUS	D	When the data provided is not enough for the user to evaluate if the compliance is full or partial.
INCONSISTENT	I	When the data provided by the organization is different from that required by GRI-G4 guidelines.

TABLE II. BASIS FOR INFORMATION CLASSIFICATION

CATEGORY: NOT SHOWN		
NOT AVAILABLE	NA	When the organization recognizes that the data required is relevant to its activities, but it still does not have conditions to provide it.
NOT APPLICABLE	NAP	When the organization recognizes that the data required is not relevant to its activities or business field.
OMITTED WITH A REASON	OR	When the organization omits the data required by GRI-G4 guidelines, presenting a reason for such omission.
OMITTED	O	When nothing is commented about the indicator, as if it did not exist.

To calculate GAPIE, the total number of Full Compliance indicators ("FC"), i.e., the total indicators that had their content reported according to what is required by the GRI guidelines, is added to the total number of indicators omitted with a reason ("OR"), i.e., the indicators that the organization omitted from its report, but presented a reason for the omission, and divided by the total number of Core indicators (which are essential indicators for sustainability reporting) subtracted by the total number of indicators that are Not Applicable, "NAP", i.e. indicators that do not apply to the organization. Figure 2 shows the formula for the calculation of this index.

$$GAPIE = \frac{\text{TOTAL INDICATORS " FC" + TOTAL INDICATORS " OR"}}{\text{TOTAL INDICATORS ESSENTIAL - TOTAL INDICATORS "NAP"}}$$

Figure 2. GAPIE Formula.

To calculate GEE, the total number of Full Compliance indicators ("FC") is divided by the total number of Core indicators subtracted by the total number of Not Applicable indicators "NAP", as shown in Figure 3.

$$GEE = \frac{\text{TOTAL INDICATORS " FC"}}{\text{TOTAL INDICATORS ESSENTIAL - TOTAL INDICATORS "NAP"}}$$

Figure 3. GEE Formula.

Another way of assessing compliance is through the use of the GRIConformity index. This index is intended to compare the data reported by organizations to the data required by the GRI guidelines. Through the use of this index, the analyst/auditor can analyze and assess whether organizations disclose sustainability data in accordance with the guidelines.

The next section presents the analytical processing operators based on these three indices, which will allow the auditing of sustainability reports based on the guidelines proposed by the GRI and the studies proposed by Dias [7] and Carvalho and Siqueira [3].

V. OPERATORS FOR THE ASSESSMENT OF COMPLIANCE

The use of tools for the analytical processing of data (OLAP) to perform strategic analyses of an organization allows assisting stakeholders in identifying trends and patterns in order to better conduct their business.

A language called LMDQL was proposed and aims to conduct analytical processing of multidimensional data expressed in XML documents connected by links [20].

LMDQL is a language derived from Multidimensional Expression (MDX) [15][26] and executes OLAP queries on relational databases and XML-based documents. OLAP queries executed in the Mondrian server generate SQL queries, which are translated into XQuery with the Sql2Xquery driver [20]. The Sql2Xquery driver enables the suitability of relational OLAP servers to XML environments. LMDQL is designed to run on a data cube, i.e. a multidimensional structure of data representation [20] - constructed from a relational database or an XML database, defined by XBRL Dimensions documents [27].

Therefore, the Audit Services layer was designed to perform analytical processing (OLAP) on sustainability reports [20]. This paper proposes the use of Mondrian server to execute OLAP queries through an extension of LMDQL language, in order to manipulate sustainability data issued in GRI/XBRL reports. To make this possible, a Web Service to access the Mondrian server is proposed [18].

LMDQL has financial analytical operators, which allow (a) the acquisition of data in linkbases, which is a characteristic of XBRL taxonomies; (b) to execute analytical queries in a set of XML documents; (c) to execute queries based on the value or structure of the XML document; (d) to create operators based on other operators created at run time, (e) to perform horizontal, vertical and separatrix analyses and also analyses based on the proximity of data values [19] [20] and (f) fraud analysis (i.e. forensic analysis) in financial reports based on Benford's Law, 3-Sigma Rule, Z Test and Chi-Square [22] [23].

For the analytical processing of a sustainability document, considering the GRI guidelines and GAPIE, GEE and GRIConformity indices, three operators were specified: GRIConformity, GRIGapie and GRIGee. The LMDQL operators for sustainability auditing are presented In Figure 4. The three operators (i.e. GRIConformity, GRIGapie and GRIGee) have a MemberSet type as a parameter, which refers to a member set of a data cube, according to the specifications of LMDQL operators.

GRIConformity (*<MemberSet>*)
GRIGapie(*<MemberSet>*)
GRIGee(*<MemberSet>*)

Figure 4. LMDQL Operators for Sustainability Auditing.

To execute an LMDQL query based on these operators, a parameter is provided referring to the sustainability element (or a set of elements) contained in the sustainability report to be assessed, that we call Element. To analyze the chosen operator, a specific element can be used according to the needs of the analyst/auditor, such as [Element].[Aspect BoundaryLimitationOutsideOrganizationDescription]). If the auditor/analyst wishes to make the analysis of a set of elements, the keyword "children" must be used (which is native to the Mondrian server [18]), referencing all children members of the "Element" dimension (contained in the database), i.e. "[Element].children". In the tests carried out in this paper, the following dimensions were specified: (i) Entity, which refers to the name of the companies that issue sustainability reports; (ii) Document, which corresponds to sustainability documents that the company issues; (iii) Element, which refers to the elements that correspond to the sustainability indicators contained in these documents and (iv) Time, the time period to which the document belongs. An example of an LMDQL query is shown in Figure 5.

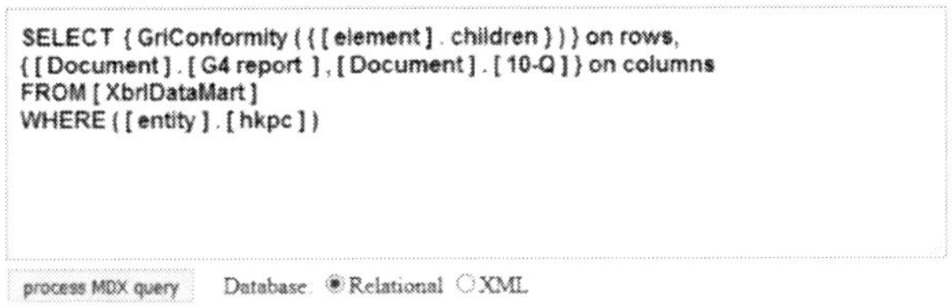

Figure 5. OLAP query using an LMDQL operator for sustainability auditing

In this query, the auditor informs which document he aims to analyze, which is specified in the Document dimension. Two types of documents have been defined, i.e. G4 Report and 10-Q, which refer to a sustainability and financial report, respectively. It is also necessary to specify the company that issued the financial report (e.g. [Entity].[hkpc], which is the company Hong Kong Productivity Council). The options "relational" and "XML" are attributes of the extension of the Mondrian server, which implements LMDQL, with which the analyst chooses on which database paradigm he wishes to execute the query [20] [22] [23].

To illustrate the use of operators in relational and XML environments, two databases are used to store sustainability reports: MySql [17], a relational database, and Exist [8], a native XML database; both were chosen for being open source and free. The logical model schema stored in the database must be informed in a mandatory XML configuration file of the Mondrian server [18].

In this example, in Figure 5, the GRIConformity operator executes a query to assess the compliance of the sustainability elements contained in XBRL/GRI documents with the elements specified by GRI as important indices for enterprise sustainability issues [10]-[12]. After executing the query, the operator classifies the elements as "yes" if they are in compliance, and "no" if they are not, as shown in Figures 6 and 7, which respectively show the result of the compliance of the documents contained in the database which belongs to the company Hong Kong Productivity Council, and the non-compliance of the documents of Facebook company. Fields containing the character "-" indicate that there are no results for the query executed by the GRIConformity operator.

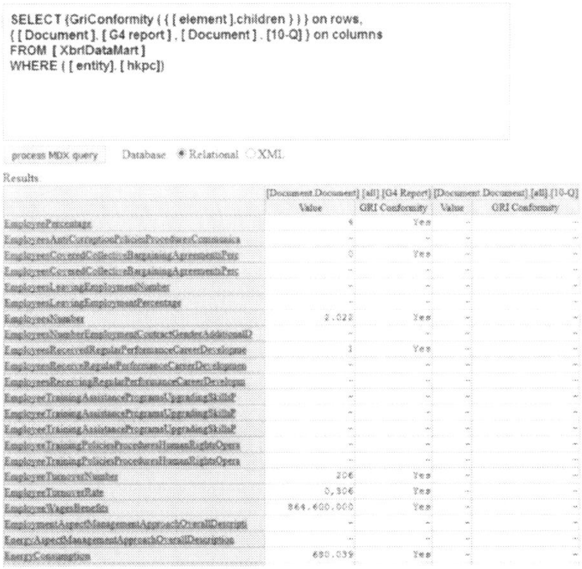

Figure 6. Example of compliance of an LMDQL query with the GRIConformity operator

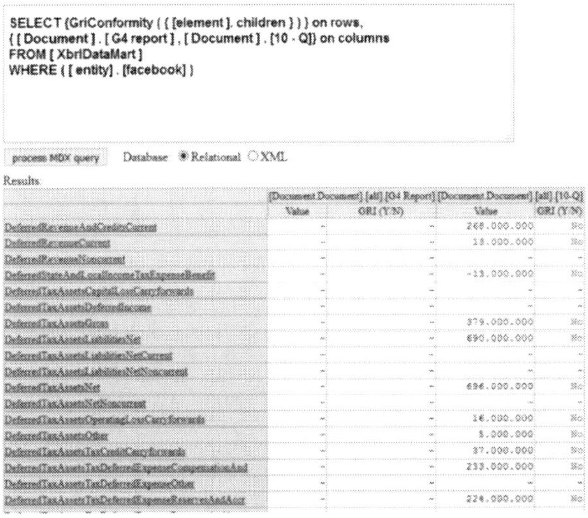

Figure 7. Example of noncompliance of an LMDQL query with the GRIConformity operator.

From the presented operators, it is possible to perform analytical processing of sustainability reports based on the XBRL-GRI taxonomy. They are therefore expected to assist in the continuous audit process of those reports, which will provide stakeholders with greater integrity of the organization's sustainability information.

VI. Conclusions and Future work

In this work, we presented a service framework to audit sustainability reports based on the GRI rules. This framework can contribute to the development of a model that is able to simplify the collection, analysis, comparison and disclosure of data related to the sustainability performance of organizations. For the analysis of reports an OLAP tool was presented, an extension of the Mondrian server [18] and LMDQL language [20], which allows the audit of XBRL reports based on the GRI guidelines, assessing their compliance, that is, if they meet the guidelines proposed. Continuous monitoring of sustainability reports of organizations can be performed with this tool. It is expected that through this work and the use of technology involving SOA and XBRL, the framework can bring greater reliability and security to stakeholders in decision-making, with regard to the fundamental dimensions of corporate sustainability that are: social, environmental and economic. This framework is a scale model that grows as the organization establishes excellence in sustainability, internationalization and standardization of data. For future work, we intend to raise the level of detail of the framework presented, in addition to implementing the GRIGapie and GRIGee operators.

References

[1] C.E. Brown, J.A. Wong, and A. A. Baldwin, "A review and analysis of the Existing Research Streams in continuous auditing, " Journal of Emerging Technologies in Accounting, vol. 4, pp. 1-28, 2007

[2] M. R. Camargos, "Análise do uso do modelo Global Reporting Initiative para elaboração do relatório de sustentabilidade das empresas de energia elétrica no Brasil," Campinas, SP, 2012.

[3] F. M. Carvalho, and J. R. M. Siqueira, "Análise da Utilização dos Indicadores Essenciais da Global Reporting Initiative nos Relatórios Sociais e Empresas Latino-Americanas". [Online]. Available from: http://www.atena.org.br/revista/ojs-2.2.3-08/index.php/pensarcontabil/article/view/113/ 2016.04.14.

[4] D. Y .Chan and, M. A. Vasarhelyi , "Innovation and practice of continuous auditing". International Journal of Accounting Information Systems, 12(2), pp.152-160, 2011.

[5] E. M. Cruz, D . Costa, and P.C . Silva , " Sustainability reports based on XBRL through a service-oriented architecture approach". In: 3rd International Conference on Challenges in Environmental Science and Computer Engineering (CESCE 2014), 2014, London. Proceedings of the 3rd International Conference on Challenges in Environmental Science and Computer Engineering (CESCE 2014).

[6] C. Qiushi, H. Zuoming, and H. Jibing , "A Collaborative Computer Auditing System under SOA-based Conceptual Model," CFO, 2013. [Online] Available from: https://www.researchgate.net/publication/258814902_A_Collaborative_Computer_Auditing_System_under_SOA-based_Conceptual_Model/ . 2016.01.20

[7] L. N. S. Dias. "Análise da Utilização dos Indicadores do Global Reporting Initiative nos Relatórios Sociais em Empresas Brasileiras, " 2006. Dissertação (Mestrado em Ciências Contábeis) - FACC/UFRJ, Rio de Janeiro, 2006. FIBRIA. Relatórios de Sustentabilidade. [Online]. Available from: http://livros01.livrosgratis.com.br/cp030028.pdf/ 2016.04.02

[8] ExistDB. *The Open Source Native XML Database*. [Online]. Available from: http://exist-db.org/exist/apps/homepage/index.html. 2016.04.03

[9] F. P. Marzullo, "SOA na Prática Inovando o seu negócio por meio de soluções orientadas a serviços". Novatec, 2009.

[10] GRI, "Directrizes para a Elaboração de Relatórios de Sustentabilidade, " Amsterdam, 2006.

[11] GRI™ (2013). *G4 XBRL Schema*. [OnLine]. Available from: http://xbrl.globalreporting.org/2014-12-01/Forms/AllItems.aspx/ 2016.04.03

[12] GRI (2014) . *For the Guide Lines and Standard Setting - G4*. [Online]. Available from: https://www.globalreporting.org/Pages/default.aspx/ 2016.04.03

[13] A. Kanellou, and C. Spathis, "Auditing in enterprise system environment: a synthesis".Journal of Enterprise Information Management, 24(6), pp.494-519, 2011.

[14] C. C. Lin, F. Lin, and D. Liang , "An analysis of using state of the art technologies to implement real-time continuous assurance, ".Proceedings - 2010 6th World Congress on Services. Miami, Flórida, 2010, pp. 415-422, ISBN: 978-1-4244-8199-6

[15] MDX. *Multidimensional Expressions (MDX) Reference*. [Online]. Available from: https://msdn.microsoft.com/en-us/library/ms145506.aspx/ 2016.04.03

[16] U. S Murthy, and S. M Groomer, "A Continuous Auditing Web Services Model for XML-based Accounting Systems," International Journal of Accounting Information Systems, No.5, pp. 139-63, 2004.

[17] MySQL. [Online]. Available from: https://www.mysql.com/. 2016.04.03

[18] Pentaho. *Logical model*. [Online] Available from: http://mondrian.pentaho.com/documentation/schema.php#Cubes_and_dimensions/ 2016.04.03

[19] P. C. Silva, and V. C. Times, "LMDQL:Link-based and Multidimensional Query Language". World Wide Web Consortium (W3C) Website (2009). [Online]. Available from: http://www.w3.org/2009/03/xbrl/soi/LMDQL.pdf/ 2016.04.03

[20] P. C. Silva, and V. C. Times , "LMDQL: Link-based and Multidimensional Query Language". In: DOLAP 09 - ACM Twelfth International Workshop on Data Warehousing and OLAP, 2009, Hong Kong. ACM Twelfth International Workshop on Data Warehousing and OLAP, 2009.

[21] P. C. Silva, and V. C. Times, R. R. Ciferri and C. D Ciferri , "Analytical Processing Over XML and XLink. International Journal of Data Warehousing and Mining (IJDWM)". Volume 8, Issue 1. IGI Global, 2012.

[22] M. A. P Silva, and P. C. Silva , "Financial Forensic Analysis".13th IADIS International Conference WWW/INTERNET (ICWI). Porto, Portugal, 2014. ISBN: 978-989-8533-24-1.[Online]. Available from: http://www.iadisportal.org/digital-library/financial-forensic-analysis/. 2016.04.03

[23] M. A. P. Silva, and P. C. Silva , "Analytical Processing for Forensic Analysis". In: 1st International Workshop on Compliance, Evolution and Security in Cross Organizational Processes (CESCOP 2014), Ulm, Germany. 18th IEEE International EDOC Conference Workshops (EDOCW'14). DOI: 10.1109/EDOCW.2014.60.

[24] S. Leibs, "Sustainability reporting: Earth in the balance sheet," CFO, 2007. [Online]. Available from: http://www.cfo.com/article.cfm/10234097/ 2016.04.03

[25] P. Sikka, S. Filling, and P. Liew , "The audit crunch: reforming auditing". ManagerialAuditing Journal, 24(2), 135-155, 2009.

[26] G . Spofford , "MDX solutions: with Microsof SQL Server Analysis Services". New York: J. Wiley, p.163, 2001.

[27] XBRL International Inc (2012). *XBRL Dimensions 1.0*.[Online]. Available from: http://www.xbrl.org/specification/dimensions/rec-2012-01-25/dimensions-rec-2006-09-18+corrected-errata-2012-01-25-clean.html/ 2016.04.03

AUTHOR INDEX

**International Academy, Research,
and Industry Association (IARIA)**
412 Derby Way
Wilmington, DE 19810

ISBN 978-1-5108-2347-1

CURRAN ASSOCIATES INC.
proceedings.com